JOURNEY

RICHARD MAGGIO

ISBN# 978-0-9861141-0-6 (Hard Cover)
ISBN# 978-0-9861141-1-3 (Soft Cover)
ISBN# 978-0-9861141-2-0 (E-book)

Dedication

I would like to dedicate this book to my wonderful wife Judy who has been married to me for 46 years.
No small feat.

TABLE OF CONTENTS

Richard Maggio

PREFACE

I have named this book "Journey" because it is my journey with the Lord for forty-five years. My journey did not start as a child, but began when I was thirty-one years old as an adult. I was a former Catholic who did not know the Lord personally as in being born again. This was a key factor for the beginning of my journey. I have been very fortunate in the past forty-five years, as you will read. God has allowed me to be involved with many people and ministries that have helped me in my journey. There was one incident that spurred me on in my life in the Lord as a young Christian.

This incident was a visit to a ministry headquarters called World Vision. As I toured their facility, I noticed a framed poster on a wall. The poster showed Jesus reaching down to feed a child (my recollection). The poster had a quote (a prayer) with the caution that said, "Unless you mean it, do not pray this prayer." I thought about it awhile and decided to pray it. The prayer was, "Break my heart for the things that break Your heart." God heard me, and thus began my journey. The rest of my story will be followed through the chapters. They will show my interest and my attention to those interests as the years go by.

This is my first and second attempt at putting a book together. I say together because I have been writing what could be considered chapters for many years as the Lord gave me the ideas and the words for each document/chapter. If they all were added to one book it would be too large for a single book.Therefore, I needed wisdom from the Lord for what you will read here. Consequently, I have divided the chapters and they will be published as two separate books. I have repeated phrases for emphasis.

I do not consider this book to be a teaching or a Bible study, however, you will learn much from what God has done with me and how have I dealt with each issue over the years. I have told people that I graduated from UA, not the University of Arizona, but the University of Adversity with a few years at the University of the Desert, a school where the Holy Spirit teaches all of the classes, and when you graduate, you will be promoted.

When I first made my commitment to Jesus Christ and accepted His saving grace for the forgiveness of my sins, I was told by a very wise and saintly lady that what had happened to me was justification and that took only an instant. She told me what would happen to me next was sanctification and that it would take the rest of my life. This book is a forty-five year piece of that process. I am not through yet, but I am on the journey.

I hope that I have given credit to the authors of all the books I have read. There are times when you read so much that you begin to own all that you know. With that said, I will apologize to all of the great authors I have read over the years; there is no way to reread or remember them all. Rather, I express deep gratitude for all of the well-known authors in the Body of Christ since many of them have taught me so much. If someone ever reads this and sees something you wrote and received no credit, I am sorry. However, I don't expect any of you fellows to ever read this work but if you do and want to copy anything, go ahead.

I want to make another statement, and that is I am not smart enough to have written anything that is earthshaking, so if it is earthshaking and it is not your work, it was the Holy Spirit who wrote it. I did not write it.

I mentioned that I had prayed a prayer that asked the Lord to break my heart with the things that broke His heart. That is what the rest of this book is about. Every chapter is a portion of my journey through my life with Jesus, the Holy Spirit and the Father as they directed me in various areas of my walk.

A Note: The titles of the chapters are for understanding only. I don't intend for them to be a teaching on the subject. I have written what I would call essays on every chapter subject that impacted me over many years and this book is a compilation of many of my writings. I say many and not all, as I have written on many more subjects.

There is a central theme in what I have chosen for this book because these subjects don't seem to be interesting to many people in the Body of Christ. They are too busy with their real life after being born again. I know I must appear to be a Johnny One Note, but I have no choice. The Lord Jesus is very interested in His people keeping their focus on Him,

His Holy Spirit and the Father, and not living like the unsaved world. He wants us to make the world jealous of us and what we have in Him. He didn't like religion from the beginning and He doesn't like it now. I believe that religion is still a tool of the enemy. I believe Mary's work is better than Martha's work. (Luke 10-38-42) I believe that even benign or good things, when they become repetitive can become a stronghold and take our focus from the Lord and are displeasing to the Lord. So, the journey begins.

Chapter One

My Testimony

I thought I should begin with my testimony to put things in perspective. I would never be in this endeavor without the change that occurred in my life. What I have written about are life-changing events in my life and the lives of my family. It is not a small thing and has been the dominant theme in and of my life and the lives of my family for forty-five years. It is not possible for me to explain how I feel about my decision made on February 7th, 1970, nor can I separate it from any part of my life. All my experiences are part of the sanctification process I mentioned in the Preface.

I will begin this testimony by citing the scripture, Romans 12:2 (NIV), "Do not conform to this world, but be transformed by the renewing of your mind. Then you will be able to test and approve what God's will is. His good, and pleasing and perfect will." I quoted this particular scripture because this is the crux of why I was on the opposite side, the worldly side, of every issue before I made my commitment to Christ.

That was the beginning of the changes in my life. I have been moving toward renewing of my mind/conforming to the Mind of Christ for years now. My mind has been renewed. I think differently on issues. I am not a mindless robot, but I sift all issues through what I know of the Word of God and what Christian perspective is for that issue.

My Testimony

It all happened on February 7th, 1970. I had just married Judy and had gone through a horrible divorce of my own making. My neighbors, Bob and Delores Anderson, lived across the street and noticed the goings on at my home. They came over and invited Judy and I to a swim party at their home. We had no friends since Judy was from another city that was a considerable distance away and our mutual friends stayed with my former wife. My mom, dad and brother were the only people we had for social and family communication.

We welcomed these neighbors. However, unbeknownst to me, they had ulterior motives. They were Baptist folks and decided to tell me about their God. They did not know that I was a Catholic. Nobody could tell as I was not living by the rules of the Catholic Church. They told me that their God was Jesus. I said that mine was as well. We agreed on the basic tenants of our faiths so that was no problem for me. Over the next six months, we built our friendship and we became very close. I asked Bob every question I could think of and he would always answer from the Bible. Bob, as a Baptist, did not know much about Catholics. He tried not to make me angry and he never did. I always wondered why this Non-Catholic knew so much about the Bible. I had erroneously thought that the Bible belonged only to Catholics, we just weren't encouraged to read it.

Bob told me that I needed to accept Jesus as my personal Savior to obtain eternal life. That was pretty foreign to me and I resisted that idea for quite a while. Bob persisted, answering my questions. I never attended Bob's church where he taught the adult Sunday school class. Delores and Judy became fast friends as well since Judy was a Baptist herself. I knew she was, but she was not evangelistic toward me. Somehow she felt that she would alienate me if she preached to me. Please do not think that Judy was living a lifestyle of sin in dating me, a married man. I had lied to her as I did to my former wife. When she finally found out she refused to see me again.

When Bob asked me what conflicts I had about being a born again Christian, he asked me if I believed that Jesus Christ was the Son of God. I knew He was, as does every Catholic. Then he wanted to know if I believed Jesus died on the cross for my sins (Good Friday). I believed that and as do all Catholics. Then he asked if I believed that Jesus rose from the dead. I believed that and so do Catholics (Easter Sunday). I began to realize that I had no conflicts, just a bunch of questions. I began to realize that by the rules of the church of which I was a member, I was on my way to Hell. I was divorced and had not fulfilled my Easter duty (Mass, confession and Communion at least once a year). I was effectively excommunicated from the Catholic Church. He then asked if I believed that I was a sinner and could not save myself. I think I answered that above.

In February Bob asked Judy and I to come to a Valentine's

Day Banquet put on by his church at a restaurant. It seemed innocent enough. A man named Lieutenant Bob Vernon, a police officer in the LAPD, was the speaker. Lt. Vernon gave a testimony about his conversion to Jesus and about how God was so real to him. After I heard him speak he gave an invitation for anyone who wanted to accept Jesus into their heart as Lord and Savior. I knew that I had a decision to make. I told God that I had a lot of questions but I would let Him answer those questions afterwards. So I repeated a little prayer recited by Lt. Vernon expressing the beliefs I listed above.

Some people tell me that they have not left their wife, have not committed adultery, have not robbed any banks, they bring their pay home and love their kids. This somehow exempts them from needing God and the redemptive work He did on the cross. I only mention this because some have told me this to suggest that I needed a savior and they do not. Anyone who thinks they have not sinned is beyond my thinking.

In any event, this is really where my story starts. Since that day my life has not been the same. I knew that I was forgiven. I literally felt a weight of guilt lift off of me. I knew that what I had done was real and that I truly was forgiven for past, present and future sins, and that when I died I would go to be with the Lord. All this was based on the Scriptures. By the way, what I realized first was that I had no questions and that the Bible was not an allegory, but was true. Every word was true and it did not contradict itself in any way. I realized that anything I did that was good had no impact on whether or not I was going to heaven. I realized the things I once liked, I no longer liked or cared to do anymore. My whole perspective began to change.

I began to have a real love for the Bible and I began to read and study it "religiously." I also memorized many passages and soon was able to teach from the Bible.

I wanted to go to the Catholic Church and teach the Bible, but God knew that I would not be kind. I would have beaten someone on the head with it. About four years later the Catholic Church asked me to teach the CCD. That is an acronym for the Confraternity of Christian Doctrine which teaches Catholic rules and traditions. I thought that I would have one high school grade, but I got all four grades, about 300 kids. I taught along with a friend who moved from a Catholic Church in Thousand Oaks into my area and was a Catholic Charismatic. We used the Bible as our only text and the Church bought the Bibles. There was a considerable uproar when it was discovered that we were considering the Bible to be absolutely true and inerrant and the only book we would use. I explained that if I had a ruler and was teaching math, we all had to have the same ruler. I also said if they thought that part of the Bible was not true, please tell me because I did not know of any false passages and we would discuss it.

That was the beginning of two years with the kids. By the end of the course we knew of none who did not believe that the Bible was true. We also did not know of any that did not accept Jesus as their personal Savior. We had many parents coming to our classes because they could not understand why their kids wanted to attend CCD when in the past they had to be bribed to attend. Many parents came to Christ as well.

Judy and I were then asked to help lead the Charismatic Renewal in our area. This renewal started in 1965 at Duquesne

University and later at Notre Dame. By 1974 was sweeping across the country. We were in charge of seven groups in the San Gabriel Valley. We met once a month at Loyola University for training and then we would meet with each of our groups each week and teach the Bible and the born again experience.

Later we began attending church at a place called Melodyland Christian Center. Judy and I felt that God was calling us to some lay ministry. I know that this will sound strange, but this chapter is not long enough to tell all that has occurred in our lives. We joined with the assistant pastor of Melodyland and were a part of helping him start a worldwide ministry. We went around the U.S. and to Australia (over most of Australia). Our ministry was healing through the power of God, teaching and moving in the gifts of the Spirit as stated in the Bible in Corinthians, chapters 12 and 14. You must understand that before I became a Christian I did not care about spiritual things. I had no interest in anything that did not benefit me. It was all about me. Since I became a Christian that has changed.

I mentioned that I had prayed a prayer and asked the Lord to break my heart with the things that broke His Heart. That is what the rest of this book is about. Every chapter is a portion of my journey through my life with Jesus, the Holy Spirit and the Father as they have directed me in various areas of my walk.

Chapter Two

Why We Believe & What We Believe

When I was saved/born again, I believed that God loved me. Did I have all the understanding of His love? No, I did not. I had a new Christian warm and fuzzy feeling regarding God's love for me. I thought that He must have loved me a great deal to send His Son to die for me for my sins, but I did not understand the reasons or ramifications of His love.

I was a newborn in the Lord. I just enjoyed my new relationship with Him like a baby would love its mother. I watched Him change my life in little things, taking certain habits out of my life and changing my likes for the things of this world to the things of His world. I was getting the Mind of Christ. I was justified, and now I was getting sanctified. I had a long way to go and I am still working on it with the Lord's help. I learned that the big things went away fairly easily, but the little things like forgiving my enemies and loving them was not as easy as it may sound. I learned that considering it all joy when trials come upon me is easier said than done and I learned that God is there to help through it all. I learned that He loves me more than I love Him. So what was next?

I thought of going to Seminary or Bible school, but I had two families to support. Consequently, God directed my interest and love toward His Word and the Holy Spirit became my teacher. He taught me some interesting things over the years. God gave me a taste of spiritual ambition. He allowed me to teach a class in a Bible school in Australia and to speak before large crowds. He allowed me to travel with and be part of a worldwide ministry. When I questioned His power, He showed it to me by healing me. When I wanted understanding in His Word, He sent His Holy Spirit to reveal what His Word meant. When I questioned the gifts of the Holy Spirit, He gave me gifts. When I did not understand how much He loved me, He let a trial come into my life.

The way I see it, if you want the rainbow, you got to put up with the rain. ~Dolly Parton

God Makes All Things New (or Being Born Again)

We often realize how much God loves us in the the valleys more than we do on the mountain tops. More revelation comes in the valleys than on the mountaintops. God's plan for us goes far beyond salvation. It is like having a natural child and not teaching him or her anything except how to birth other babies. In the natural we can see how ludicrous that would be. They would be growing older but not growing up.

When I was born again I submitted myself to God with all I had as a baby. As I started to grow, I continued to submit myself to God as my final teacher. I say that because I was exposed to many passing teachings and movements. I tested all of those teachings in the light of the Word under the revelation of the Holy Spirit for conformation or rejection. He was always faithful to tell me which way to go. I was exposed to many teachings such as the faith movement, the discipleship movement, the name it and claim it movement and the Y2K movement.

I was also exposed to the Baptism in the Holy Spirit and the Pentecostal/Charismatic movement. I did the same testing by subjecting all the claims to the standard of the Word. I soon realized that these last movements were in the Word of God and had started back at the birthday of the Church. This caused me to check further and to wonder why they were showing up in the 19th and 20th century and where had they gone since the first century and why. That question has bothered me for many years because I was a bit naïve and did not understand how anyone could reject such a wonderful gift from God. However, God was patient and helped me deal with it personally over the years.

Baptism in the Holy Spirit

I personally sought the Baptism in the Holy Spirit as a second work after salvation (See Acts 19: 1-7). This, along with many other Scriptures, caused me to ask Jesus for the Baptism in the Holy Spirit (See Luke11: 11-13). A pastor friend laid hands on me and I began to speak in tongues. It was not a prophetic message needing an interpretation, it was a sign (evidence) of my Baptism in the Spirit. That was forty-four years ago. When I was born again my life changed dramatically, but this baptism in the Spirit was a disruptive change, as it was for the Apostles on the Day of Pentecost. They had Jesus, but they were in fear of the Romans and the Jews and they were hiding.

When they received the Baptism they received a power that they did not have the day before. Before they received the Spirit, they were hiding, afraid of everyone and everything. As Disciples of Jesus, they were afraid they were next to go to the cross. Then when they where filled with the Holy Spirit they were not afraid anymore. They began to preach about Jesus without fear and with boldness, thus the Church was born.

I have experienced the power to pray in the Spirit and to teach and preach in the Spirit. We call it an anointing in the Holy Spirit. It isn't natural, it is supernatural. It is help to do what God wants to do through you or I. Jesus said that He was sending another comforter to us. Jesus was a comforter and now He was sending the Holy Spirit. Jesus said that the Holy Spirit would hear from Him and tell us what He heard (See John15: 26). Why would anyone ever reject this offer from the author of the Bible itself?

My life in the Lord in these last forty-five years has been an exciting time to say the least. Jesus has called me His friend. He has said that he wants me to love Him with all my heart, soul and mind (See Matt. 22: 36-38, Deut. 6: 5). No one taught me how to do this even though Jesus started this command by saying, "You shall love the Lord your God."

The Lord had to teach me how to love Him with all my heart and soul and mind and strength. He started with telling me that I had to ask for this intimate relationship with Him, just as we must ask for salvation. Then He said I had to pray without ceasing. That has been a challenge because even without an agenda or laundry list of requests to receive from God, I still needed to learn to pray without asking for something. Since prayer is communication, I had to learn to listen instead of only talking, to listen to God's small voice as He whispers to me or speaks to my heart. He said I must worship Him with abandon as David did so He taught me how to worship Him without saying a word or singing a word. He also said He wanted me to be free to worship in all manner, to sing, dance, jump, shake, with hands raised or not raised and anything else that made sense or didn't make sense, like King David with clothes or without.

I had to learn how to trust Him which was one of the hardest things I have ever done and it did not happen quickly but over time, a little at a time. I learned that I had to go through trials if I was going to mature as a Christian, if I was going to build character and learn to trust Him (See James1: 1-18 & 1st Peter 4: 12-17). Other people look at us Christians whether we're in a trial or being blessed, and they want to see how we handle trouble in our life or how we handle blessing or wealth. I trusted God for a little and then He gave me more to trust Him with and I don't mean that He always gave me more blessing. I didn't need to trust much in times of blessings. I don't want anyone reading this to think that I have arrived because I have not. I have a lot of life to go and each day is a day of doing and failing and doing and learning. I never studied

Greek or Hebrew to read the Bible but I read the Bible in the Holy Spirit and the revelation He gives. After all, He wrote the Bible and He surely knows how to explain what I need to know.

I could tell many stories of how Jesus spoke to me in so many ways, but there is no time to tell them all. I will relate one story. One morning while driving to work Jesus spoke to me concerning me trusting Him and not on my own resources. That morning my wife, Judy, mentioned to me that our refrigerator was not working. I told her to call the warranty people. She said that we might need to pay a deductible fee of $100. I said fine and drove off to work. A short time later the Lord spoke to me and said, "It's interesting that you are not concerned about your refrigerator because you have a warranty and you have the $100 in your bank account. What if I take away your resources, will you trust me then?" I have been doing my best trying to trust God in all things, not only issues regarding resources, but also all the issues of life, God, family, work, church and relationships.

Someone might wonder why I have written this testimony of sorts. Well, it occurred to me in my ongoing quest for why anyone would not accept the Holy Spirit in all His fullness. Then I wondered how and where I would be if I had gone to Bible school or seminary. I thought I might have become a professional preacher or teacher. I soon realized that what could have happened is that I would have gained an agenda. I would now be a product of the denomination that owned or ran the school or seminary that I attended. I would have been indoctrinated with their "religion", their biases and their thinking on many issues formed many years ago. Their doctrines, traditions and beliefs would have formed my thinking. They would have taught and retaught until I became so entrenched in their philosophy and doctrine that even if it was heresy no one could change me, not even Jesus Himself. Then I would have become a product of that thinking.

I would not have believed that the Holy Spirit is for our day and age. I would have passed off the miracles as fakes as well as those who moved in them. I would no longer hear the Holy Spirit beyond the need for Jesus to save me. I would not read any Bible translations except the King James Version in many cases. Depending on the school I attended, I also would be writing off over 700 million of my brothers and sisters as being out of the mainstream, when in fact the opposite is the case.

I believe that these schools have produced the Pharisees of today. They are the very people of Jesus' day who would not even recognize Him and would not change anything that conflicted with their religious doctrines and traditions. Their traditions are more important to them than God Himself. I believe that God dislikes this form of Christianity. He did not like it in His days walking the Earth. He preached against it then and I don't believe He likes it now. Anything that takes our focus away from the full purposes of God and focuses on a form of godliness, but denies His power is not God (See 2 Tim3: 5).

When I would have graduated from one of these schools or seminaries, I would have followed him. I would do everything he did and I would emulate him in every way. If you are thinking that I mean Jesus Christ, you are wrong. I would be following and doing everything the leading pastor in my denomination was doing, the one who has the largest church. After all, how can Jesus compete with the potential of drawing 10 or 20 thousand people to my church? It's so easy to think that with that many people, I am doing the will of God.

As one of those graduates I would be supporting the most ineffective missionaries and evangelists in the Body of Christ. I would have missed hearing the voice of God in a prophetic word because I would have been taught that prophecy is really preaching or teaching. I would forsake real teaching for an evangelistic service each Sunday. I would experience "no change equals no change." I would remain the same nominal Christian I was after I received the Lord. I would have missed Matthew 22: 36 in favor of verse 39. I would also follow my brethren and enter into a competition to build the largest church with the most staff and programs and the most volunteers working hard until Jesus comes back. When it is all said and done, I would have to escape this form of Christianity so I could find Jesus again.

I recently heard a preacher say that he did not want to come to California to take a church because he was comfortable in another state. He said that he had a good church and that he and his family were happy and secure there. But he said that God wanted him to come to California and take this particular church. He thought that he needed to give back to God and to take a demotion and come. First of all, I don't think that coming to California is a demotion. I also don't think taking a large church with a fairly new church building with low debt and a large congregation as giving anything up for the Lord. I can talk about this because I know the church.

What if he decided to embrace the Holy Spirit in His fullness and get into the real main stream and started preaching the Pentecostal beliefs and put his profession on the line, forsaking his seminary bias and seeking the Lord for direction instead of his taught doctrinal bias? What if he started looking at the Bible through the eyes of his heart with revelation from the Holy Spirit? What if he started really believing that God is the same yesterday, today and forever? What if he stopped following the largest church building format? What if his purpose changed from purpose driven to Holy Spirit driven? What if he shook off his form of godliness and stopped denying the power? That would be giving up something for the Lord. It would be leaving all his brethren and many friends, losing much of his congregation and facing ridicule. That would be opening your hands face up and telling God, take me and use me for Your Kingdom and not my kingdom.

Long ago the Holy Spirit told me that He did not want me to listen to what other people said about what He said, but He alone wanted to tell me what He said. I understand I cannot create or change the Word of God or create doctrine. Revelatory word (Rhema) must always agree with the written word (Logos). I am not trying to be a wise guy and I am not unteachable. I have been studying the Word of God and teaching it for many years as well. I have no degrees from a Bible College or University or even a ministerial institution. However, I am ordained and have pastored. I only say this to show my lack of anything formal as it pertains to Bible knowledge. My total Biblical education consists of the school of the Spirit.

My thinking is somewhat different than most of the teachers I know. I believe that God gives all of us a different bent or as we may call it, our particular destiny. If I were to try to identify my bent, it is more to and for the Body of Christ as it affects the Church. However, along with it God has given me insights possibly unique to me. I have been able to put much of what I have learned on paper for the edification of the body of believers. I think what I am trying to say is that I have learned things from the Holy Spirit and have walked in those things for many years without reprimand from God. I am not saying that I am perfect, far from it. However, I am teachable. I am able to listen to others' opinions without getting angry just because someone disagrees with me. I also do not follow every wind of doctrine.

I have a sincere desire to understand the answers to my questions about specific scriptures. I do not want to hear statements that declare another answer, but rather a detailed explanation using other scriptures that could expose the truth. I do not neccesarily want to hear from someone from the 3rd, 4th or 15th century. We have enough revelation from God today and many honest Bible scholars can speak to some of these issues.

I believe these issues are key to much of what I believe and to what many others should consider. We cannot be told that there is only one way to find salvation and then hear from someone that there is another way, or that the way we have believed in and trusted in can be lost through sin. Romans 8: 1 is clear.

Chapter Three

The Power of God Comes With a Price

This observation is not specific to any church or any one person or group in particular. It is just a general spiritual observation of the Church today as I see it and feel that the Holy Spirit has shown me. I am not saying that this is the Word of the Lord. I am saying that as I look at the condition of the Church locally, I have felt the Lord confirming to me that my observations are correct. I stand open to correction at anytime by elders that would offer a differing view.

The Church may not enter the realm of the Spirit at all, or it may stay on the fringe of the working of the Spirit or it may go fully into seeking the power and manifestations of the Spirit. However, there are consequences with each choice. Only the church leadership can make the choice. Individual believers can also make their own choice, as I have done.

If we stay out of the realm of the Spirit, we will remain safe from criticism from our brothers and sisters who are devoid of any movement of the Spirit of God beyond His work in salvation. Another expanded and accepted version of this is the "talk about but don't allow" the Spirit to work as some seeker friendly churches do for the purpose of attracting anyone who would be fooled by this pretense. They are not really seeking the works of the Holy Spirit, and truthfully, they are not willing to let Him move freely. I have seen this formula all over Orange County, California where I reside. God is not fooled by this ploy. It reminds me of a restaurant that offers Mexican food, Italian food and any other ethnic food to attract all customers. Its good for a restaurant to do but does not work in a church.

If a church seeks the evidence of His presence in its meetings with real worship, it could invite criticism from people even in its own fellowship who do not understand and are afraid. They are afraid of anything new. They do not understand why you want to change what they have been doing for years. This lack of belief hinders the freedom of the Holy Spirit to move in corporate meetings, and it hinders God's ability to do miraculous acts in our midst. It also fits in a phrase I use a lot "no change equals no change."

The Pharisees hated Jesus because He was changing the established system. They questioned why He would want to change everything and threaten their authority, their position, their hierarchy and cause them to get out of their comfort zone. He exposed their sin. When the Holy Spirit comes He exposes our sin and makes sinners uncomfortable.

That's part of His job. John 16: 8 (NKJV), "And when He has come, He will convict the world of sin, and of righteousness, and of judgment." Some people are taught that when they are saved they have all the Holy Spirit they can get and this attitude and lack of belief keeps it that way. Leadership perpetuates this by using the authority that they have to frustrate the goal of allowing the church to become a Spirit filled church. This has caused splits in fellowships over the years.

"Do not be hasty in the laying of hands, and do not share in the sins of others. Keep yourself pure." When the local church doesn't follow 1 Tim. 5:22 and elects elders that are not mature or do not believe in the entire Bible and do not believe that it is relevant for today, it will be impossible to move in the Spirit. The Scripture that says do not be unequally yoked with unbelievers applies here as well. There will be confusion, a lack of unity and an environment in which the Holy Spirit is unlikely to move. 2 Corinthians 6:14 (NKJV), "Do not be unequally yoked with unbelievers." Do not make mismatched alliances with them or come under a different yoke with them, inconsistent with your faith. As an aside I want to say we may never have a church in total unity. When the Apostles were in the upper room waiting on the Holy Spirit, "They were in one accord" and The Holy Spirit fell on them with power." Matthew 9: 23-26 (NIV), "When Jesus entered the synagogue leader's house and saw the noisy crowd and people playing pipes, he said, 'Go away. The girl is not dead but asleep.' But they laughed at him. After the crowd had been put outside, he went in and took the girl by the hand, and she got up. News of this spread throughout that region." I believe the key word was "go away" because they had no faith or belief. I have seen this sort of lack today.

One caution here , Isaiah 53:4-5 (NKJV)says, ". . . By His stripes we are healed." I believe that this scripture says that healing is the inheritance of the believer. Now that Jesus has resurrected, faith for personal healing may not be required for the believer. However, to move a mountain will require faith. After saying both Statements, God is still in control. I also do not believe that if you have 4 people each with 25% faith for healing this assures success. I have been in prayer meetings where that was present, but God is still sovereign. I have been requested to attend a meeting for a Christian friend's daughter for prayer and the requirement was please bring someone who believes in healing. His words were "that can pray." His daughter was healed. God is still sovereign.

I spontaneously prayed for an employee of mine who had been diagnosed with 29 tumors on his lungs. I called him into my boardroom and shut the door. I had no faith to heal cancer at all. I did not touch him, I just put my hands in front of him and said to Jesus, "You're God and I am not." The Lord slammed him against the wall, steam came out of his body and he was healed. That was 6 years ago and he is still healed. God is sovereign. Seventy percent of the Bible consists of radical visitations, trances, dreams, visions, signs, wonders, angelic encounters and supernatural accounts! We need to go back to the Bible. If God is not a respecter of persons, could it be that God might want to radically meet with you? This is a word from Jill Austin who was a recognized prophetess and international speaker. Jill is with the Lord now.

Teaching is necessary today on Biblical proof that the Holy Spirit is still on the Earth and working in the lives of

Christians. We sometimes think that our brothers and sisters are where we are in the things of the Spirit, but they may not be. We think because they are hard workers in the church, that they are mature in such things. No, they are just hard workers. If they are born again in a strict evangelical environment, their paradigm needs to change regarding the Holy Spirit. If the goal is to have a Spirit-filled church, these people should not be put into positions of authority.

On a personal note of explanation, my definition of Evangelical may be different than yours, but since this is "My Journey" this is my definition. I consider all non-charismatic churches Baptist style churches. The dictionary defines Evangelical as Protestant Christianity emphasizing the authority of the Bible, personal conversion, and the doctrine of salvation by faith in the Atonement. I realize there are other denominations that follow the Baptist style of beliefs. I know why the dictionary doesn't mention the Baptism in the Holy Spirit in this definition! It is because Evangelical doctrine does not believe in it. Their term is dispensationalist or cessationist belief.

I prefer teaching to preaching. Preaching means to declare, to pronounce or to announce. To teach means to train and instruct for change. Preaching doesn't change people. It gives information and convicts. Teaching gives understanding and people will not change until they understand. You cannot grow until you have understanding. That's why Jesus taught the Disciples and He never preached to the Disciples. Jesus taught the Disciples Kingdom principles but He announced the Kingdom to the multitudes. I have entreated the Lord to show me why the Holy Spirit does not respond here in America as I have seen Him do in other places. I know we understand how the Spirit works today and we are sincere in asking for God to move in a mighty way. Why doesn't He move? Is it because of unbelief? If God does move in a powerful and miraculous way among people who do not believe that it is possible then a decision must be made. The status quo is a powerful thing. The Pharisees operated in it. It is a large tool for the devil to block the power of God.

Sometimes rejection is the price that comes with an "I surrender all" seeking of the Holy Spirit and allowing the gifts to operate. People who have only heard about speaking in tongues do not understand anything about it because they have only heard about it from people who know nothing about it and are trying to protect their doctrine. No one seems to understand Word of Knowledge or Word of Wisdom or how they function, or that there are nine gifts of the Holy Spirit set in the body for the building up of the Body.

The gifts mentioned in Romans 12: 4-8 (NKJV) have always confused non-charismatic people. "For as we have many members in one body, but all the members do not have the same function, so we, being many, are one body in Christ, and individually members of one another. Having then gifts differing according to the grace that is given to us, let us use them: if prophecy, let us prophesy in proportion to our faith; or ministry, let us use it in our ministering; he who teaches, in teaching; he who exhorts, in exhortation; he who gives, with liberality; he who leads, with diligence; he who shows mercy, with cheerfulness."

The nine gifts of the Spirit are very specific: I Cor. 12:7-11 7(NKJV), "But the manifestation of the Spirit is given to each one for the profit of all: for to one is given the word of wisdom through the Spirit, to another the word of knowledge through the same Spirit, to another faith by the same Spirit, to another gifts of healings by the same Spirit, to another the working of miracles, to another prophecy, to another discerning of spirits, to another different kinds of tongues, to another the interpretation of tongues. But one and the same Spirit works all these things, distributing to each one individually as He wills."

People will automatically think that if they are not Spirit filled they will be thought of as second-class Christians. Love, prayer and teaching are needed. God put the love chapter between the two chapters on the gifts. People can't love what they fear, they can't know what they haven't been taught and all must be explained in love. God will meet us every step of the way. As our faith increases, He will prove and reward our faith. However, we must leave room for God to move sovereignly in whatever manner He wishes as He does in many meetings.

I once was asked to participate in praying for a friend who was speaking at a Full Gospel Businessmen meeting at a restaurant. As we gathered in the kitchen and laid hands on my friend to pray, all the brothers began to speak in tongues (their prayer language, no interpretation required). I was a little embarrassed because the kitchen was full of waiters and cooks and I thought that was not a good thing to do. What a surprise I got when the Holy Spirit fell on all of us as we prayed in tongues in front of all these non-believers. My comment to the Lord was "You must like this." God is Sovereign.

People tend to attribute more power to the devil than to Jesus Himself. They feel comfortable with that. Its almost like God is supposed to stay in Heaven, but the devil may roam around the Earth doing black magic. Methodical Biblical teaching where people can ask any question they want will help dispel any erroneous teaching from non-Spirit filled teachers. This type of teaching will dispel the confusion about tongues and other gifts. The reasons why Pentecostals believe that the Baptism in the Holy Spirit or the infilling is considered a second work can be discussed. It can be explained that it is not important what we call it one-way or the other. Open discussion on areas of confusion will dispel rumors and half-truths taught by people who have never experienced the Baptism in the Holy Spirit (See Acts19: 1-7).

Prior to the Azusa Street revival in 1906, Frank Bartleman, a holiness evangelist was so excited about the revival in Wales, that he wrote Evan Roberts to get instructions on how to experience a move of God in Los Angeles. Roberts wrote back, "Congregate the people who are willing to make a total surrender. Pray and wait. Believe God's promises. Hold daily meetings. May God bless you is my earnest prayer."

When the Azusa Street visitation/revival took place in 1906, it started the modern-day Pentecostal movement. It was not until that revival however, that Pentecostalism achieved worldwide attention. An African-American preacher, William Joseph Seymour, started the Azusa Street Revival in Los Angeles. He learned about the baptism with tongues following, and he started the historic meeting in April 1906 in a Black

Holiness Church, a former African Methodist Episcopal church building located at 312 Azusa Street in downtown Los Angeles, CA. The Holy Spirit visited them and the rest is history.

The Azusa Street Apostolic Faith Mission conducted three services a day, seven days a week, with thousands of people seeking the Baptism in the Holy Spirit received the baptism with tongues following. Even though segregation existed in the United States, Blacks and Whites worshiped together under a Black pastor. The color line was washed away in the Blood of Jesus in Los Angeles.

At Azusa Street, besides the baptism with the accompanying manifestation of tongues, there was joy, praise and worship to the Lord and service to each other. The worship and praise included shouting and dancing. This mixture of tongues and other gifts combined with Black music and worship styles creating a new and indigenous form of Pentecostalism that was to prove extremely attractive to people, both in America and around the world. From Azusa Street, Pentecostalism spread rapidly around the world and begun its advance toward becoming a major force in Christendom. It has been said that at that time the Azusa Street address was more famous than any other address in America or Europe.

Those brothers had nowhere to go for guidance but the Bible. They established a Spirit filled movement that has lasted more than 100 years and is still going strong today. The Spirit filled movement has produced the most effective missionaries, evangelists and church movements in Christendom. When the Catholic Charismatic Renewal started in 1967 at Duquesne

University, it started with a few Catholic Christians having a prayer meeting. They began to experience the same things that the Apostles at Pentecost and the Christians at Azusa Street experienced. They, however, were able to call for guidance from the Pentecostals as well as the Word of God. In fact, they called on David DuPlessis known as Mr. Pentecost for advice on their new experience. The partnership was terrific and the Catholic movement continues today worldwide.

My wife and I got involved in 1976 in what was considered its heyday. We stayed involved in teaching their prayer groups in the San Gabriel Valley California for about 3 years. By 1993 it touched the lives of over 70 million Catholics in over 120 nations. Episcopal Pastor Dennis Bennett, one of the early Protestant leaders in the Charismatic renewal of the late sixties and early seventies with his book "9 O'Clock in the Morning", is credited with starting the Protestant Charismatic renewal in Van Nuys, California. Anyone wanting to duplicate the Pentecostal experience will find many books on the subject. Pastor Jack Hayford is head of the Foursquare Denomination, pastor of Church on the Way in Van Nuys and president of The King's University, has written many. Jack Deere, a former Baptist theologian, who taught opposition to the Pentecostal and Charismatic movement until he realized that his position was wrong, has written some very scholarly works as well.

There are many great writers, however, my personal favorite is Jack Hayford. He is recognized for his balance in preaching the Word and avoiding extremes while not diluting or compromising the truth. His manner is one of graciously revealing the heart of God. He is Biblically sound and accepted by his Pentecostal as well as non-Pentecostal peers. He is a most prolific writer on this subject and others, having written over 36 books. Jack's books are available on Amazon and Church on the Way's website. I have about 10 of Jack's books on many issues on this subject.

I feel that teaching on this subject will bring people along and lead them to a new paradigm of thinking on the Holy Spirit. Again, I believe we need to leave room for the Holy Spirit to move sovereignly on these individuals. As people get correct instruction on the kind of praise and worship that the Scriptures teach, they will respond. We have seen this already in teaching, such as Psalm 100, entering His gates with thanksgiving and into His courts with praise. We also need teaching on how King David worshipped God and what God thought of his worship. I recently saw worship in South Africa on a video. I saw dancing before the Lord and I saw African Christians dancing. I thought that they would never do that in our fellowships in America, and if they did most of the people would not understand and leave. Dancing can be done as I saw in the video with a lot of laughing and joy. It can also be quiet and respectful, something like you might expect to do before a King. I might add that in the church my wife and I attend, led by the Lord, you may worship anyway you like.

Someone asked me why I raise my hands during worship. My answer is that I never raise my hands during worship unless I can't keep them down. Someone also told me that they wanted to speak in tongues (a prayer language), but I don't see them entering in worship with hands raised or with any other expression of worship beyond sitting on their hands. My answer was you will never be able to praise and worship in a new language if you can't worship in your native tongue (my opinion). I also don't mean to make a religion out of anything including raising hands. Just as we seek out books and authors to learn from their experiences, anyone involved in musical worship teams must humble themselves and seek Holy Spirit type worshipers in fellowships that have had experience in this type of worship for years. Some music chases away demoniac spirits and activity (1 Samuel 16:23) and some music invites the Holy Spirit into our meetings.

We need to change the thinking that we are entertaining the people sitting in front of the worship team when we are really worshipping God. These are just habits formed over time in churches that have not taught their people that the music and singing in the church is not entertainment, should not be performances, but should be praise and worship directed to God. Worship teams with their music, words and instruments are supposed to help lead us into deeper praise and worship, not entertain us. Teaching and instruction in this area will help the Body of Christ here. Our audience is an audience of one, God Himself.

Churches and their people sometimes fall into a Kiwanis Club mode. The Kiwanis have meetings, they help the poor, they have civic programs and have social times together. Some churches and their leadership seem to forget that the Church belongs to Jesus and He is the only one they should be worshipping with all their activities. The longer this wrong activity goes on, the harder it is to change and enter into a mode of real worship and praise to God. This is a problem especially if they have an issue with the Holy Spirit because He is someone they are afraid of. They give Him lip service but they feel more comfortable if He is not mentioned at all.

In conclusion, an interest in the Holy Spirit is definitely for people who want to move on with the Lord. As Evan Roberts said, "People who are willing to surrender all." If this is not a person's interest or passion, we may not be able to get them to go deeper into the things of the Spirit. Some people go to church for social reasons, some because they think it is an acceptable thing to do in a civilized society and some love God, but only on their terms and some because their spouse drags them. If it gets too spiritual they will bolt and run to a more comfortable church, to a seeker friendly church. I believe seeker friendly means don't do anything if it disturbs or offends anyone or if it stops them from giving or, sin of all sins, causes them to leave and go to another church. When we ask God to come down in power in our midst, we should be prepared to see people leave and take their checkbooks with them. Once we have come to the place that we can accept the loss of people and income, and can trust the Lord for all, I believe He will come into the life of our church. He will then be free to bless and multiply.

A friend of mine wanted to experience the move of the Holy Spirit like he had been hearing about so he attended a fully charismatic church meeting. As prepared as he was, he was not able to handle what he saw. He told me he experienced the power of God and the manifestations of the Spirit. He also saw the manifestations of the flesh. Control is key to order. The oversight of a meeting or the pastor must take control. If it's the flesh it must be pastored and told that what was happening was not the Spirit and must stop. I have seen this done and it works very well. If it's the devil it can be cast out and put under control. I have done this myself and it works well. If it's the Spirit of God, He is free to do anything He wants to do. The key in this case reminds me of an old saying, "don't throw out the baby with the bath water."

So teach, pray, wait on the Lord and listen for direction and expect to be persecuted personally and corporately, to be called weird and a kook who believes in all kinds of things, even things you don't believe in and be ready to trust the Lord with your reputation and everything else, then you are ready for a visitation from God. Jeremiah 29:13 (HCSB), "You will seek Me and find Me when you search for Me with all your heart."

Chapter Four

A Message to the American Churches

The Church has in many ways abdicated its responsibility as a parent to new believers as well as the shepherd of old believers. The pastors are so interested in building their kingdoms that they are even remiss in telling their members that they must vote and not shirk from their civic duty . They will not talk about voting and they will not talk about political issues which are not really political, but issues of sin and morality. They are afraid of reprisal by losing their tax-exempt status.

Some say that the blood of the martyrs is the seed of the Church. If that's true, then we have no seed in the American church. I pray that the Lord doesn't send the same persecution that the Church has in Egypt or China to reseed the American church. I am so amazed that the Christians in China and other oppressed countries are willing and not afraid to give up their lives for the Gospel, while the American churches are afraid to risk their tax-exempt status . The Church of Jesus Christ was born in the fire of affliction and persecution, but the American church has become lukewarm. The Lord had much to say about a lukewarm church (See Revelation 3: 16 and and Zechariah 10: 3).

The seeker friendly phrase used in the American church today has a lot to do with money. It is used as an excuse to keep people comfortable so they won't leave and take their checkbooks with them. They say that the phrase is an evangelistic tool to win souls and to build the Kingdom, but it's not the Kingdom of God, it's the kingdom of man. I wonder how much money would come into the Church if the government would not allow a tax write-off? I fear that the pastors believe, not much. There must be some correlation between commitment and maturity. This lack falls at the feet of the pastors and teachers in the American church. I once taught my Bible study that we should not be hindered in our giving to the Lord's work if we could not receive a tax write-off. The Lord quickly made me put my money where my mouth was, and for a period of time He would not allow me to give money and take a tax write-off.

The Church should mature the body in their care to be so committed that they are willing to give without a return from the government. If we only give because the government blesses us with a tax write-off and we do not teach the Body of Christ what to believe, what is sin, what is immoral and we do not tell them to apply that Christian ethic and vote, then there will be a day when the Church's worst fears will come upon it. We will have a government with leaders that are opposed to anything Christian and we will be forced into accepting sin into our churches as political correctness and law directs. Soon we will need to meet underground as the Chinese Christians do. Then the Church and the Body of Christ will grow and mature. I had written this a few years ago and now it has come to pass before our very eyes. We are commanded to pray for our leaders, but wouldn't it be easier to pray for our leaders when they believe what we believe, rather than for a leader who is opposed to everything we believe? Once laws and rules like abortion become the law of the land it is more difficult to change than before it became the law. Can any blame be put at the feet of the American church for not opposing many of the laws now in effect? If so, then it better get prepared because it hasn't seen anything yet (See Zech. 10:3). Acts 14: 22 states that through many tribulations we must enter the Kingdom of God. This is because troubles always lead us to seek the Lord because He is the solution to every human problem. A friend said to me that in the same way, the Great Tribulation would be the doorway through which the whole world enters the Kingdom. The Great Tribulation is basically the result of mankind trying to run the world without God.

Name Above All Names Now Deemed Offensive

Navy Chaplain's Corps. Lt. Gordon Klingenschmitt, the devout Protestant chaplain who defied an order not to "pray in Jesus' name" because it might offend non-believers and those of other faiths, has gotten the boot. He is being kicked out of the Navy after almost sixteen years of service with no pension. His career has been destroyed. It's no secret that many liberals and atheists don't want to see or hear anything Christian. The mere mention of Jesus' name raises questions that atheists do not want answered. Below is a true message from an active duty Navy Chaplain. He states, "I'm still striving to faithfully serve as a chaplain in the U.S. Navy, appealing a court-martial verdict that will cost my family and me everything. You see, the Navy just ordered me to separate from the service by 31 January 2007. They are hoping to permanently end my career after 15.5 years of award-winning evaluations. I'm losing my pension, and my family is now being evicted from military housing, without health care benefits." Criminalization of Christianity has officially begun! The liberals and atheists will not be satisfied until America is a Jesus-free zone. Are we aiding these liberals and atheists by our inaction and our hiding behind the thin walls of a few rules that still give a little protection? Don't be fooled. Persecution awaits us all, even you and me. My advice to the American church is keep it up church, keep it up pastors, keep it up teachers. Don't teach and the government will teach for you and then the church will grow and thrive under the persecution the Church had in the first century. Or repent, pray, listen to the prophets, do what God commands in His Word, love one another, be of one accord, accept the Holy Spirit in His fullness and stop building the kingdom of man. The end of the world will come after the Gospel of the Kingdom of God is preached throughout the world (See Matt. 24: 14). We have preached the Gospel of salvation and in many cases the gospel of the kingdom of man, but not the Gospel of the Kingdom of God. All earthly kingdoms will fall before the Kingdom of God, so why build your kingdom?

The Church and Politics

It's okay pastors, don't tell your people to vote, it may

be too late anyway because it has already started. These two paragraphs below are more proof from the American Family Association (Oct 28, 2006), and it is just the beginning. Soon you will be forced to hire homosexuals as staff in your churches and agree to marry same sex persons. Be prepared to hire a homosexual to teach Sunday school or lose tax-exempt status. If your meetings are held in a public venue like a high school, they will end without compliance. Democrats have gone on the record in support of homosexual marriage. Activists pushing for legalizing of homosexual marriage say they will not stop with just homosexual marriage. They demand more. They want government and societal acceptance, approval and financial support for many kinds of relationships, including polygamy. The Democratic Party says it will help them achieve their goal. Activists say that marriage is not the only worthy form of family or relationship. The Church is under judgment. (1 Peter 4:17 NIV) I believe it is the Church and not the world. The world is already under judgment without Jesus. The scripture 2 Chronicles 7:14 states, "If My people will humble themselves. . . ," not the world. If that is true, how did we get here? Our silence on issues of sin and our lack of unity have contributed, see John 17: 23. How can any army fight an enemy when they are fighting each other over doctrine and traditions? We focus on things we want until they become idols and replace God in our lives. Sports, both the activity and watching sports on television, have taken over family time. Look at the statistics on divorce, alcoholism and drug addition. Under our watch 56 million abortions have taken place. We have left God. He judged the Hebrews for less (See Jeremiah 29:10).

Chapter Five

The Church is the Enemy of the Church:
Let's Move on to Maturity

A few days ago the Lord awakened me with a short word that I believe to be a prophetic word. The Lord said to me "The church is the enemy of the Church." His meaning was clear to me. Notice that I have a lower case c versus a capitol C. That is the essence of the word. What the Holy Spirit is saying is that the local church is the enemy of the Body of Christ. Then the next day He awakened me with the scripture below. Those words have prompted me to write this. I have sought the Holy Spirit for direction, so here it is. Hebrews 6:1-3(NLT), "So let us stop going over the basics of Christianity again and again. Let us go on instead and become mature in our understanding. Surely we don't need to start all over again with the importance of turning away from evil deeds and placing our faith in God. You don't need further instruction about baptisms, the laying on of hands, the resurrection of the dead, and eternal judgment. And so, God willing, we will move forward to further understanding."

Why do many churches not honor or obey this scripture? Why do they hold the believers hostage in the nursery? Is there some reason for this? The Catholic Church has kept their members bound by a philosophy and traditions and a set of rules held tightly by fear of damnation if broken. They call this formula the propagation of the faith. The dictionary says it means the spreading of the faith. I believe a better translation would be the continuation of the faith by fear and intimidation. It is not so much evangelistic as it is keeping their membership from straying. This works very well, as it is a mix of a lack of knowledge of the things of God and the Scriptures and the ever-present fear of excommunication for breaking of certain rules. So why does the evangelical church continue to preach the basics of the faith over and over and not teach their members to move on to maturity? I believe that they are doing it for the same reason the Catholics are doing it. They don't have a distant leader like the Pope who has supreme authority whom the Catholics both respect and fear. We chide the Catholics for almost worshiping the Pope, yet the evangelicals use the Holy Scriptures as a substitute for a supreme authority and they almost worship them. However, they are very selective according to their needs. They will just take what they want and forget that the rest is scripture. They have found that if scriptures are chosen carefully, they can make them do exactly what they want. For example, if only the evangelistic scriptures and the Great Commission are preached they will be the main focus of the church and everyone will be committed to that course. The church can forsake all else, including personal growth as well as a lack of concern for sin in the life of the believers.

Evangelism breeds evangelism because the more people that are saved the more people there are to continue to evangelize and that exposes the real reason that the local church has moved away from Hebrews 6:1-3 and Matt 22:36-38. What is that reason? It is to become bigger and bigger, to have a bigger and better facility, a larger staff and all that comes with a megachurch. They are not building the Kingdom of God. They are building the kingdom of man. This type of church is trapped into a continuing need for money. No money is wasted on the needs of the believer. Whatever the believer wants, he pays for. Every event and every meeting is an occasion to ask for money for the latest project or program. All is used for the real goal of the church. It has ceased to be God's church and has become an extension of the needs and wants of the leadership.

Some think that the local church is a democracy and they get to vote. However, you will quickly be told that it is a theocracy, but if that were the case then only God could vote. Sadly He cannot vote either. The vote goes to one or two people who really control and direct this private kingdom. At this point I want to mention the traditional denominational churches who may preach a social gospel , a heretical gospel or a politically correct gospel allowing every sort of sin and perversion to exist in their churches. These cannot even be counted in the number of churches called the Church or the Body of Christ. Who really knows who is saved and who is not saved in those churches? I don't know whether or not God counts them as the Bride or not, but I will not for this illustration. However, I realize that certain branches of some of these denominations are correctly preaching the Gospel of Jesus Christ, and in some cases these branches have split from the errant groups causing great suffering, ridicule and persecution .

I will relate a letter sent to me from a woman and her husband. She confessed to me that she and her husband were drinking each day more than they should, and could not stop. They knew the Lord wanted them to stop, but they had tried many times but could not stop. Her biggest concern was that they would lose their salvation and were very concerned they would not go to Heaven, but to Hell. Wow! I thought that divorce was the unforgivable sin. It is in the Catholic Church. Anything as basic as this that has not been dealt with in their church is the bigger sin. The first issue is not being tought regarding the security of their salvation and the second is not helping with their addiction. However, all this could have been eliminated if the church would not try to manage sin after the fact but give proper teaching to prevent sin. It is much more difficult to cure alcoholism with an AA group than to prevent it in the first place. I like divorce recovery programs, but the same advice applies. The answer falls at the feet of the pastor/ shepherds of the local churches. The Lord will hold them responsible. Zec.10: 3, "My anger burns against the shepherds." The phrase shepherd care has been reversed to mean the sheep take care of the shepherd. All the needs of the church are put on the back of the believer, even the support of missionaries. Please do not think I am against evangelism because I am not. However, I am opposed to evangelism being used as a tool to build a large church with no care for the believers other than to use them. I am not opposed to parents having many children. But just as I would not like children to be birthed for an ulterior motive such as exploitation as is done in some countries, I feel that the new believer is being birthed for exploitation and not for the benefits of being a child of God. They are not taught the full Gospel and there is no progression to maturity. I understand this is a bit general as some are better than I am projecting here and not all Christian churches fall into this group I am describing.

I just read where a Spirit-filled evangelist had a meeting in Africa and had 1.2million people attend the meetings with 400,000 Africans giving their lives to the Lord. I know that there are some thousands of indigenous Christian churches in Africa and India to care for many new believers, as we have sent missionaries there with the power of God. I believe that Jesus and the Holy Spirit will care for much of this flock as well. If the new believers in our churches are taught that God has a plan for their lives and it includes more than fire insurance and a job at the local church, they would desire a relationship more than a series of church programs that feed the desire of the leadership.

God wants His kids to be different than the world's kids. He wants them to know that He has a way for them to lead a better life, to have a happy marriage and that He will not forsake them in times of trouble. They must be taught that the Body of Christ, the Church, was born for the storms, the storms that we believers find ourselves in most of the time. This is kept from the believer. When was the last time we heard a sermon on that subject? God wants new believers. It's His greatest desire, after all, He died for them, but He doesn't want them for the reason many churches want them. He did not die for people just to gain workers for His Church or Kingdom. He has a true and wonderful motive. In Mathew 22:36 Jesus says that the Greatest Commandment a believer has and must follow is to love the Lord his God with all his heart and soul and mind. What does God want the Church to look like? Well, first Jesus said that His house would be called a house of prayer, but we modern day Pharisees have done what the Pharisees of old did, we have made it a den of thieves.

There are two churches; the local church and the Body of Christ, the Bride of Christ or the Church. Jesus said that He would return for His Bride and that she would be without spot or wrinkle. Jesus left this job to certain offices in the body which are pastor, teacher, evangelist, prophet and apostle. The local church should be a house of prayer and the expression of these offices, sometimes known as the five-fold ministry.

If done correctly the evangelist will bring in the new souls, the pastor/shepherd will be responsible to care for the new and older believers, the teacher will be responsible for their maturity and the prophet will hear from Jesus through the Holy Spirit and guide and direct the local church. Prophets proclaim the word of the Lord and that could be considered teaching as well. The apostle is one sent with a special message so he oversees the church to determine that it is not in error and acts as an emissary of the Lord. Ephesians 4:11-13 (NIV), "So Christ himself gave the apostles, the prophets, the evangelists, the pastors and teachers, to equip his people for works of service, so that the body of Christ may be built up until we all reach unity in the faith and in the knowledge of the Son of God and become mature, attaining to the whole measure of the fullness of Christ."

I have a question. In Ephesians 4 God says that He is sending the five-fold ministry to the Church. If we do not have a specific pattern for the Church like the ones that we all attend, then it would seem that we should appropriate those offices as needed. The best definition of church that I like is a a body of believers. The next time you are tempted to pass ministry responsibility to your pastor, remember what Ephesians 4 says. After all, there are no part-time Christians in His Kingdom. We may get our income from secular jobs, but our ministry as Christians is full-time. There are obviously requirements to become a pastor, teacher, prophet and apostle. However, we are all considered full time evangelists. How many are teaching the people in the church you attend about these offices? I want to add that it is not about titles, it is about the Body of Christ being built up until we all reach unity in the faith in the knowledge of the Son of God and become mature, attaining to the whole measure of the fullness of Christ.(Eph 4:11- 16) .

The Bride is not without spot. She is not much better than the world she lives in. What would be the point for Jesus to come for a bride that was not transformed in His image and looked very much like the rest of the unregenerated world? What would Christ's death on the Cross have accomplished? When I say without spot or wrinkle I mean a believer who has the mind of Christ and has taken the full advantage of the life God has made available for us, a person who images Christ. The Bride is the large "C." The small "c" is the local church. I have found no model in the scriptures for the local church, at least not the model we are seeing across our country. The Book of Acts is the birthday of the Church and from that point on the leaders have been making their own version of what the Church should be and look like. Jesus never changed what He wants His Church to look like. The Scriptures are full of what the individual believer who is a microcosm of the Church should look like. Jesus still has compassion for His people who are not being shepherded, but are being exploited for other agendas. He had no interest in buildings and property and various programs put in place by the leadership of the local church. His interest was and is people and their spiritual and physical health. He wants a closer relationship with His people, closer than is typically provided by the North American church. We have been turned into workers for the moneychanger's tables. To repeat myself, Jesus did not like them in His day and I don't believe He likes them now. Jesus turned over the moneychanger's tables and said in Matthew 21:13 (NKJV), "My house shall be called a house of prayer, but you have made it a den of thieves. " I believe the two statements Jesus made that day are relevant to each other. In fact, becoming a house of prayer is very important because if we follow that directive, the other will disappear. Prayer is communication with God and communication is a two-way street. If we listen as well as talk, God will tell us what He wants us to know and do. Why were the Pharisees so opposed to Jesus? I believe it was because He threatened their authority and agenda. I believe that situation exists today in the local church. If the church submitted to Jesus and His agenda He may ask them to change a few things that have become idols. The church would say it is for God we do these things. I can hear the moneychangers saying the same thing.

I don't think that Jesus is interested in whether we did a good job working in the parking lot, information booth or helped in the nursery, if we have not found a way to love our wives, raise our kids in the nurture and admonition of the Lord, or overcome our problem of sin in our lives. I am not talking about perfection, I am talking about a close and intimate walk with God, looking to Him for our needs, and I don't just mean our laundry list of needs. I am referring to the problem of committing the same sin over and over again, like loosing our temper time and time again. The scripture in Revelation says to all of the churches "to them who overcome will be given." We all want to be overcomers, but we don't want to overcome anything. We want to have it done for us without any pain from us. Those who do not overcome will not inherit the promises of God, as James says in James 1:12 (NIV).

We don't often hear to count it all joy when we encounter various trials. It seems that it is not politically correct, but it is sound Biblical truth. If we run every time we encounter opposition we will never mature as the scripture says in James 1:4, "Let perseverance finish its work." Real soldiers run toward the battle not away from it. Whenever we receive resistance when we are trying get close to God, we can be sure it is from the enemy of our soul. He does not want us to receive or understand the purposes of God for our life. James 4:7-8 (ESV), " Submit therefore to God. Resist the devil and he will flee from you. Draw near to God and He will draw near to you." It is the responsibility of the individual believer to do what he can to attain maturity. If your church does not teach you how to have a closer relationship with God you must seek ministry outside your local church. God has raised up extra Church ministries for this reason. It is easier to have a religion than a relationship. This is true even for a church. Programs are easier and more profitable for the church than teaching on think it all joy when you have trials, but if they do not teach this, the result is a stagnated Christian walk. You will never know the real power, joy and provision available to you as a child of God if you remain immature. This may be an oversimplification, but accurate nonethless .

Growing Old Instead of Growing Up

It is easier to grow old in the pew than grow up. The scripture says, "My people perish for the lack of knowledge" (Hosea 4:6). I believe that the Lord's purpose for the Church has been frustrated. The Church at best looks more like a service club and at worst, the unregenerate world. Because the Church in America is mostly made up of local churches, as the local churches go so goes the Body of Christ. If a vast majority of the believers in the local church do not understand the Scriptures, then the Body of Christ will not understand how to use the Scriptures for life's issues. If the vast majority of the pew sitters may not really be saved then the Church is in serious trouble, and we have been lying to God and the world. Saying a prayer does not mean you have committed your life to Christ. Jesus is not Santa Claus. He is the God of the universe and He was serious about going to the Cross and giving up His rights to forgive us of our sins and teach us how to have His mind. He died to teach us a new way to live, not just on Sunday, but all week long. Philippians 2: 6 (NIV), "Who, being in very nature [a] God, did not consider equality with God something to be used to his own advantage; . . ." The shepherds of these local churches have not even told its sheep that there is an enemy, the devil, and that he has a plan for their lives that is not for their good. Hardly anyone knows that our warfare is not carnal, but spiritual. Not many know we have weapons of war that are not guns and knives, or how to use them. I'm copying Ephesians 6 because it is what I have been talking about. Ephesians 6:10 (NIV), "Finally, be strong in the Lord and in his mighty power. Put on the full armor of God so that you can take your stand against the devil's schemes. For our struggle is not against flesh and blood, but against the rulers, against the authorities, against the powers of this dark world and against the spiritual forces of evil in the heavenly realms. Therefore put on the full armor of God, so that when the day of evil comes, you may be able to stand your ground, and after you have done everything, to stand. Stand firm then, with the belt of truth buckled around your waist, with the breastplate of righteousness in place, and with your feet fitted with the readiness that comes from the gospel of peace. In addition to all this, take up the shield of faith, with which you can extinguish all the flaming arrows of the evil one. Take the helmet of salvation and the sword of the Spirit, which is the word of God. And pray in the Spirit on all occasions with all kinds of prayers and requests. With this in mind, be alert and always keep on praying for all the saints. Pray also for me, that whenever I open my mouth, words may be given me so that I will fearlessly make known the mystery of the gospel, for which I am an ambassador in chains. Pray that I may declare it fearlessly, as I should."

This is not taught much if at all in the local church. It just doesn't fit the evangelical model of the seeker friendly church in America. I realize that there are churches that teach the full Gospel of God. My wife and I attend such a church . This includes the armor of God, the baptism in the Holy Spirit, healing and the other eight gifts found in 1 Cor. 12 and 1 Cor. 14. These churches don't confuse the gifts mentioned in Romans 12 because their focus is on the Holy Spirit, and not only on service gifts, which include being a cheerful giver. I am not minimizing the service gifts in any way. The church that my wife and I attend has a large commitment to feeding the poor on an everyday year round basis in our surrounding community. Our people meet the need for salvation and healing as well as food and clothing. It sounds like the Book of Acts to me. I just know that the power, revelatory and vocal gifts in 1 Corinthians 12 and 14 are totally ignored by many elements of the local church that are focused on building their church into the next megachurch. They must focus on service gifts to further their agenda. Even though there are some spiritual gifts in this group they are never encouraged, e.g. prophesying, even though the Scripture says in 1 Corinthians 14:39 (NIV), "Therefore, my brothers, be eager to prophesy, and do not forbid speaking in tongues." In the Book of Romans (NIV), chapter 12 speaks of, "We have different gifts, according to the grace given us. If a man's gift is prophesying, let him use it in proportion to his faith. If it is serving, let him serve; if it is teaching, let him teach; if it is encouraging, let him encourage; if it is contributing to the needs of others, let him give generously; if it is leadership, let him govern diligently; if it is showing mercy, let him do it cheerfully."

What is the Answer?

I believe the pastors who control the local churches need to have an encounter with the Holy Spirit, e.g. the Baptism in the Holy Spirit. They need to give up their goal of copying the mega- church in their area, as though it is Jesus' goal for them. I believe that God may have called a megachurch into existence, but I do not believe that He called every other church to copy it. I recently interviewed a member of a local and very famous megachurch with an equally well-known pastor. The person I interviewed was concerned that speaking in tongues was not encouraged in her church. She said that the Senior Pastor was her pastor and after much protesting to his assistants, she finally got to speak to him. His answer to her was, "I know what you want, but you will not find it here, as we are focused only on evangelism," and then he told her what church she could go to. I wonder if Jesus would have said that He was not going to seek the fullness of the Holy Spirit because it did not fit His agenda? Would Jesus say that evangelism was His goal and speaking in tongues would be confusing or would scare seeker friendly people away? Would He have suggested she go to a different church?

They Make a lot of Converts But Few Disciples.

I believe pastors of any size church need to seek the Lord and ask what He would like them to do before He returns. I also believe that pastors need to stop using the Great Commission as an excuse to build a large church. The Great Commission in Matthew28:19-20(NIV) says to, "Therefore, go and make disciples and teach them to obey all that I have commanded you. . ." They make a lot of converts, but few disciples. They also need to build the Kingdom of God, not the kingdom of the pastor. A member of a local church asked me why the church was always asking for money and why a church I know very well asked the congregation for a large sum of money to refurbish the pews and carpet and much more? The person also asked me why the church only received a very small amount of the money needed? My answer was that the people were tired of paying for edifices and staff and for growth and programs not needed. Once a church or a pastor gets on the treadmill of growth as a measure of his or his church's success it may choke out everything of God. It will make priorities of anything that raises money for his kingdom. Sometimes they seem so innocent, like let's have a seminar on how to gain and keep wealth or how to manage your money, but they are thinly disguised ways of getting more money from the believers.The excuse is furthering the kingdom of God through evangelism or missions. The mission faith promise is safe for the church because it costs the church nothing if the people are talked into a faith promise arraignment meaning that the believer makes a faith commitment to pay for missions beyond their tithe. This leaves the tithe intact for the churches to use for whatever it wants.

Someone suggested that only about 10% of Christians in the churches in North America are really committed to Christ. If that percentage is remotely accurate who is doing anything about that? The local church could do all that is necessary to bring the church to full maturity or a good semblance of it and they could do it without building another building or buying another sound system or any more pews. What use is it to have a great evangelistic program when nothing is being done about the souls already saved? What benefit is it to add more souls to the pile when the same evangelistic program brought the last weak Christians into the church? It is as though mothers and fathers are birthing children but not providing care or education for them. There is no glory in birthing kids, physical or spiritual. There is an old saying, "It's easier to have kids than to raise them." That is also true for spiritual kids. They still need to be raised. It is not easy or fun to teach or preach the hard stuff that may cause some to leave, but there is no excuse for not doing it. Jesus did it and we need to do it. There is so much more to the Christian life than salvation. The close relationship with Jesus, I mean the intimate one, is wonderful and no one is taught how to achieve it. Hardly anyone has it. We are taught how to enter through the door and enter into the entryway, but we are not taught and even prevented from entering any further because of our doctrines and philosophies. When we try, we are asked to leave the church, not the larger Body of Christ because we do not have the power or authority to do that though I sometimes think that if we did we would. I believe that many of the pastors of the local evangelical churches are modern day Pharisees. They have a form of godliness, but deny the power thereof, and the scripture warns to turn away from them. 2 Timothy 3:5 (NKJV), "Having a form of godliness, but denying the power thereof: from such turn away." Believers should seek the Lord as much as they can, but people sometimes feel that they are going against their pastor , because the pastors are who they trust to teach and train them in the Word. This scenario reminds me of the scripture in Matthew 23:13-15 (TLB), "Woe to you, Pharisees, and you other religious leaders. Hypocrites! For you won't let others enter the Kingdom of Heaven and won't go in yourselves. And you pretend to be holy, with all your long, public prayers in the streets, while you are evicting widows from their homes. Hypocrites! Yes, woe upon you hypocrites. For you go to all lengths to make one convert, and then turn him into twice the son of hell you are yourselves." I was concerned because I felt that the Lord could not soon come back for a church without spot or wrinkle with the lack of maturity that exists in the Body of Christ. Then the Lord gave me this scripture. Zechariah 10:3 (NIV), "My anger burns against the shepherds, and I will punish the leaders; for the Lord Almighty will care for his flock, the people of Judah, and make them like a proud horse in battle". That scripture says that the Lord will mature His Church and make it holy and spotless for His return.

Chapter Six

My Joseph Story

You'll really never know the strength and reality of your faith until you experience difficulty in life. You'll never know for sure whether God can be trusted or if you'll fall to temptation. You won't know what you can expect from God or how you will do unless you are given a trial in your life. Trials are not fun, but necessary if you expect to mature in your relationship with God. I have always likened God trials to boot camp. Boot camp is one of the hardest things anyone can do short of fighting a war. However, in the war of life we need boot camps, plural. If we do not complete our trial or fail it, we will need to repeat again.

As I experienced Marine boot camp, the worst fear for a recruit was failing enough times that you would be sent back to square one to complete the same things you had already completed. Now you had to leave your current friends and return to the beginning to repeat everything again. This will happen in your walk with the Lord. God did not want to punish Joseph but God knew Joseph was not ready to accomplish the work God had for him.

Genesis 37: 3, ". Now as it happened, Israel loved Joseph more than any of his other children, because Joseph was born to him in his old age." Joseph had a special call on his life. Has anyone said to you that you have a Joseph anointing? If so, look out, if you do have such an anointing you may be required to follow in a similar tortuous path that Joseph did. This was said of me. So this is the story of Joseph's life and mine under the same anointing. Joseph was a little arrogant and prideful, but not to worry as God would take care of that later in his life. The story of Joseph is a familiar one and I won't go through it again here; however, I will mention parts of it and I want to talk about why Joseph went to prison and what he did there.

It seems that because God is the same yesterday and forever, He works in all of us in a similar fashion regarding certain things. He wants to perfect our lives before He can or we can fulfill what calling or destiny He has in mind for us. The test seems to be proportionally connected in some way with the magnitude of the call. In Joseph's case, his was a great call, to save the Hebrew people from starvation. Therefore, the test was of equal magnitude. I call it a test because it is a test. If we just needed to sleep through a trial without any conscious involvement on our part what would be the advantage of the trial? The Scripture tells us that Jesus even though He was the Son of God learned obedience through His suffering. Hebrews 5:8 (TLB), "And even though Jesus was God's Son, he had to learn from experience what it was like to obey when obeying meant suffering." So Joseph's first test was his coat of many colors and his dream that his mom, dad and brothers would bow down before him, not to mention the sun the moon and the stars (See Gen 37:9). Maybe I should add that he was a little stupid as well. God must have said, "We have a long way to go with this kid. Let's start with the pit." God knew that there was potential in Joseph, that he would learn and the end would be better than the beginning. However, it was going to be painful for Joseph.

Someone said to me that I had a Joseph anointing. It was a prophetic person with a solid reputation. I did not know what to expect at the time. I thought like Joseph it was to help with resources for various ministries. I was already doing that so I felt okay with the prophetic word.

Let's go back to Joseph. Here he is in the pit sold by his brothers but God did not allow him to be killed, as was their first choice. That would have frustrated God's plan. This is significant and I will talk about it later. The Word does not say much about the pit experience. I feel it was a transition time to go to the next test. Again, significant, because even Joseph's brother Reuben's plan to save him could not happen. I think this shows us that God was in this the entire time.

We know the rest of the story. Joseph is sold into slavery and resold to Potiphar, one of Pharaoh's officers. Potiphar was captain of the palace guard and a fellow hand picked by God as part of the plan. Now we find out that Joseph was a pretty good kid. He was seventeen years old and handsome. He had a good work ethic, was intelligent and ultimately showed honesty, integrity and loyalty. I would think that would be good enough for God's plan to use Joseph before the rest of the testing, but apparently not. His ways are higher than our ways.

Potiphar's wife soon began to lust after Joseph. I believe that Potiphar knew that Joseph was innocent, because he knew that God was with him (See Gen. 39: 2). It was part of God's plan to get Joseph into prison for thirteen years. This is where the real trial, perfection and promotion would take place. So now we know why he was in prison, now what does he do while there? The Scripture is not telling us much. I believe it goes back a way and it has to do with forgiveness. Joseph needed to forgive his brothers, the slave traders, Potiphar, Potiphar's wife and Pharaoh's cupbearer and baker. It is worth putting the scripture in at this point because God now had Joseph right where He wanted him. God didn't just leave him in prison for thirteen years and not work with him. Genesis 39: 21-23 (NKJV), "But the Lord was with Joseph and showed him mercy, and He gave him favor in the sight of the keeper of the prison. And the keeper of the prison committed to Joseph's hand all the prisoners who were in the prison; whatever they did there, it was his doing. The keeper of the prison did not look into anything that was under Joseph's authority, because the Lord was with him; and whatever he did, the Lord made it prosper." God caused everything Joseph did to succeed. He had the Lord's favor because the work that needed to be done in Joseph was not how he handled prison life, how he handled his time in the pit or in Potiphar's home. Joseph got all the way to Egypt's prison for doing nothing wrong. I believe it was how Joseph handled his time in prison. How would you or I handle thirteen years in prison being innocent? Would we be mad at God? Would we forget God? Would we feel abandoned by

God? Would we forgive God? I suspect Joseph was allowed to wallow in unforgiveness and self-pity for a few years while in prison. However, there is no mention of it and I do not want to imply that he did, but it would seem that if not, he would have been out a lot sooner.

It is very difficult being punished for being innocent. It is hard being taken advantage of when you have done nothing wrong. I have experienced that very thing. I called for justice, "Lord I want justice, Lord you promised justice." The second question to the Lord was, "why me?" Psalm 9:16 (NIV) says, "The Lord is known by his acts of justice; the wicked are ensnared by the work of their hands." and Psalm 89:14(NIV) says, that, "Righteousness and justice are the foundation of your throne; love and faithfulness go before you." So where is my justice? Why am I in this prison? How long will I be in here? Is this the way you treat your kids? Yes, I have said these things and I suspect Joseph did as well. Can God use a servant with this attitude? Yes, but could God have used Joseph to save the Hebrews with that attitude? I don't know. I think that he may not have had the correct attitude if he was harboring resentment for all the wrong that had happened to him.

I recently read of a person who was incarcerated for nineteen years for something he did not do. When DNA finally proved his innocence he was released. His attitude was not vengeful. I wonder if we would feel vengeful? If Joseph wasn't vengeful what did he learn from his experiences? He learned to handle personal attacks, fear, unexpected situations, unjust accusations, perseverance, disappointments, injustice and he gained patience. He also learned that God was in every step of the way and that he was in prison for something greater than himself. Do these lessons sound familiar?

Joseph also had experienced tremendous disappointment with the expectation of release when he performed a great feat through God in the interpreting of the dream of the Baker and Cupbearer. When their promise was forgotten, that was a very important thing. Joseph experienced a deep betrayal. Another test? I would say yes and probably the worst of all. I believe that all of the trials Joseph endured were from the fruit of the betrayals he suffered. I will talk more about it here later. If our trials are proportional to the promotion we receive, then Joseph was ready at the end of his imprisonment to save the known world from starvation, and he did. Forgiving those who betray you, especially ones whom you love or are related to you is graduate level Christianity.

Why do we need to go into a desert or valley experience? If we are serious about our commitment to the Lord we need to be trained. So into training we go. Does this mean that God does not love us or that He will not rescue us from the training? I joined the U.S. Marine Corps when I was a young man. When I arrived at boot camp in Quantico, Virginia, I thought I had made a mistake. I thought boot camp was never going to end. However, as time went on I realized I would have been a very poor Marine had I not gone through what at that time was the hardest thing in my life. It was all worth it when I graduated. I was now allowed to be called a U.S. Marine for the rest of my life and I inherited a brotherhood of millions of other Marines. I also learned to use the weapons of warfare.

Our entrance to the Kingdom of God through Jesus' work

on the Cross is much like entering into the Marines without going through the Lord's boot camp. I guess you can see where I am going with this analogy. God's boot camps are the valleys and deserts were we are trained to use the weapons of our warfare to fight the enemies of the Lord. Our weapons are not flesh and blood; there are two scriptures that speak to this: 2 Corinthians 6:7 (NIV), "In truthful speech and in the power of God; with weapons of righteousness in the right hand and in the left. And 2 Corinthians 10:4, "The weapons we fight with are not the weapons of the world. On the contrary, they have divine power to demolish strongholds." So how do we learn to use these wonderful weapons the Lord has provided for us without training? In the Marines you can stare at complicated weapons, but without training they will be useless to you. God's boot camp at times can feel brutal, but when the training is complete you graduate and can then move on to the plan God has for your life. Psalm 144: 1 (NIV), "Praise be to the lord my Rock, who trains my hands for war, my fingers for battle." However, there is another issue to consider. We are in training with the things of the Lord our whole life and if we want to continue to move in the plan of God, we go from glory to glory. 2 Corinthians 3:18 (AMP), "And all of us, as with unveiled face, (because we) continued to behold (in the Word of God) as in a mirror the glory of the Lord, are constantly being transfigured into His very own image in ever increasing splendor and from one degree of glory to another; (for this comes) from the Lord (Who is) the Spirit." This scripture speaks of a continuous training. But take heart, God is a wonderful and loving drill instructor. It seems we hear a lot about Josephs and the Joseph anointing from many teachers these days. What does this mean for us? Does God have a lot of Joseph types in boot camp ready for the war to start? I believe that may be the case. A Joseph in today's world can do a thousand times what the Joseph of the Bible did from a chariot in the desert. We are able fly all around the world to minister; we go on TV, we can muster resources etc. We do not know what God has in store at the end. Do you want to be a Joseph? Joseph is not the only patriarch that had trials. David waited many years after the promise of God that he would be king. Abraham waited until he was a hundred years old for the promise of God. Moses was another deliverer of God's people who had to wait forty years in the desert tending sheep before God would let him wait another forty years in the desert and still did not let him enter into the promise. Waiting is difficult.

Perseverance is refusing to quit. It's falling down and getting back up again and again. Perseverance is not a matter of us making things happen. It is a matter of us waiting on the Lord as long as it takes before God chooses to help us to overcome. That is also part of our training, because without learning to trust God you won't wait. I have forced a few doors open and suffered for it. I know this is just information, not much comfort in the midst of a trial. That is a trap we can fall into and we must be aware of it when we want to complete our destiny. It is an easy one to fall into, because we have help. The help comes from the enemy of our soul who hates God, but he can't touch God so he attacks the apples of God's eye. However, David did not fall nor did Joseph, but Abraham did. It is called making the promise happen yourself. This is known as "making an Ishmael." Ishmaels never work out because they circumvent God's original plan; He will let us do it, but we will be sorry that we did. Sometimes making Ishmaels looks like we are helping God, but that is because we have not learned some of the things Joseph learned by going through to the end of his trial. Do you think that if David had killed Saul when he had the chance that God would have let him become king? I don't know, but God's time is God's time and God's ways are God's ways and they are not our ways. David was in a trial just like Joseph and like you and me. God does not want us to make an Ishmael or kill Saul or try to get out of prison before our time.

I want to talk about the issue of betrayal that Joseph experienced. I realized that David and Moses also experienced betrayal, as did Daniel as well. It seems whenever you are trying to do God's will someone will betray you to stop the move of God in your life. David did nothing to hurt Saul, yet he threw a spear at him and wanted to kill him all the rest of his life. That was betrayal. David also had a very personal betrayal from his son Absalom who tried to steal the kingdom from him. Moses tried to defend a Hebrew slave by killing an Egyptian soldier and a Hebrew turned him in. King Darius of Babylon (See Daniel 6: 1) made a rule that no worship was allowed to any god but him, so Daniel was betrayed to the lion's den by the jealous Satraps. It seems to me that the devil likes to use jealousy to help because we are so willing to be partners in betrayal. I have experienced betrayal from many people in my life but the worst was from a close friend. It was devastating to my wife and I and I did not know how to handle it correctly. I went to the Lord and cried, "I have been betrayed." Jesus answered me rather quickly with the words, "I am familiar with betrayal." I realized He was talking about Judas and Peter. Judas' betrayal of Jesus led to His death on the Cross. Even though it was His destiny and He knew it, still it was hard to endure from a close friend. My wife and I were able by the grace of God to break the pain that was before us and move in forgiveness. I knew that this was a foothold that the devil could turn into a stronghold in our lives if we let it fester and build into ongoing hatred. Jesus wants us to follow in His footsteps. He was in the world and we are in the world. He was betrayed and we will be betrayed, and Jesus wants us to handle it the same way. Is it easy to bear? What did Jesus do? From the Cross in His physical pain, He forgave His betrayers. Jesus is a hard act to follow, but we must if we want what God wants for our life as followers.

While talking with the Lord about this betrayal and forgiveness, the Lord said that there were other people we needed to forgive as well. He told us to make a list of all the people who had cheated us or otherwise hurt us where we were completely innocent. The Lord gave us the scripture 1 Corinthians 6:7, "Now therefore there is utterly a fault among you, because ye go to law one with another. Why do ye not rather take wrong? Why do ye not rather suffer yourselves to be defrauded?" He said take the list and forgive each one of these people. There were 39 on the list and we did that. However, the Lord came back with another request. He said to take each name from the list and add it to your morning prayer list and pray and bless that person for a week, and do this until all the names have been put on the prayer list and have been prayed for. We completed the list. I am not saying that your trial has anything to do with forgiveness, but it may. God gives us trials to test our faith and trust in Him for a promotion to another level in our relationship with Him.

I knew two Christian brothers who experienced betrayal. Both died from cancer and I believe it could be the result of the destruction that was caused in their bodies from their lack of forgiveness to the people that they felt betrayed them. It is said that when you forgive a person someone is released from prison, and that someone is you. It has also been said that when you do not forgive, you are taking poison yourself and expecting the other person to die.There is an interesting story that goes along with these two people mentioned above. Both were betrayed by the same person, a Christian brother. However, the betrayal was not considered a betrayal by the person accused of it because the particular ministry involved became unwieldy and needed to be reorganized. The reorganizing was devastating to these two men because close personal relationships were unsympathetically severed, causing great pain. Their lives were so intertwined in the ministry that asking them to step down and change close relationships and take lesser positions was more than they could bear or understand. They both had changed their lives, moved from their homes, and one gave his pastorate to another to become involved in this ministry.

There is a story that Corrie Ten Boom tells of her forgiving the Germans for killing her family in the concentration camps. She tells of the time when she was preaching on forgiveness in a church in Germany many years after the war. This had become her ministry. She had finished preaching and the people were filing out of the church when a man began walking down the aisle toward her. He was crying as he came, and Corrie recognized him immediately. It was the guard who was responsible for the death of her sister. He stuck his hand out and said, " God has forgiven me, but I have no peace until you forgive me". Corrie said it was a lot easier to teach on forgiveness than to reach for this man's hand and say, "you are forgiven". She hesitated for a while and then reached for his hand and forgave him. I think what Jesus did on the Cross trumps this as He said, "Forgive them Father for they know not what they do." I wonder how long it took Joseph to forgive all the people that betrayed him? I do not think he could have done it right away. I realize that God used this situation and set it up to show Joseph that before his dream of everyone bowing before him would come to pass he needed to become a forgiving, compassionate and loving person, to be able to justly handle the power, promotion and destiny he was about to be given. God already knew how Joseph would do when he came out of his pit prison ordeal but Joseph didn't. Learning forgiveness and learning to let yourself be defrauded is part of our faith and trust as the Holy Spirit applies the blood of Jesus to our sins, and gives us the ability and example to forgive. This is why we all must go through our own valleys and desert experiences with tests of learning, trusting and faith building. God knows how we will do when we come out and He knows how long the desert needs to be to make it happen to fulfill our destiny. It took Joseph thirteen years to be ready to fulfill the destiny that God had planned for him.

Is it always about forgiveness? No, not just forgiveness, it's also about wholeheartedly trusting God for provision. In adversity, it is about loving God, learning Biblical principles and having faith in God in spite of our circumstances. We cannot pray our way out of a learning trial. This only comes through our valleys, pits and desert experiences. The mountaintop teaches little, with the exception of Romans 2: 4,

"It's the goodness of God that leads men to repentance." Before I end this example, the Lord gave this word to me that speaks specifically of why we need to be tested and taught the ways of God. God needs to test us. He knows how we will act in a crisis situation. However, He also knows that we won't act in faith without having a record or personal experience of what God can and will do in our extreme need. So God wants us to know what He knows about us. Once we have been tested in battle and have acted in faith and trust, God can then send us out to do His will with confidence. In the Marines we call it taking the "Point." It is dangerous on the point because you are the first to confront the enemy.

I sound like God doesn't know all, not true, He does, but He does not want us to fail. We can fail even after coming out of our prison, but the likelihood would be greater if we came out untested. Even Moses failed after spending many years in a closer contact with God than almost anyone. We are flesh and blood and we are weak and God knows it. He doesn't expect more from us than we can do. But the soldier that goes into battle being properly trained has a better chance of completing his mission and protecting his people than if he was not properly trained and tested.

I am reminded of the time that David decided to count his horses and chariots and what we would consider a minor infraction, God considered a betrayal. David never lost a battle. After experiencing the faithfulness of God by trusting Him in many battles, and seeing His provision, then counting his horses, chariots, swords and troops was a grave mistrust in his God. While giving David a choice, God still killed 70,000 innocent Hebrews. The Word says in Psalm 20:7 (NIV), "Some trust in chariots and some in horses, but we trust in the name of the LORD our God." Isaiah 31:1, "woe to those who rely on Egypt. Woe to those who go down to Egypt for help, who rely on horses, who trust in the multitude of their chariots and in the great strength of their horsemen, but do not look to the Holy One of Israel, or seek help from the Lord."

In 2 Samuel 24:10-17, David realized immediately that he had done a great wrong and was remorseful. It seems that many times when we sin others pay for our mistakes. David asked the Lord to punish him instead of the innocent sheep as he called them. When a soldier makes a mistake many times others die.

In Revelation 2 and 3, the Lord lists the things that are disappointing to Him in each of the seven churches, but to each He says to him who overcomes that He will grant various blessings. As I have mentioned before, we all want to be overcomers, but we don't want to overcome anything because it is difficult. God has had me in a twelve year desert experience and only He knows what He wants me to learn and why. I have agonized over what is next, but God spoke to me and said that, "Joseph did not know when he would get out of his thirteen year ordeal or what he would do when he got out, and so, neither will you know when or what." I have gained intimacy with God during this time as I am sure Joseph did , so I have learned to trust Him and be resolute to God's will for my life. I have also learned that God is faithful to perform it.

Chapter Seven

In the Beginning

The first Adam separated us from God; Jesus, the second Adam, restored us to God. The Word of God is a very beautiful and an informative book, but sometimes it can be difficult to understand. I don't mean the story in general, but specific verses. However, when you are born-again, if you have had no experience with the Bible with the exception of the Christmas story or Easter, you really don't know what God had in mind regarding the New and Old Testament. As a Catholic I was one of those people. When I was born-again I began to go to Bible classes and find Bible teachers whom I could understand and I began to learn.

After you are in the family of God a while and you read the scriptures like Roman 1: 1-6 (NIV), "Paul, a servant of Christ Jesus, called to be an apostle and set apart for the gospel of God— the gospel he promised beforehand through his prophets in the Holy Scriptures regarding his Son, who as to his human nature was a descendant of David, and who through the Spirit of holiness was declared with power to be the Son of God by his resurrection from the dead: Jesus Christ our Lord. Through him and for his name's sake, we received grace and apostleship to call people from among all the Gentiles to the obedience that comes from faith. And you also are among those who are called to belong to Jesus Christ." You will understand what the Gospel is about as you hear from many sources. You will begin to understand why Jesus had to go to the Cross. You are told that without the shedding of blood there is no remission of sin. You realize that God's plan in the beginning was to cover sin by some sort of blood sacrifice, a firstborn male lamb without spot or blemish, a bull of the same ilk and so on. You soon realize that Jesus fills this requirement perfectly. You are introduced to Abraham, Isaac and Jacob, the major and minor prophets, King Saul, King David, Solomon and the Book of Psalms and Proverbs.

Soon you begin to understand how the Old and New Testaments are tied together. Finally, you are introduced fully to the New Testament. Now you understand what was just a nice story of a baby being born in a manger and that business about Jesus being raised from the dead, has changed to a real understanding, albeit a cursory one. You are now beginning to realize it is a new way of life with rules that are sometimes difficult, like forgive 70 times 70 and love your enemies. You soon realize that if you do not read and study you will not fully understand what you believe or how to live this new life as a Christian.

I don't want to confuse what happens to the believer when he becomes born-again which is a sovereign work of God with the adventure you will have when you begin studying the Scriptures. You will begin the slow renewing of your mind (Ephesians 1:9) if you follow the Lord and stay in the Word, you will be transformed and receive the mind of Christ regarding sin and the love of the brethren and the fruit of the Spirit. What I am referring to is Ephesians 1:17-18, "That the God of our Lord Jesus Christ the Father of Glory may give you a Spirit of Wisdom and Revelation in the knowledge of Him; having the eyes of your heart enlightened, that you may know what is the hope of His calling, what the riches of the glory of His inheritance in the saints." This is the advanced understanding that only comes from studying the Word of God and waiting on the Holy Spirit to open certain scriptures to your understanding, scriptures that were heretofore a mystery to you. This enlightening is spoken of in Ephesians 1:18b that speaks of there being more to our salvation than just our going to Heaven when we die. We won't understand it all unless the Holy Spirit opens it up to us. When this happens we will be entering into a realm of enlightenment in the Scriptures that will make ordinary Bible study seem boring. You will not be satisfied unless the Holy Spirit opens the Word to you. If this type of Bible study has not been part of your life, please do not distrust what I am saying, speak to other Spirit-filled people and ask them.

Some people relate being Spirit-filled with hearing God's voice. I agree. Remember when you were not Spirit-filled, but you were dead in your sins, God, the Holy Spirit spoke to you and told you to receive Christ. If you responded, you heard the voice of the Holy Spirit and were born again. You may not speak in tongues but that doesn't mean it doesn't exist, and if I speak in tongues and you don't it does not mean it doesn't exist. I have repeated that phrase because it is a stumbling block to many until they understand it. By the way, speaking in tongues is not a prerequisite to hearing God's voice or being filled with the Holy Spirit, but it is a wonderful indication and fulfillment of the promise of Jesus to send the Holy Spirit to us. Most of the things regarding the Holy Spirit, the gifts of the Spirit, speaking in tongues, prophetic words and healing are not accepted in a part of the Body of Christ, mostly the evangelicals. Granted there is much confusion, I believe brought on by unbelief. I need to explain my focus and why I have written this. The Lord is not happy with what some denominations have adopted as a doctrine that will not recognize the Comforter Jesus said He would send in John 14: 16-18. Over the last forty plus years I have been associated with the Catholics, Pentecostals, Charismatics and Evangelicals. I have been concerned about the lack of teaching among Evangelicals in the Body of Christ, specifically the heresy they teach in their cessationist/dispensational doctrine that teaches that the Holy Spirit does not interact with believers beyond salvation since the Cannon of Scripture was completed. This teaching has been very successful in keeping large numbers of Christians from the Holy Spirit, gifts, healing, personal revelation, corporate prophetic word and freedom of understanding worship among other things. Some churches do not want to be associated with "word of faith," so they should be called "word of unbelief" churches due to the fact that their main focus is on building large churches and filling their pews. I call this lack of belief in the work of the Holy Spirit a heresy because the devil alone wants the Body of Christ powerless. Without faith it is impossible to please God and the evangelicals have worked hand in hand with the purposes of the enemy of God and His Church. Paul says in 1 Corinthians 2:4-5, "And my speech and my preaching was not with enticing words of man's wisdom, but in demonstration of the Spirit and of power: That your faith should not stand in the wisdom of men, but in the power of God." If they call themselves the keepers of the Word, I believe it is only part of the Word.

I feel that the converts are exploited, and teaching is forgotten. Churches have fallen in love with their ministries, but it's better to fall in love with our God and to choose intimacy with Him. I mentioned earlier in this book that some groups are called the Father, Son and Holy Word people. Some would say they already have an intimate relationship with the Word. I know Jesus is the Word; however, that is not my point here. To accept the written word (Logos) over the person of God is a ploy of the enemy. If we come to the place where we can love the Lord with all our heart, soul, mind and strength, we will not have a problem with anything taking the place of that relationship, whether it is sin, our church or our denominations, or special interpretation of the Scriptures. We will let nothing take the place of our relationship with the Lord our God.

Unity in the Body of Christ

I believe that the lack of unity in the Body of Christ is a big part of what is holding back the return of the Lord (See John 17: 23). He is looking for unity in His body. I believe that unity and the lack of disciples are the two main hindrances for the Lord's return. When I speak of the lack of disciples, I am speaking of the lack of maturity displayed in the individual convert. The Church is not teaching the believer the Word. The Great Commission wants disciples, not just converts. I am trying to not repeat myself; however, I may have already. It is important that we realize our problems and what is causing them and how to fix them. Why are our statistics on sin as high or higher than unbelievers? You will read much more in this book regarding the lack of unity and teaching, the reasons for it and the results the Church/ Body of Christ will have because of that lack. I mentioned in my testimony that I prayed a prayer that I wanted my heart broken for the same things that break God's Heart. This issue is one that the Lord used to break my heart because His heart was broken over the non- acceptance of the Holy Spirit in the Church. This has been my Journey.

Chapter Eight

Our Quest for Fellowship

God created man to have fellowship with Him. After the fall of Adam, God sent Jesus to restore what we lost through Adam's sin. We will have even more than Adam had. He walked with God, but we have God living in us and have the ability to have an intimate relationship with Jesus. Jesus did not die to have workers tend a New Testament garden. He died to restore what was lost and to restore the ability for both of us, man and Jesus, to have a close relationship again. This is true, however, there are requirements for us. Just receiving Jesus gives us fire insurance from Hell's fire, but there is more that is needed from us. Jesus' death on the Cross and His resurrection is complete and needs nothing, but to walk with God like Adam, Abraham and Enoch did requires something more from us. Jesus going to the Cross opened the door, not only to salvation, but also to the ability for us to have the relationship that the above three humans had with God. The other reason Jesus needed to go to the Cross was to repair the breach made by Adam. God did it with the Second Adam, a human without sin. This repaired the breach. Now that the gate to intimacy is unlocked we can walk through it anytime we like or when the Lord likes for fellowship.

I have read Matthew 22:36-39 many times, as I am sure you have. I was beginning to read a Christian book, "Passion for Jesus", by Mike Bickel with the forward by Jack Deere. I read this verse in the forward to this book. As I read it the Holy Spirit opened this verse to me. What happened was He opened the eyes of my heart. I began to see what that verse meant to me and to the whole Body of Christ. I immediately became convicted because I did not have an intimate relationship with the Lord. I had not understood it before. I had a lot of work to do regarding this Scripture in my own life in order to share it with others who would listen. I loved God and my conversion was a radical one. I started to work with God and the Holy Spirit. The key word is work. I thought that I had it all covered until I read the scripture this last time.

The Scripture says (if you have not read it): "What is the greatest commandment? 'That you shall love the Lord your God with all your heart, mind and soul. This is the first and the second is like it. Thou shalt love your neighbor as yourself and on these two hang all the law and the prophets.'" Deuteronomy 6: 4-9 (NIV), Love the Lord your God with all your soul and all your strength. Impress them on your children. Talk about them when you sit at home and when you walk along the road, when you lie down and when you get up. Tie them as symbols on your hands and bind them on your foreheads. Write them on the doorframes of your houses and on your gates." As you can see God was pretty serious about this particular Scripture.

When I read it this time with my heart eyes opened, what I saw right away were five things: (1) This was something I was not doing and that I needed to do. (2) I did not know how to do it. (3) It was not a suggestion because of the word shall and the phrase write them on your hearts. (4) Much of the Church was not doing it either. (5) Jesus was displeased with us for not doing it. Matthew 22: 36-38 speaks of the entire goal for Jesus coming to Earth as a man (the second Adam)was to restore what was lost because of original sin. Jesus wanted to walk with Adam in the cool of the evening, and he wants the same intimate ability with each of us. He didn't create Adam to tend the Garden, and the Father didn't send Jesus to get workers for the Church.

The Great Commission vs. The Great Commandment

When the church or a believer tries to fulfill the Great Commission without having followed the Lord's command, "Thou shall Love the Lord your God with all your heart soul, and mind" called the Greatest Commamdment they often do it for the wrong reasons. They become belt notching, self serving, pew filling and unloving builders of the kingdom of man. We cannot do the Great Commission properly without having followed the directions of the Greatest Commandment. I believe that part of the Great Commission is integral to the second greatest commandment in the scriptures, "Love your neighbor as yourself." I don't believe we can love our neighbor as ourselves until we have learned to love the Lord with all our strength, mind and soul. In fact, the Lord told me to learn verses 37-38 first.

Disciples are different than converts. Converts have fire insurance; they know the Lord in salvation only. They understand that their sins are forgiven, and that the Father loved them enough to send His one and only Son to die for their sins, but they are usually not taught much more. Hebrews 5:12-13 (NIV), "In fact, though by this time you ought to be teachers, you need someone to teach you the elementary truths of God's word all over again. You need milk, not solid food! Anyone who lives on milk, being still an infant, is not acquainted with the teaching about righteousness." I believe that so many of our converts fit this scripture so well because they are never discipled. I know that is a generality, but the evidential fruit does not show much more, either from the convert or the church that brought them into the Kingdom. Discipleship is the next step after salvation. It is the job of the Church universal and the church local, in union with the Holy Spirit, to equip the (Saints) converts; however, if the convert is commissioned to work in the church, his or her ongoing growth will not be a priority of the church. God raises up extra-church ministries to cover the lack of maturing in the local Body of Christ. Extra-church ministries are good teaching ministries outside of the local church, but many times they are considered competition for the resources of the church, so the local church resists them, and the Christians suffers from everlasting spiritual mediocrity.

Distinctions Between Evangelicals and Charismatics

I want to make a distinction between evangelicals and charismatic converts. The evangelical part of the Body of Christ is primarily the group I am writing about. That is not to say they are the only ones unaware of the commands in Matthew 22 and I use myself as evidence. I have been a Charismatic Christian for many years and for 38 of them I did not know that I needed to have an intimate relationship with Jesus. I have attributed this to two things: First, to my recollection, no one ever taught on that Scripture, and second, the Holy Spirit never revealed it to me in the way I understand it now. However, in some of the latter day Charismatic meetings, I believe that the Holy Spirit has apprehended people who became so immersed in the Spirit in their worship that they have became quite intimate with Jesus and less interested in being just a laborer for the Lord.

Mary vs. Martha

It is amazing how much the Holy Spirit can input in your Spirit in a matter of seconds when He opens the eyes of your heart! Another thing that happens when God opens a verse to you is that He usually opens more verses to help you understand what He wants you to know. This was the case with this verse. I learned of another verse that came from this same book I was reading in Luke 10:40-42. The story begins with Jesus and His Disciples relaxing with Mary, Martha and Lazarus in their home. Martha was cooking dinner and her sister Mary was sitting at Jesus' feet. Martha got mad because Mary wasn't helping in the kitchen. Jesus told Martha that Mary had chosen the better thing and that it would not be taken from her. I don't know about you, but I never understood why Jesus did this. After all it seemed that Martha was doing something that needed to be done, they needed to eat. Based on the Matthew 22 scripture, Jesus was telling Martha that Mary had the Matthew 22 or at that time a Deuteronomy 6: 5 relationship with Him and that was better than cooking dinner, or as I supposed later, better than many other good works that we do. It seemed that Mary was doing something good and it wasn't going to be taken from her. Consequently, it would seem that what Martha was doing was not the best thing. Intimacy with the Lord holds that position. Sometimes it is easier to do work for God without intimacy with God. This is a challenge to my own walk with God. It is easy for me to fall into this trap of working so hard for Jesus that I forget to work with Jesus. Jesus desires intimacy more than works. He tells us in John 15:5 (NIV), "I am the vine; you are the branches. If a man remains in me and I in him, he will bear much fruit; apart from me you can do nothing. If anyone does not remain in me, he is like a branch that is thrown away and withers; such branches are picked up, thrown into the fire and burned." Whatever we do for the Lord must be with Jesus and not just for Jesus.

The Prodigal Son

In the story of the prodigal son, the son that stayed and worked did not understand the love his father had for him and his brother. He thought that it was based on the quantity and quality of his work. Since he stayed and did good work he thought that made him more acceptable for his father's love. How many times have we done this very thing? We feel that if we tithe and we work faithfully at the church, we are more acceptable than the one who does nothing. The church is guilty of perpetuating this. It feels if it has a large staff, offers many programs and it supports many missionaries, then they have done what is needed to be totally acceptable to God. This is how legalism develops in believers and churches. "Who does more work for the Lord, who has more programs etc.," they ask? Then they become angry with Mary, the Prodigal Son and church members who do not meet their criteria for acceptance. As I said before they have fallen in love with ministry when they should have fallen in love with their Father. The correct attitude is to understand that our acceptance by our heavenly Father is regardless of our works and righteousness; it is because of what Jesus did on the Cross. But it is more than that, it is because the Father loves us so much that He sent Jesus. The love He showed towards us was while we were yet sinners, not while we were doing good deeds because our good deeds (righteousness) are as filthy rags (Isaiah 64: 6).

I guess you can see what's coming? God was showing me that the good work that Martha was doing was not as good and pleasing to Him as what Mary was doing. Let's look at it carefully. If we look at the Church we can say the same thing. The good works it does and we do corporately and individually are not as pleasing to Jesus as loving Him with all our heart and soul and mind. I mentioned this to an evangelical pastor friend who agreed with me, but he said that the Church needed Martha's work as well as Mary's. I agreed at that moment until I thought about it and then I realized that was the church speaking and it was speaking to the need to build the church. However, after saying that there is nothing wrong with working in the church as long as the motivations are pure, and I do not mean the motivations of the believer, I mean that of the local church and the motivation of the pastor. It matters whether he is building the Kingdom of God or his own kingdom. I believe Martha's input is needed and acceptable if it is related to Jesus in the Matthew 22:36-38 way, as Mary's was. Otherwise, the scary verse of Matt. 7- 21-23 would apply , " Not everyone who says to me Lord Lord will enter into the Kingdom of Heaven only those who do the will of my Father. They will say did we not do good works in your name…" This scripture above is very difficult to undertand in my opinion. I am not a Biblical scholar. I don't know Greek or Hebrew and you can see by reading this I have my trouble with English. Another scripture that gives me difficulty is Matthew 25:11-12 (NKJV), " Afterward the other virgins came also, saying, 'Lord, Lord, open to us!' But he answered and said, 'Assuredly, I say to you, I do not know you.' "

Jesus Died For A Relationship With Us

It's almost like saying to us that if we don't have the relationship of Matthew 22:36-38 and if we or the church begin doing the second greatest commandment before we learn how to do the first, He will treat our works as He did Martha's and will not accept them, no matter how good they may seem to us. Jesus seems to be more interested in an intimate relationship with us than He is in our good works. This scripture seems pretty harsh, but clear.

I want to mention one work that the church considers good, but I put it in because I believe it is an illegal relationship with the Word of God. Some do today in the church what it could not do in Jesus' day. That is to love the Word of God more than God Himself. Some believers today have become a people of Word worshipers instead of God worshipers. God never intended us to worship His written word. I understand that Jesus is the Word, but you know what I mean. He intended for us to worship His Son who came in the flesh, suffered and died on a cross for our sins and rose from the dead and now sits at the right hand of the Father, ever to make intercession for us. A great book on the power and the concern that the Father has for the Blood of Jesus and His sacrifice on the Cross is, 'The Power of the Blood " by Bob Sorge.

To Obey Is Better Than Sacrifice

1 Samuel 15:22 (NIV) is another scripture we don't hear quoted very much, "Obedience is better than sacrifice. But Samuel replied: 'Does the Lord delight in burnt offerings and sacrifices as much as in obeying the voice of the Lord? To obey is better than sacrifice, and to heed is better than the fat of rams.' "

Can you guess what kind of other good works the Church does today that are not as pleasing to Jesus as loving Him with all our heart soul and mind? Let me write about what I think we do individually and corporately that displeases the Lord as well. I will start with something that the Church does not do. It does not teach us how to love God with our whole heart and soul and mind.1 Samuel 15:22 means that many times we, individually as well as the Church corporately, do things that we believe are more of a sacrifice than doing what God has commanded us to do. Because of the nature of the work and the inherent good it accomplishes, we think it will suffice instead of doing what God commands . We think we know better than

God how to run His Church. For example, God might say, stop drinking, stop smoking or go on a diet to certain individuals. We say, "'I believe I will double tithe". God laughs! If the Church does this it is more critical because it leads sheep away from God's commands and His will for them. But the Church says let's have an evangelistic conference. Let's invite a national evangelist. An individual might say to that same command I will make a missionary trip to Africa. Jesus is not pleased. He doesn't want our sacrifice, He wants our obedience. Matthew 7: 21-23 (NIV), "Not everyone who says to me, 'Lord, Lord,' will enter the kingdom of heaven, but only he who does the will of my Father who is in heaven. Many will say to me on that day, 'Lord, Lord, did we not prophesy in your name, and in your name drive out demons and perform many miracles?' Then I will tell them plainly, 'I never knew you. Away from me, you evildoers!' " Here's that difficult scripture again.

Again, I do not believe that these scriptures have anything to do with salvation. Bill Johnson, a Bible teacher and pastor of Bethel Church Redding, California said, "I believe God judges us individually and the Church corporately on the level of light and revelation rejected rather than on inequity," and I say inequity, after all, was taken care of at Calvary. Light or revelation rejected has to do with obedience and our walk and progress in the Lord.

God Speaks To Us Through His Word

The Holy Spirit opened one other Scripture to me regarding this issue of an intimate relationship with Him: John 11:20-26, "Then Martha, as soon as she heard that Jesus was coming, went and met him: but Mary remained inside the house. Then said Martha unto Jesus, Lord, if thou had been here, my brother had not died. But I know, that even now, whatsoever thou wilt ask of God, God will give it thee. Jesus saith unto her, 'Thy brother shall rise again.' Martha saith unto him, 'I know that he shall rise again in the resurrection at the last day.' Jesus said unto her, 'I am the resurrection, and the life: he that believeth in me, though he were dead, yet shall he live: And whosoever liveth and believeth in me shall never die. Believest thou this?' " Jesus purposely delayed His coming to His friend Lazarus as he was dying. When He arrived Martha said, "If you had been here my brother would be alive." Jesus said to Martha what I believe is the best theological statement in the Scriptures, "I am the resurrection and the life he who believes in me will live and not die and any one who dies will live." Then when He met Mary at the tomb, she said the very words Martha said but Jesus did not give her a theological answer. The Scripture says in John 11: 35, ". . . that Jesus wept." What a difference when we have a special relationship with the Lord! Mary's pain moved Him to tears. To Martha's pain He almost sounded irritated. It hardly seemed like a time to give Martha a teaching. After all this, I was left with a very jealous heart for the relationship that Mary had with Jesus. Now how do I do it? I can't quite wash His feet and dry them with my hair . So how does the Father want us to achieve this feat with Jesus? I began to ask the Father how to do this. Through His Holy Spirit, He was very faithful to tell me and also He wants me to share it. I emphasize here that He gave it to me for me to apply to my life, but to share it as well, but first I want to lay some groundwork.

Did You Ever Hear God Speak?

When I say, "He said", I don't mean I heard an audible voice, not to say God can't speak audibly if He wants to. Just because He didn't speak audibly that does not mean He did not speak. Part of what God wants from us is to learn to hear His inaudible voice, His still quiet voice. 1 Kings 19:12(KJ21), "and after the earthquake a fire, but the LORD was not in the fire; and after the fire a still small voice." You can do it, you just need to practice. Most of us don't stop talking long enough to hear anything. One way to start is to remember when God spoke and what He said to you the last time He spoke to you. I covered this earlier. You don't think the Holy Spirit ever spoke to you? Who told you to receive Christ as Lord? I don't mean who gave you the Gospel of Salvation; I mean who spoke to your heart and said receive? It was the Holy Spirit. That's His job. Was it audible? Probably not, but you heard it. I know of people when it was audible. I have heard my name called.

Secrets In The Mansion

This is a word the Lord gave to me. The Scripture and the comments are below:

John 15:15 (NASB), "No longer do I call you slaves, for the slave does not know what his master is doing; but I have called you friends, for all things that I have heard from My Father I have made known to you." But all you want to talk about is your salvation, your fire insurance. When was the last time you thanked your insurance company for your home fire insurance? Jesus is saying, at your salvation you were given the keys to a mansion. You inherited a very large mansion

(The Kingdom of God) full of secrets and all sorts of goodies. You were given permission to enter through the door. You enter, but never go past the entryway. The entryway speaks of salvation. You keep thanking God for your entry into the mansion and you keep admiring the entryway or salvation, and you bring others in and you keep telling others about the entryway, but never about the rest of the mansion and all that they will inherit. Consequently none of you receive all that God has for you in the mansion. Isaiah 29:13 (NLT), says, "And so the Lord says, 'These people say they are mine. They honor me with their lips, but their hearts are far from me. And their worship of me is nothing but man-made rules learned by rote.' " This scripture is a pretty good description of the modern day believer, who says he is a Christian, goes to church, but leaves church after the Sunday service to go back to their real life watching football, baseball etc.. He wants no more of God than the Sunday service. They are not interested in searching out more of God in the mansion or finding more in this life. I believe that God judges His people for this lack of interest in the things of God. When I say judges, I do not mean sin. I mean our fellowship with Jesus is weakened.

Search for the Secrets and Treasures of God

Did you ever explore in an attic or a basement? I have. My brother and I lived in a hundred year old house when we were kids. The house had an attic on both sides of the upstairs rooms; we would go through the boxes and old trunks with great expectation hoping to find a treasure. We did, we found a blunderbuss rifle with a funnel end, probably well over a hundred years old. That is the expectation we should have as we live in the Kingdom of God. God says He has treasures in the basement and the attic in our mansion, secrets which we do not know of. Jeremiah 33:3 (NIV), "Call to me and I will answer you and tell you great and unsearchable things you do not know.' " The unsearchable things are unsearchable outside of the Kingdom of God. He says He will tell us, but we can't hear Him in the entryway, we must enter into the mansion to hear. That's the intimate relationship. God has revealed more to me regarding the mansion, but that is for another time or book. Did I go off track? Well if I did let's get back on track. If we want to learn how to talk to God which is all that praying really is, read the Psalms. David had it figured out. We must consider God in everything we do all day long. That means our life becomes a prayer. Communication with God is talking and listening, mostly listening.

How To Love The Lord Your God

Let's go back to the point I was making about how to love the Lord with all your heart, mind and soul. We live a pressurized hurry-up life, and we made it that way ourselves. We have built a lifestyle for ourselves and our family based on what we think is best for all. I saw a license plate on a Cadillac SUV that said "Taxi Cad". That had to be a mother screaming for help in a humorous way. Soon we become slaves to the things we own and the lifestyle we want to maintain. We may know God, we may love God with the revelation we have and we may go to a church that is busy building their idea of what church should be. If we want to get closer to God we help in the bookstore or the information booth or become an usher. We feel like we are closer to God if we are not sinning and we are doing a good thing. A teacher I know said, "My ministry was leading Christians to Christ." Another Bible teacher Steve Thompson says, " You may need to leave the church to find Christ". Notice I use lower case for the local church. If I mean the Body of Christ or the Church corporate, it appears in upper case.

When Jesus approached the Temple and saw the moneychangers, He overturned their tables and said, "My church will be a house of prayer and you have made it a den of thieves"(Matt. 21:11-13). I believe the moneychangers are back and have recruited us to work the tables. It takes a revelation from the Holy Spirit to even know that attending the megachurch in your area and working for the church is not making you closer to Jesus in the way He wants.

Our church attendance and our lifestyles do not help us get closer to Jesus in the way I am writing about here. When most people have extra time they do fun things or have a hobby that takes up their time. The first Adam separated us from God. Jesus, the second Adam, restores us to God.

Chapter Nine

Jesus Our Model

When we have a need for healing we want God to do what He promised He would. We have been taught that God will answer when we call. As a Christian for many years and through many trials I have discovered that there is a higher call to God than to just heal my diseases. Our desire should be to seek His face not His hand, and His grace and His closeness to us when we are in pain. We should want to receive more than just healing when we are experiencing pain. Jesus knows and feels our pain. God is a loving father administering comfort and love to us. I have experienced instantaneous healing and it is almost perfunctory with no intimacy. Yes we thank God but it is like having a doctor fixing your broken arm with a cast and you say thank you and you are grateful but there is no intimacy there. I believe Jesus wants us to have our relationship with Him be the main attraction. I think if any of the bible heroes who could have prayed their way out of their problems, would have frustrated God's plans for their lives, and changed biblical history.

His presence will deliver the joy and peace we need. I have a short example of what I mean: a friend who travels a lot told me when he would come home from a trip he always brought candy and put it in his pockets. Each time he arrived home his young kids ran to him and rifled his pockets. After a few return trips he did not know whether his kids loved the candy or Him. I believe we can substitute that word with healing. Does God think that way about you? God has more for us than our healing. Seek the Lord with all your heart and you will find Him. You will discover that God can and wants to do more than just heal your diseases. He wants intimacy with you and me. He also has a plan for your life *Jeremiah 29:11 for I know the plans I have for you* **James1: 2-5** *"Consider it pure joy, my brothers, whenever you face trials of many kinds, because you know that the testing of your faith develops perseverance. Perseverance must finish its work so that you may be mature and complete, not lacking anything" (James 1:2-5) NIV God often allows pain to ignite destiny in our lives. Without motivation, many of us would never fulfill the purposes for which God created us. Often times a measured assault invades our life and creates a depth of pain that all we know to do is press into God with all our being.* When was the Last time you heard a sermon on the above scripture? If you are a minister did you ever preach a sermon on this scripture? This scripture is saying don't think that it is not absolutely normal if we experience problems in our walk with God. God's goal is to mature us. He wants a personal relationship with us, not just to give us salvation and to answer every need we have, but a close intimate relationship with us, and us with Him. He wants more from us than only our needs. Yes there is healing in the atonement, as stated in Isaiah 53:4-5. We are healed by his stripes, however, all are not healed. God, often will walk beside us while we are in a painful trial to draw us closer to Him and build character. How does a Christian become salty? Saltiness comes from our trials. God will measure our character by how we handle our trials. A life of no difficulties and full of all the things we want, does not make us salty or build character. Character is built like muscles are built, by exercise in the spiritual sense. We know what Jesus said about salt, "if it is tasteless it is no good for anything but to be trampled underfoot". Matthew 5:13 If we want to be salty we must embrace our trials and pains.

Your goal might be when you feel pain you pray to have God remove it. If these scriptures I have quoted above are what you do, I believe you are a normal American Christian. Why do I say that? It is because we who believe that God heals want to immediately alleviate any pain we have. If we have a headache we quickly take a pill, anything more severe than a headache we go to a miracle meeting. I personally felt the same way about a headache or any pain or illness we may have. I was guilty myself of immediately trying to correct the issue. I have since learned to not be so eager to get the pain taken away. I want to listen to what God wants from me, not what I want from Him. There is an old saying; "if a light flashes on your car's dash board there may be something wrong under the hood". God may want to look under our hood. If we unplug the light we may cause a bigger problem. Jesus is more than a healer of our diseases. He has other roles and desires for us. Why doesn't Jesus heal every time we pray to Him for healing since it is a promise and our inheritance? Isaiah 53:4-5. God is sovereign and He heals as he pleases. That may sound cruel, but it is not, it is a father's love for us. Our character is important to God. He measures us by our response to our trials.

Hebrews 5:8 *this scripture is clear; Jesus learned obedience from the things He suffered.* So what are we to do? We seem to be taught from childhood to scream if we are in pain, and our mommy will make it all go away. Now that is ok. We loved having our moms relieving our pain and meeting our every need. As we grew we still may have had our needs met by our parents. All very good, but soon as we matured we were left on our own to cover our pains in the areas mentioned above. Now as adults, what do we do about them? It seems that we quickly find a healing meeting. Some of our pains are not always physical; they can be emotional, financial, relational or psychological. I have had some of the above, and each has it's own pain that screams for help, which we want now. After all we are only human. However, Jesus was also human in the aspect of feeling the same kind of pain we feel. Yet Hebrews 5: 8 says He endured the pain and gained obedience through the pain. Jesus should be our model.

I want to ask a few questions: Is it a sin to seek a doctor when you are sick (need healing)? Does it show a lack of faith in God to go to a doctor? Is it a lack of faith to seek alternative measures for healing? The answer to all of these questions is basically no, but we should still seek Him first. If you chose to seek God for your healing even that does not guarantee you will be healed. God may have another plan for your healing as He did for many in the scriptures. I was involved in a healing ministry in my early years as a Charismatic Christian; we saw many healings and many who were not healed. God has His master plan for our lives. After saying this I believe when we are ill we should seek the Lord for what He may want from this healing. Questions like, "Father is this a training, a place for me to find greater intimacy with you"?

This problem in the Charismatic fellowships is common even among leaders. When asked if you are seeing a doctor and if so are you following a course the doctor is recommending, the answer many times is I am trusting in the Lord. There is an opposite scenario among non-charismatic Christians. They will see a doctor and he will offer a course of action. At this point the doctor becomes their god. They will not try any other remedy (with the exception of prayer), usually all will accept prayer, possibly because it won't interfere with their current doctor prescribed medication. So praying is always safe to try. I want to mention a caveat to these healing thoughts. I believe that when a person is on his or her deathbed or has been in an accident etc. and time is of the essence God may be likely to heal. I have seen many testimonies of that situation. Again God is sovereign and can do what He feels necessary. This subject is very complex and I do not claim to have many answers.

Before I leave this part of this chapter I want to mention that I am a person who searches the Internet to see what others have done with my type of illness. I look for remedies that have worked; I look for any information that may help. If God is not helping me, I need to be the one looking for my need. I want to say that this is not a sin and not a lack of faith. In my search I recently found a product that seems to cure many types of cancers. It is an all natural product that has been around for years and comes with a CD full of personal testimonies. I gave a bottle to someone with stage 4 cancer that the doctors had given up on and now this person is free of this disease.

I Was Healed

I want to share some personal testimony: I want to mention that I have been miraculously and instantaneously healed twice. When I say that I mean that it was not a headache or something that could be fixed, there was no known cure for one of my problems and the other one would have cost $50,000 and much re-habilitation. Both cures were instantaneous and at different times and without the need for any rehab. God did it. I wonder sometimes, why He did it? I don't mean the general reason as to why, I know that God loves me and he has the power to heal me anytime I call for healing. I also have the faith for healing based on this experience and also praying for others.

So why did He heal me? Why does He heal some instantly after one prayer? I do not know. Besides the obvious reasons of me being His favorite son, and that He has the power and that Isaiah 53:4-5 says that we are healed by His stripes, and his wounds. This makes our healing as Christians our inheritance. That seems like enough to heal us each time we ask for healing. So why am I not healed every time? Why are you not healed every time? By the way what is this in Hebrews 5:8 about? Jesus had all the power in the world and when He was the Father's favorite Son. Yet, instead of the Father healing Him Jesus learned obedience from his pain. Do we think that God wants us to experience obedience like Jesus did instead of healing everytime we call for healing? Sometimes is my best answer. Again, obedience is better than sacrifice and Jesus is our model.

I want to add a little more scripture for some explanation. *1Peter 4:1-2 NIV Therefore, since Christ suffered in his body, arm yourselves also with the same attitude, because whoever suffers in the body is done with sin. 2 As a result, they do not live the rest of their earthly lives for evil human desires, but rather for the will of God.* This sound a lot like God wants character building from us.

It would appear that there is some benefit for not receiving the healing we want so badly, it would also seem that healing is not the be all and end all of our Christian life… Would your charismatic pastor agree or would he want you to come for healing repeatedly? Sometimes God will give you what you want but you may not like it.

I want to tell of an experience that would be considered an issue for prayer the same as prayer for physical healing. It is a combination of a financial problem and a betrayal. Many times we do not think of these sorts of problems in the same category as physical problems. However, they can be just as devastating and lead to physical needs in the end. The problem I will mention is one that happened to me. I had come up with a new invention and I received a US, CN and Mexico patent for it. It was good enough to change a complete industry. When that happens it is designated as "disruptive technology". I have had other patents that did very well but nothing as life changing to a complete industry as this was. I had a very successful business as I introduced this new product nationwide. I needed to produce the product all across America and I had four factories manufacturing the product. At this point I needed a sales force to market the product. So I took on a partner. The partner was a very large national corporation, who quickly decided to copy my product and destroy my company.

I won't be more specific as more specifics are not important to this writing. What is important is that this was as devastating as a serious illness to me and to my family who worked with me. So I treated it as I would any illness that I would have had. I prayed to the Lord. I mentioned to the Lord that I was betrayed. The Lord quickly said, "I am familiar with betrayal"… Again specifics are not important here now. What I learned through all of this was, that I needed help from the Lord, and a solution from the Lord.

When we pray we do not expect half a healing. We expect all of a healing. My point is that God wants to train us like He does with many of His kids. Remember Moses received a 40-year training in the desert tending sheep before he could deal with Pharaoh, and another 40years before his people could enter the Promised Land. Don't forget Joseph who got a13-year boot camp training in prison before he was released to rule and become the second most powerful man in the ancient world, God trains his kids. If you are one of His kids you can expect some training. Training from our God is not designed to kill you it is designed to TRAIN YOU.

I want to say that I think sometimes praying for a healing may be contrary to God's plan for you or me. This could be a valley of testing or training for you. We may not get healed because God wants to train us to be mature and to align our character to His. Remember the 2 scriptures above Hebrews5: 8 and 1Peter4: 1-2 Jesus is our example. Is it wrong to pray everyday for your healing? The Bible doesn't say much on this subject Paul says, *2 Cor12: 8-9 (NIV) Three times I pleaded with the Lord to take it away from me. 9 But he said to me "My grace is sufficient for you, for my power is made perfect in weakness."*
It sounds to me like God is telling Paul forget the thorn in your flesh and get on with your job that I gave you.

It sounds to me like we are to endure our pain like Jesus did, to gain obedience, and build our character. God may want us to do what He has in mind for our good, or for His glory. We sing a song "Be Glorified." Who do we think will do the glorifying, you and me or someone else? *1Sam15: 22 NLT but Samuel replied, "What is more pleasing to the LORD: your burnt offerings and sacrifices or your **obedience to his voice** Listen! Obedience is better than sacrifice, and submission is better than offering the fat of rams.*

I am not saying that it is wrong to pray for your healing, however, you may be missing out on a lot of things the Lord has for you if you spend all your time going to healing meetings every Saturday, Sunday, Monday and Wednesday. If you believe

God has the power to heal you, and you believe God loves you enough to go to Calvary and die for you even if you were the only one on the earth, then why do you keep begging for healing like you don't believe? Why do you stand up, go down to the front where you perceive there is some sort of magic every week? Do you think that God can't find you or won't heal you if you do not raise your hands or standup or go to the front when asked to acknowledge your illness to God? Do you think that you need to help Jesus to heal you? Do you think that Jesus sacrifice on the cross was not enough to heal you… and you must help? What if God wanted to give you a ministry in something new that He knows you would be terrific doing, but like Joseph you need training? Do you think you may be bordering on unbelief doing all those things each time you have a need?

I want to go back to my testimony regarding the betrayal and how God answered my cry for help. God allowed my partner to take my business. It was not a disease, as we think of healings. I had to endure the suffering of losing my business. I was left with a lot of equipment and machinery plus many employees and a lot of debt.

The Lord comforted me by telling me that Joseph and King David suffered but in the end they were better off than before. He told me I would be better off as well. It was a longer story but suffice to say I knew I was in God's hands.

How did God do it? I had to sell everything as that is what the situation required. I called someone I knew on the East Coast who bought and sold equipment like mine. He quickly said I have someone in CA now and he is looking for your type of equipment. I said send him to me. He came and after seeing the equipment I said I wanted to sell the company and also my patents and molds, he said he would buy the company as well. I took him to the trade show just in time before it ended, to acquaint him with the industry. He liked what he saw and said he wanted to buy the company and hire me as a consultant. Then he said something that can only be God. He said that he wanted to give me a royalty on every one of my products that his company sold for the remainder of the patents 17 years. I don't know anyone as generous as this man, except God. This man is a Christian as well.

Now I have the benefits of my company again only I don't need to work for it or in it. The buyer of my company was not an employee of his company as I originally thought, he was and is the owner who just "happened" to be in my neighborhood when I had exactly what he needed, and I needed what he could provide. He has 6000 employees, and He said, "Your product will be bigger than anything we have". So far all is well and he is also an honorable man. Sometimes God doesn't want us to be healed the way we want to be healed, and we need to give God room to move on our behalf. His way is always better. Guess who needed to forgive the company that betrayed me? I had to forgive long before God moved on my behalf.

Why should Christians suffer?

1Peter4: 12-13
12 Dear friends, do not be surprised at the fiery ordeal that has

come on you to test you, as though something strange were hap-
*pening to you. **13 But rejoice inasmuch as you participate in***
the sufferings of Christ, so that you may be overjoyed when his
glory is revealed.

I was going to end this chapter here, however, I think I should mention that I have a disease that is not curable by man's standards. My immune system is overactive and thinks my body is a germ and trys to kill it. It is called Myasthemia Gravis, MG it is an autoimmune disease. I know nothing is impossible for our God. I do not know when I got it; I believe it was around the time when I was dealing with the betrayal from my partner. Even though I have prayed for the Lord to heal it He has not decided to heal me yet. Although the disease is manageable, and I am stable and can do almost everything a man my age can do. Would it be good to have God heal me completely? Yes it would but I have told God that I am ok if He does and ok if He doesn't. A complete healing would be the cure of both my betrayal and my MG. So my point is made regarding we Christians may only receive half a healing. God is sovereign!

I don't go up for healing each time there is a call for such but I am always open for what God wants. He knows me, He loves me, He is concerned about me and He knows that I love and trust Him and Have an intimate relationship with Him. Matt22: 36-8.

Chapter Ten

America Needs Revival

I wanted to change thinking and talk about a something that has been on my mind for quite a while. The first thing I would like to discuss are the words revival and awakening and their meanings in the context I am referring to. There have been revivals in the past and awakenings as well, and I believe that at times these events have been misnamed. The dictionary definitions those words as follows:

Revival: (noun), an improvement in the condition or strength of something: a revival in the fortunes of the party | an economic revival, an instance of something becoming popular, active, or important again: cross-country skiing is enjoying a revival.

Awakening: (noun) an act or moment of becoming suddenly aware of something: The war came as a rude awakening to the hardships of life. The formal act of waking from sleep: The beginning or rousing of something: the awakening of democracy in Eastern Europe. (Adjective) coming into existence or awareness: his awakening desire | an awakening conscience. Awaken (verb): rouse from sleep; cause to stop sleeping: Anna was awakened by the telephone. To awaken someone to, make someone aware of (something) for the first time: the healings helped to awaken the people to the love of God. In researching the Welsh Revival of 1904-1905, a Welsh newspaper wrote in September a conference was held in Blaenannerch. It was reported that "massive blessing" was upon this conference and the news quickly spread throughout the area and beyond. The South Wales Daily News noticed the events and reported, "The third great revival was afoot through the nation!"— The other two revivals being the Welsh Methodist revival and the 1859 Methodist Revival. I want to add the Catholic Charismatic Revival, mostly called the Catholic Charismatic Renewal. This renewal has been going for almost fifty years and is now worldwide. It is not as dramatic and instantaneous as some revivals, nonetheless, millions have been revived, healed and filled with the Holy Spirit. I am familiar with this movement of God as my wife and I were involved for a few years in the early 1970's teaching salvation and the Baptism in the Holy Spirit, called "Life in the Spirit Seminars" (LSS).

I am putting a little information on the Welsh Revival as a point of understanding my premise in "America Needs Revival." I feel I must clarify what I mean and what is needed in America. I feel America and the American Church needs an awakening/ renewal that will bring about revival and bring America back to our first love, Jesus. There have been stories of men on ships while still out at sea heading toward the Welsh shore, falling on their knees and repenting of their sins, knowing nothing of what was happening on shore. This is a sovereign work of God. This is what I mean when I say America needs a revival/awakening. It is the goodness of God that leads men to repentance (Romans 2: 4). A feature of the Welsh revival that was not seen in any other revival prior to 1904 was the role of the media. The Western Mail and the South Wales Daily News, the Wales' daily Newspapers, spread news of conversions and generated an air of excitement about the Revival that helped to fuel it further. Western Mail in particular gave extensive coverage to Evan Robert's meetings in the city of Loughor. It is believed that at least 150,000 people made Christian commitments during the movement during the revival. (http://truthinhistory.org/the-welsh- revival-of-1904-1905.html) "It has been argued by some conservative Christian historians that the 1904–1905 revival lacked the depth of previous revivals in terms of nurturing the newly converted Christians in Biblical teaching.However, many modern Pentecostal ("Charismatic") Christians reflect on this period as being critical in developing a larger (Awakening) understanding of the Holy Spirit in the greater Church, and what it was lacking during this period."

I believe my point here is that some of the meetings that we have in the Church today affect many locations beyond the meeting locations and are further pushed on by satellite television and other mass communication. We see healings and we begin to name the meetings a Revival. Following are some examples: John Arnott's meetings in Toronto, Canada that have been ongoing daily for fifteen years. Steven Hill's Brownsville meetings in Texas, Todd Bentley's Lakeland meetings in Florida and John Kilpatrick's Bay of the Holy Spirit have all been called Revivals. Some have called these meetings Awakenings. Sometimes these words are used interchangeably. I would like to use them that way as well to make my points, however, I will refer mostly to the one word revival since I named the chapter "America Needs Revival."

I want to clear up my definition of the word revival. When I speak of revival in the Church I do not mean that God will do something specific to change or cure or wake up the Church with a miraculous event. I believe when God does a miraculous event called a revival it is to awaken the people who are dead in their sins to be born again into life in the Lord. I believe that we have used the word to mean an event that may be a meeting that a church or ministry puts on and God shows up and causes healings and salvations. I do not mean that in "The Church Needs Revival." I mean that the Church in America must get its act together and stop doing their thing and start doing God's thing. I don't believe that God will create a specific event to accomplish that need. We already have the Word to show us what God wants from His Church.

I believe that a true revival does include healings, but many meetings that include healings do not initiate revival. The healings I am speaking of seem to be specific to the particular meeting, even if it occurred while viewing of the meetings from home on television. I am saying that a true revival will include healings to "awaken" the fact that there is a God to the unbeliever and then that will cause a turning to God or "back to God" for the spiritually asleep Christian. Since revive means to awake someone or a thing up from a sleep this is the essence of revival. I believe a revival can also be a spontaneous move of

God initiated by the awakening of the people by God, causing people to turn to God (Jesus), turn from their wicked ways of greed, debauchery, and lust thereby producing the fruit of revival.

Who Needs Revival?

My statement that, "America needs Revival" is not the same as the American Church needs revival. I will deal with that later. I believe that they are both connected and have been the cause for each being in this state of need.

One of my frustrations with liberal thinkers and writers is that they never have any solutions, only criticisms. It's an easy trap to fall into. The reason they are always in that mode is that they have no solutions because their agenda is just to change the control of the power in our country. They do not have true sympathy or care for the real problems of our land. So let me begin with a few thoughts. America has become a greedy, selfish, prideful, arrogant, thieving, lying, stealing, uncaring, Godless, pleasure loving, rude and thankless nation. Our sense of good and evil is seriously flawed. Our conscience is not functioning. Every person has a sense of morality. The problem is that it is not spiritual, it is secular. Many times people say they believe certain things, but when it comes down to practicing or defending the morality they say they believe, they fail. It is time to seek God, for Christians as well as non-Christians.Christians must stop their religiosity, their doing "for" Jesus and start doing what Jesus wants them to do. It's time to stop having church as usual and it's time to seek the Lord. Most churches in America will keep you so busy doing good works that you could lose your relationship with the God of the Church. Good works and programs, no matter how good they are, will not mature a person or cause them to lead a moral life. Almost all that is done in the Church is not spontaneous like helping a needy person. It must be part of a program. Jesus had no programs, He just helped as He came upon a need. How do we help the Church return to the correct relationship with the Lord?

A Revival Makes Us Think Of People Being Saved En Masse

I am not talking about this kind of revival. In Matthew 9:35-38 (NIV), "Jesus went through all the towns and villages, teaching in their synagogues, proclaiming the good news of the kingdom and healing every disease and sickness. When he saw the crowds, he had compassion on them, because they were harassed and helpless, like sheep without a shepherd. Then he said to his disciples, 'The harvest is plentiful but the workers are few. Ask the Lord of the harvest, therefore, to send out workers into his harvest field.' "I am one who thinks that the Church has misused this scripture to make more converts. I believe that the Lord in stating this was not looking for more evangelists to bring in more converts to the sheepfold that was already crowded. I believe since he was talking about Jews and they were harassed and helpless and had no shepherds, He felt compassion. What did Jesus want? He wanted them to be taken care of by a shepherd. That is the kind of the revival the American church needs now. That is the revival I am talking about.We have become fire insurance salesmen. Jesus wants His sheep to affect the world like He did. The world is affecting His sheep instead. We seem to think that a mass sale of fire insurance will save the world, but it will not. Salvation is personal. When I have my hellfire protection it does not protect my neighbor; he must buy his own. I don't want to lose my point here, my born-again experience in my life will do nothing to convert the world if I am not trained and make the world jealous of it. Romans 11:11(NIV), says, "Again I ask: Did they stumble so as to fall beyond recovery? Not at all! Rather, because of their transgression, salvation has come to the Gentiles to make Israel envious." We will not make anyone envious of having Jesus by being involved in church activities. The world wants to see commitment. They want to see something worth living for. Perhaps then we might see revival.

Has The Church Failed?

YWAM, Youth with a Mission, said it best, "We have more Christians today per capita with less impact on the culture than ever before. We are big and we are weak." To me, it sounds like the entire American Church is the Church of Laodicea mentioned in Revelation 3:15-17 (NIV), "I know your deeds, that you are neither cold nor hot. I wish you were either one or the other! So, because you are lukewarm, neither hot nor cold, I acquired wealth and do not need a thing.' But you do not realize that you are wretched, pitiful, poor, blind and naked."

Choices are made based on our personal desires, agenda, ethnicity or our sexual or political bias. I only share what follows to show the heart of the Lord. A number of years ago I was on a business trip in another state. I was with my son,

Scott and his wife. My wife was with us as well. The business was a trade show so the family was planning on doing some shopping and sightseeing. We were having breakfast in a coffee shop rather early in the morning. There was a man sweeping the floor in the restaurant; he stopped sweeping and went to the pay phone and made a call. He called a local church for some help; it seemed he needed money for a bus ticket to get to his father's funeral. Apparently, he had called the night before and was told to call in the morning as though he could get a hotel room. He asked the restaurant, an all night place, if he could sweep the floors and sleep there until morning. The restaurant agreed and now my family and I entered into this scenario. We heard the man say on the phone, "But you are a church and a pastor and you told me to call in the morning." That's all we heard, but we heard enough to know he was not going to get any help. I said to my family, "we will help." As soon as we said we would help, the most powerful anointing of the Holy Spirit I have ever felt fell on the entire restaurant, on us as well as the waitresses. My son asked, "what is that?" I can't stop crying and I feel a strange power around us." I called the waitress over to us as the restaurant was not crowded. I said we were going to help the man and gave her a handfull of money and I said, "Don't say where it came from." She was already in tears as well and said that the waitresses were going to help too. If you are reading this and feel an anointing please know that I feel it as I am writing. This is another confirmation of the heart of God. This was many years ago. I received the compassion of Jesus that morning and I still have it today. There is a great scripture I should put in here now: Zechariah 7:6-10 (TLB), "And even now in your holy feasts to God, you don't think of me, but

only of the food and fellowship and fun. Long years ago, when Jerusalem was prosperous and her southern suburbs out along the plain were filled with people, the prophets warned them that this attitude would surely lead to ruin, as it has.'" Then this message from the Lord came to Zechariah. "Tell them to be honest and fair—and not to take bribes—and to be merciful and kind to everyone. Tell them to stop oppressing widows and orphans, foreigners and poor people, and to stop plotting evil against each other."

Who Should Tell Us How To Live?

"This is what the LORD says… 'Your Redeemer, the Holy One of Israel: I am the LORD your God, who teaches you what is best for you, who directs you in the way you should go.' "(Isaiah 48:17 NIV) Enough said, for Christians at least. The world does not understand this yet. It has been our job to tell them through word and deed. We have failed, especially through deed. Saint Francis of Assisi said, "Preach the Gospel at all times, use words when necessary."

In Conclusion

My statements are quite an indictment and you might think that they don't fit America. I would challenge you to call any service-oriented company and talk to any one of their employees. Try the phone company, if that does not convince you, go to your nearest bank and try to get service. Go to the post office and ask for a little service, that's all you'll get, "a little service". There was a study done as to which industry was the most criminally corrupt. The number one corrupt industry, much to my surprise, was shown to be the banking industry. These are the very people we trust with our money, our home loans etc. When I wrote this our country had not yet experienced the banking crisis. However, now we know how corrupt the banking industry is. When I wrote this no one knew that the banking industry would be a major player in the next almost depression. Now in 2015 it is very evident to most of us. I recently got a finance charge on a credit card I use. I always pay the monthly charges as soon as I receive the bill, even the same day if I am home when the mailman arrives. I even joke that if the mailman waits, he can take the payment with him. The dates on this particular statement were manipulated to charge me a penalty and interest. I went to my bank to complain and a bank employee told me that many of their customers had the same problem and had cancelled their card. So did I.

It's Open Season on Fellow Americans

No one cares about your problem and no one wants to help. No one takes the time to understand your problem; they just pass it on to someone else. We have become a nation of "buck passers." A friend of mine once said, "We live in a wonderfully complex technically advanced time. We have terrific and very complicated goodies, gadgets and products, but they don't work and no one knows how to fix them." Think he was kidding? Just take your laptop computer in for repair, with the exception of the Apple Company, no one can tell you what's wrong or how to fix it.

Our teenagers will not work. We are dependent on foreign workers at every restaurant, and at every fast food franchise. No one speaks fluent English at any franchise. In construction, all the cement work is done by Hispanics, most of the masonry work is done by Hispanics, and all plastic factories are totally run by foreign workers. We have become a mentally, spiritually, and physically lazy country. Victor Davis Hanson's book, "Mexifornia", describes how dependent we are on foreign workers and what the end will look like in just a few years. I have a business in Santa Ana, California and English has become a second language there. Most of my workers are temporary. They are transients; they come and go as they please and they have no roots. They live two and three families together; they probably entered the U.S. illegally, they don't speak English and sometimes they don't care about their jobs or how they perform in them. The last statement is slightly exaggerated, some do care and are good employees. The statement that is put out by our liberal government is that these foreign workers are taking jobs from Americans. Find me Americans. There are no American workers that will do difficult work for low income. Some jobs cannot pay $20.00 an hour. If I need workers I must hire the migrants or shut my doors, as there are no US citizens willing to work and I start all my workers above minimum wage with insurance.

I don't want you to think that I am breaking the law hiring undocumented workers. They all have social security cards and all I must do is photocopy them and place them in a file with their name. There is no way to verify the honesty of the card; I am not permitted to do more than photocopy them. A while back a state agent came in to my business and asked if I had any undocumented workers. I said, "you tell me", and handed him my files. He looked at the phony cards and walked out.

I say phony because some come in for a job with cards with obvious girl's names on them. We tell them to go away. A few days later they come back with a better card. You may wonder why the government likes these semi-documented workers. The reason is I withhold taxes from their pay and file forms and send the money to the government; the workers are afraid to file taxes, so the government keeps all the money.

Does God Care About Our Work?

Our surveys reveal that 90-97% of Christians have never heard a sermon relating Biblical principles to their work life. Doug Sherman, author of , "Your Work Matters to God", in a San Francisco radio station survey revealed an 80% employee dissatisfaction rate with their work. A Wall Street Journal survey revealed a 50% dissatisfaction rate among executives and 80% dissatisfaction rate among general workplace population. Bill McCartney of Promise Keepers says, "The early Church began in the marketplace where the Apostles rubbed shoulders with the lost." Evangelism is pure in the workplace (marketplace). Usually there are no denominational hindrances because the goal is universal, to affect the lost. Then why doesn't it work? Why are we not effective? One reason the Body of Christ has nothing to say is because though they may not be as bad as the world, they are bad enough to be ineffective and the world knows it. The devil uses it to keep our message from going forth. Ed Silvoso of Anointed for Business Harvest Evangelism says, "The most common self-inflicted put-down is, 'I am not a pastor,I am just a layperson.' This is all part of a clever satanic scheme to neutralize apostles, prophets, evangelists, pastors and teachers along with the entire army of disciples, already positioned in the marketplace."

The people of God must stop going into "church work" as their natural course of action and go into farming, industry, law, education, banking, and journalism with the same zeal previously given to evangelism or to pastoral and missionary work. I see so many Christians going into fields of ministry with enough zeal to build a great business that could impact the Kingdom of God ten-fold more than a duplication of someone else's ministry. We in the business world need to say, "I am a Christian, Bible teacher or evangelist masquerading as a business person."

In much of our witness to the world, we have a long way to go. Our problem is inside the organized church in preparing the witnesses to witness. It has nothing to do with form or technique. Life change is what will draw the world to Jesus. I believe we need to leave the church to find the Gospel. If we take a survey and ask believers what the Gospel is I believe that they will say it is accepting Jesus as Savior. True, but the Good News (the Gospel) is more than saying a prayer and inviting Jesus into your heart. That part is forgiveness of our sins, promises of eternal life, of healing and Heaven when we die. But we think that the Gospel is only what God does for us. The rest of the Gospel is what we must do for God. We cannot live the same old life we lived before we prayed that prayer. Jesus says take up your cross and follow Me.

God came to the Earth and suffered and died on a Cross to provide a perfect sacrifice for our sins, past, present and future. But there is more. We need help to change America and ourselves. If the churches won't help, we will inherit what we see before our eyes today. We may need to leave the American form of church and adopt the Chinese underground method to grow the church and make disciples. That form is not chosen but forced upon Christians. America is close to this because the unsaved world can say to us that they do as good or better than you without Jesus, so why do we need Jesus? Try to answer that question when witnessing to an unbeliever. I am sorry if you do not like this, but it is true and we need to face it and find a way to change it before it is too late. I heard Brother Yun, one of the leaders in the underground church in China (he visited my church) say he spent most of his life in prison for his faith in Jesus. He said, "We don't pray for acceptance by the government because we grow at 15,000 converts a day underground." He has proved the saying, "The blood of the martyrs is the seed of the Church." Brother Yun's book is "Heavenly Man".

Chapter Eleven

Open Season on Fellow Americans-
Can We Get Justice In America?

Try calling the police for anything short of murder and you will be put off. You will be pushed off to an uncaring pre-recorded tape to tell your story and file your report. File that report for a theft and you will discover there is no help for you. You won't even see a policeman. Justice doesn't exist any longer in America. Go to court and watch the police lie before your very eyes to get the conviction they want. I can state a couple of situations and you will think I am not telling you all the truth but I am.

One of the most troubling issues is how attorneys operate in American. I want to say I have many attorneys that are personal friends and many of them know the Lord and attend church just as I do. It is difficult for me to be friends with some of them because of the manner in which they work and think of people's needs. When I think of a person's needs I just want to help and so did Jesus. It seems to me some say what's in it for me? I feel that that sometimes attorneys are more interested in money than justice.

It reminds me of the story of the turtle and the snake crossing the river. The snake asked the turtle to let him hop on his back to cross the river. The turtle said, "No, you will bite me." The snake said, "No, I won't, I will drown too." So the turtle agreed. Just before they reached the opposite shore the snake bit the turtle. The turtle said, "But you said you wouldn't bite me." The snake said, "I'm sorry I'm a snake; it's what I do." I feel that some attorneys do not care who wins as long as they can bill hours. I apologize to all my attorney friends, but facts are facts, truth is truth and it is hard to find those in a courtroom today.

I recently saw an attorney friend of mine with a new "toy" costing over $110,000. I had a hard time congratulating him because I knew how he got it. His excuse is he helped a person in need and won the case. I wonder if the person in need was able to buy an $110,000 toy. I also know that my insurance rates may go up because of his windfall, or at least by the cumulative successes of his and his attorney friends. I think what bothers me is when I can afford to buy an $110,000 toy, it doesn't hurt anyone else. Attorneys are running rampant over the country. Many are merciless. They will do pro bono (free work) for anything degenerate or anti-Christian, but you and I must pay. You can be accused of a simple crime of which you are innocent, but your attorneys will still bankrupt you and your family to get you any justice at all. Judges and district attorneys will not put the real criminals in prison, but they will put you in jail and destroy your life without a thought. They will claim that you must be treated the same as everyone else. The problem is they don't put the "everyone else" in jail; they will allow them to lie about other people and use those lies to get a conviction to add to their portfolio, or what is worse, to get even with a defendant to let the real criminal off. There is nothing worse than a lying or corrupt attorney. They used to say that there was honor among thieves but that's not true; they will turn on each other and lie and make up stories to get just one day off of their sentence. The police and attorneys know this and they take advantage of it. Recently on the news a man who was accused of a murder and incarcerated for nineteen years, begged the district attorney who tried him to test his DNA when DNA became accepted for guilt or innocence in trials. He was repeatedly refused until a judge forced the issue, and the man was proved innocent. The D.A. did not care that the man may have been innocent or that he spent nineteen years in jail. He did not want his record marred by a reversed conviction. The fact that a man's life was being ruined did not seem to matter. In my opinion, the District Attorney should take this guy's place in his cell. Selfish greed and injustice have become commonplace in our country. I can tell you that you will not receive justice in a secular world, but Jesus will give you justice and He will give you mercy. If He gave you and me what we deserve, we would not like what we get. He gave us salvation when we were guilty and did not deserve it.

I was recently in court for another matter (now I sound like an attorney) and while there I saw seven young Hispanics being sentenced. Each was a multiple offender and it was obvious they would not be able to pay the large fines due after their jail time. They will be back again. I realized that Hispanics who are legal aliens or have been born in America are quite different from the illegal Hispanics. The illegal ones only want to work for money while the legal ones are very similar to the regular American youth who don't want to work. The illegal ones would never even break the traffic laws let alone steal a car or get involved with drugs for fear of being deported.However, it doesn't seem to take a long time once they become legal to adopt the American lazy, greedy, immoral and lawless lifestyle.

Another situation I want to relate to make my point involves my close friend who was robbed by his friend. This fellow told some of his friends whom he had spent time with in prison that my friend had a lot of cash in his safe at his office. The amount stolen was considerable along with gold coins (my friend collected rare gold coins). My friend tells the story that he realized that his "so-called friend" had something to do with the robbery the moment he discovered that the safe was broken open because he was the only one who knew the money was in the safe. He confronted the friend with the words, "Why did you do this to me?" The friend denied he had anything to do with the crime. At this point my friend said, "Don't lie, I have you on videotape." The friend confessed and handed over $30,000 and some gold coins. My friend said that the money was only a small part of the money stolen. He called the police and had him arrested. Now the rest of this story is not believable. The district attorney would not charge this convicted felon with this crime, and he did not spend a day in jail. He lied and said my friend held a gun to his head and made him confess. The return of a small portion of the loot did not seem to show guilt to this D.A. My friend, then in frustration, wrote letters to as many officials he could think of in his county and city. After about three months he received a call from an official from the county saying that my friend's letters had gotten much attention and that they were going to prosecute this criminal and get justice for my friend. After another three months, the trial started and lasted five days. My friend's attorney (paid by my friend, more thousands of dollars) said to him, "Although he has confessed, you are still going to lose because the jury is just like the defendant; they have no money and you do and they are glad that he robbed you". The criminal went free. My friend called and told me this story and said the system is flawed. He rhetorically asked, "How do I get out of this country"?

I say the judicial system is corrupt, along with the IRS and most of the government. If you think I am wrong, you will have a harder job proving your position than I will. Our judicial system needs a revival. I don't want to forget large corporations. Is there any difference between a person breaking into a store during a time of civil crisis and looting TV's and other items, and the oil companies looting Americans at the gas pumps, crying the storm, the storm, while posting the largest profits in history at the same time? The answer is NO.

What Did God Say About a Dishonest Justice System?

This is what God says He will do and what we should do about a corrupt judicial system: Amos 5:11-15 (NLT), "You trample the poor, stealing their grain through taxes and unfair rent. Therefore, though you build beautiful stone houses,you will never live in them. Though you plant lush vineyards, you will never drink wine from them. For I know the vast number of your sins and the depth of your rebellions. You oppress good people by taking bribes and deprive the poor of justice in the courts. So those who are smart keep their mouths shut, for it is an evil time. Do what is good and run from evil so that you may live! Then the Lord God of Heaven's Armies will be your helper, just as you have claimed. Hate evil and love what is good; turn your courts into true halls of justice. Perhaps even yet the Lord God of Heaven's Armies will have mercy on the remnant of his people." Habakkuk, the Old Testament prophet, had a complaint about the injustice of his time. This sounds too familiar. Habakkuk 1:2-4 (NLT), "How long, O Lord, must I call for help? But you do not listen! "Violence is everywhere!" I cry, but you do not come to save. Must I forever see these evil deeds? Why must I watch all this misery? Wherever I look, I see destruction and violence. I am surrounded by people who love to argue and fight. The law has become paralyzed, and there is no justice in the courts. The wicked far outnumber the righteous, so that justice has become perverted." When I wrote this we had not experienced the sort of punishment we are seeing against Christians now in Iraq by a group of people called ISIS. Will these people come to America? Does what they do sound like the description of the Babylonians that God describes in Habakkuk 1: 2-4? They were notorious for their violent cruelty. Who will march across the world and conquer ISIS? The Lord replied,"Look around at the nations; look and be amazed! For I am doing something in your own day, something you wouldn't believe even if someone told you about it. I am raising up the Babylonians, a cruel and violent people. They will march across the world and conquer other lands. They are notorious for their cruelty and do whatever they like. Their horses are swifter than cheetahs and fiercer than wolves at dusk. Their charioteers charge from far away. Like eagles, they swoop down to devour their prey. On they come, all bent on violence. Their hordes advance like a desert wind, sweeping captives ahead of them like sand.They scoff at kings and princes and scorn all their fortresses. They simply pile ramps of earth against their walls and capture them! They sweep past like the wind and are gone. But they are deeply guilty, for their own strength is their god."

Is what we are seeing in Iraq by the Muslim hordes the judgment of God? If not, we can change the name of who God will raise up to punish the unjust, the greedy and the lawless this time. It may be Muslims or whomever we fear the most. Some people exemplify a lack of fear of God. I have concluded that the lawless, most of Hollywood and the East coast elite do not fear God.I look at the deeds done by merciless attorneys, IRS agents, greedy corporations and criminals who will rob you and then for no reason kill you, they have no fear of a spiritual retribution from a just God. We have come so far that people do not fear a God they cannot see.

Has Our Government Become Our Enemy?

I do not mean for any of my criticisms and questions to be rhetorical. I want to provide solutions to them if I can. Why are we a target to be exploited by every governmental agency and there is nothing we can do about it? I believe that we who work and provide the taxes for the programs and entitlements are becoming smaller and smaller in number and are able to be out voted by the millions and millions who are on the take from these programs. We are bankrupt and the government looks to us to solve their problem. They will use the police by giving tickets for some minor infraction and then the fine does not fit the infraction. It will be high enough to put some people out of their homes. The government does not care. Its them against us and they have all the aces. We always lose and they always win.

Many Americans are Wonderful Givers

I want to change horses and talk about some of the people in our country. Since I began writing this, the country has been going through horrible hurricanes, tornados, floods, oil spills and earthquakes with innocent sounding names like Katrina and Hurricane Sandy. The country has turned into the help mode, and the churches have begun to give help as best they can. This is heartening and seems contradictory to my premise. However, Matthew 22:39 is not the premise of this book. This has been Church's finest hour as related to me by a minister whose church was restored after the Katrina flood. The Christian Broadcasting Network (CBN) through their Operation Blessing fed thousands for months along with medical and construction help and more. Other ministries like Samaritan's Purse did the same mercy work, while the Red Cross left the scene after the news people left.

Why Has The Government Become Our Enemy?

In California we must balance the budget. Our governor wanted to and he said we are taking in $1.30 and spending $2.00 and it had to stop. You would think teacher's unions and other federal and state unions would understand that simple math, well maybe not. Any honest government leader will have a tough fight because the gimmes are out numbering the givees. The state of California has just enacted a new tax on limited liability companies, LLCs. My business is an LLC and the tax is about as unfair as it can be. It is a tax on revenue. It is not on profit - it is on revenue, whether you made any money or not. It is a percentage of the revenue. Mine was $6,000. In January, 6 months in advance and in June, they want another $6,000 for the rest of the year in advance. America needs a revival.

Since this is an ongoing work I can now tell you that our governor has not been reelected because he has succumbed to the pressure of the aforementioned groups and the state of California is bankrupt. Now liberal people have elected a former governor who was possibly the worst ever. Now even he sees that the state is bankrupt. We are seeing that many U.S. states are bankrupt and cities as well. We have turmoil in the streets. The people who don't understand simple math think that if we can just raise taxes, everything will be ok. It's difficult to ascribe greediness to an entity, but our government is greedy. It's greedy for power and money and it will do anything to get and keep both. We see that the power and control that it already has it makes it easier for it to get more. The government makes unholy alliances with agencies, with the media, with people on the dole and with private and public companies that will push their agenda for a promise of their share of the power and wealth. We taxpayers are powerless to stop the blackmail because of votes that keep it going.

This brings up another subject. Well, it is the same subject except it involves the government at the federal level. I am speaking of the Hispanic vote. The Federal Government understands that if they give amnesty to all the illegal Hispanics in the country then they will vote for the party that gave them amnesty. This is the biggest power grab ever in our country.We don't gerrymander anymore, we now give amnesty to a entire population who will be so grateful that they will keep the party in office who was so generous to them.Our government has learned the Santa Claus principle. Who wouldn't vote for Santa Claus? Everybody wants a gift. Someone mentioned to me that people who illegally come to America always vote Democrat because they do not understand. They think they came to a democratic country and should vote Democrat. Makes sense, but conservatives lose again.

Why Has Our Two Party System Failed?

I recently rented a building to start a new business. I paid three months rent before I got an occupancy permit from uncaring bureaucrats. I was also surprised to find out that I had to read a 33 page document of rules to enable me to put a simple $100.00 sign on the building. I also needed to pay a $500 fee. I have no sign on the building yet. Delivery people are having a hard time finding me.

Take the confirmation of our Supreme Court Justices. The Democrat Party does not care if we have a qualified person as a nominee or, in fact , a sitting justice. They only want their supposed power in the courts to continue. The word ethics could not be mentioned in the conformation process in any way. Without mentioning any names, the Democratic Party has done virtually nothing in the last year except to try to stop President Bush's appointees and find a way to get the president impeached. Now that we have a new President, Mr. Obama with both houses in the democratic majority, we are in for problems we can't even imagine. Now, some years after I wrote that, thank God we have been able to take back the House and the Senate as well. We have seen six full years of the Obama presidency and our country is in the worst shape since the 1929 Depression. This time we are without God as the foundation of our Constitution and country, and the Ten Commandments are now banned from every public building. So the premise of this chapter that America needs a spiritual revival is more needed than ever before. If we think having a Republican majority in the Senate and the House of Representatives will save us, we are fooling ourselves. We need a spiritual revival because we need a heart change in the people and the government and that speaks of God taking over or nothing will save us from the future.

The blatant lying being put forth in TV adds with cooperation by the liberal media is evidence of the loss of ethics in the highest places in our country. When we see this misguided agenda within a political party in our country that almost half of the lawmakers are in, their silence is quiet acceptance of all the unethical practices taking place by their party. They have joined in the theft of the largesse of the country. We are in serious trouble. Now that the country is faced with a conservative House and Senate and a liberal president, they fight each other on every issue. When God created the heavens and the Earth, the Bible says there was chaos on the face of the Earth. I believe we have gone back to chaos and God needs to deal with it again.

The IRS is Out of Control

I realize that I sound pretty discouraged, and that's because I am. I have been fighting an IRS audit and lawsuit for 14 years now. It has cost my brother and I hundreds of thousands of dollars in attorneys' fees. Oh by way, the IRS just sent me a letter in October, 2013, stating that we owe them nothing. By the way, you may know that there is a statue of limitations on tax audits. However, the IRS came to me just before the 7 year limit. They asked me to sign a paper to extend the limit and I said no. They said then we will make a decision on your case now, so I extended it for 7 more years. Remember that I was judged innocent of all fees and penalties, but suffered seven more years of attorney fees, and the unknown fear of what may be put upon us. The IRS is out of control and no one can do anything about it. The IRS is told by a greedy Congress to go after the businesses and the rich people because they are all crooks. While there is greed and lack of ethics in many businesses and many people try to avoid paying their taxes, Congress and the IRS are accusing us of the same greed and lack of ethics that are blatant in congress and the tax system. Nothing is more difficult than fighting a corrupt tax system being encouraged by a greedy Congress who know that more money means more power for them. The battle for the soul of America is a spiritual one; do not think it that can be won with guns and bullets, it cannot. I had written this before the latest

IRS debacle perpetrated on all 501C3 new charitable groups and conservative groups in general. Since I have written this we are seeing more IRS corruption than we could have imagined.

We Need Revival In Our Churches, Courts, Cities And States

To continue my expose' of all that's wrong with America, unlike those on the opposite side of these issues who only complain but have no answers, I have answers and you will read them all throughout this book. They are all spiritual cures and fall at the feet of our American pastors. I keep quoting Zechariah 10:3 that the Lord is angry with the shepherds and He will punish.

Chapter Twelve

Little Farm Towns Are Not Safe Any More

This next story can be put in either the column marked issues of injustice or in the column marked issues of greed. My close friend has a heavy equipment company in the Grand Rapids area of Michigan. While transferring his crane through a town in Michigan, his driver was given a ticket by a local policeman for not having a permit to drive through this particular town (all of these towns are 99% country farmland). He did not think much of the ticket because the cost of the permit is $8.00. No mistake, just $8.00. He went to pay the ticket after the city notified him that he had neglected to pay it. They told him that there would be a fine for not paying it. The fine was $25,000.00 and that is not a typo. He thought that it was a typo but soon found it was not and that the court was not kidding. He told the judge that he was considering bankruptcy, which was true. The judge did not care. They just wanted their money. My friend did not think he would need an attorney for such a small infraction. However, he did need one. He hired an attorney and the attorney was able to get the fine reduced to $6,000.00 payable at $100.00 per month.

Now let me see if I have this straight. In Michigan there is no limit on fines for any infraction of their laws? God forbid you should commit a real crime. Does this remind you of a bad TV show where the main character drives into this small town with big city thinking, commits a small infraction and is locked up with no hope of justice because all the officials that are part of the scheme? The justice in that town is nonexistent just like it is in this little town in Michigan. The only problem is that this is a real story and this is a real town. My friend, with the help of his family, is paying the fine and is trying to sell his company. He will take the fine with him if he sells as a little reminder of the greed and in- justice in America. I would like to add that there is a church on just about every corner in the Michigan farm country. They are mostly conservative Bible believing non-charismatic churches. The church needs Revival as well. I have a current update to this story. My friend has gone out of business and has left that town in Michigan and found work in another state. To keep his wife and their three children from losing their home, it will take all of his family and be a work of God. What a country! I have used many personal examples from my family and myself, as I know them firsthand.

Corporate America is Greedy

If I, as a businessman, got together with a competitor and decided to set prices on our products, we would be charged with price fixing and charged with violation of the Sherman

Antitrust Laws or the Robinson-Patman Act. Yet every gas station in America has been fixing prices or at least the oil companies have been fixing prices to the extent that they are bankrupting the small businessman, the single mom, the student and anyone on a fixed income or no income and the government says nothing.

Today I saw a gas station selling premium gas for $4.09 and regular was $3.95. I wonder what it will go up to before long if someone doesn't stop it? Ever wondered why the government does nothing about this situation? As the gas price goes up the government gets their share as increased sales tax on a higher sale. In the state of California there is a .041¢ tax on every gallon of gas sold in the state, but that is deceiving. Observe this scenario 18.1¢ Federal 7.75% sales tax and a county tax of 4.5¢ all based on 1 gallon. Including sales tax on a typical sale, California would receive an increase on every penny of increase from the oil companies. If we pay $3.00, California gets .23¢ per gallon for sales tax. When the gas was $2.35, California only got around .18¢. Guess what gas price California likes better? By the way, after receiving all the tax money from the gas sales, the citizens of California voted to raise the sales tax to 8.75%. Don't believe that the oil companies are hurting from any natural disaster. The Mobil Exxon Company just posted the largest profits in their history, 9 billion for one quarter. I wonder how it got that high? Is this any different than looting stores during a crisis? Those oils guys are too old to carry TV's.

The drug companies are financially raping the poor, the sick and even the insurance companies. The hospitals are doing the same to the insurance companies, but don't feel sorry for the insurance companies. They are raping the doctors and the people who need to buy insurance. Prices on medical insurance are going up. Coverages are going down and guess who is caught in the middle? It's the same people who are always in the middle. Nothing seems to touch the consciousness of these companies. They are not touched by the needs of the people. Now with Obamacare, God help us. We are seeing the government getting into the insurance business. The government knows how much money the insurance companies make, so it is just logical for the government to want a piece of their action. There is a big difference in that they will not have any competition from other insurance companies, so they will do what all monopolies do, they will cut services and raise premiums. No services mean that they will not pay for anything that reduces their bottom line even if it kills us.

There have been discoveries that will cure many diseases, and many of those cures have been natural cures. The drug companies along with the FDA have kept them from being sold to the public because the drug companies make money on the medicine that does not cure. It addresses symptoms, but needs to be taken daily all your life with disastrous side effects. Did I already mention the insurance companies who sold insurance in New Orleans have left the people with nothing claiming that the coverage was for wind and not water damage?

I recently had an insurance claim for a leak in my cement floor in my bedroom. I called a plumber and they had me turn the water off (it was the middle of the night). In the morning they came and used some electronic device, found the leak and destroyed my wall on both sides of my bedroom and bathroom under my cabinets and fixed the pipe. They came in at 9am and left at 1pm with $1,700.00 of my money. That is without the wall repaired. Four hours of work for $1,700. That's $425.00 per hour. That's more than my doctor makes. Now the fun starts. I called the insurance company to put in a claim. They said that they stopped covering cement leaks in floors because lots of homes get them. That would make sense if you are an insurance company and do not want to pay claims, just collect premiums. They did say that they would pay for fixing my holes in the walls and the cabinetry. This sounded good until they reminded me that I had $2,500.00 deductible. I estimated that it will probably cost around $2,000 and it did.

The Insurance, Drug Companies And The FDA Need Revival

The FDA does not approve a natural product to lower cholesterol, but approves products that destroy our liver and kidneys.Eli Lilly Company invented insulin back in the early 1900's and in almost 100 years has not made an improvement in the cure for the disease that won't hurt your organs. They have changed and improved the medication and continued collecting money on insulin and the improved types of medication. I know of a natural remedy for diabetes, but the FDA won't tell anyone about it and barely allows it to be made. I just noticed a class action lawsuit against Eli Lilly for $700 million dollars for their drug Zyprexa. Another suit is underway is for their drug Prozac for neglecting to state the dangers on the label. It's a terrible thing when the class action lawyers are the consciences of the drug companies. It makes it difficult and confusing as to who the enemy really is, the drug companies or the lawyers.... uhh not really. Mr. Rockefeller, when asked how much money is enough, said, "Just a little more." Greed breeds greed.

Drug Companies Want Money, Not Cures

Los Angeles (Aug. 25) - California's Attorney General has just said that the state has filed a lawsuit accusing 39 pharmaceutical companies of bilking the state's Medicaid program of hundreds of millions of dollars by inflating drug prices. After writing about the drug companies this article appeared in the newspaper listed below:

Calif. Attorney General Bill Lockyer said he has added companies including Amgen Inc.(AMGN.O) and GlaxoSmithKline Plc (GSK.L) to a previous complaint accusing Abbott Laboratories (ABT.N) and Wyeth (WYE.N) of hiding the true costs of their drugs so that payments from Medi-Cal, California's health insurance program for the poor, would be artificially inflated. Medi-Cal is the name for California's Medicaid program for the indigent, which is financed by the state and federal government. "We're dragging these drug companies into the court of law because they're gouging the public on basic life necessities,"' Lockyer said.

Egalitarianism is Dead in America

What happened to our egalitarian spirit in America? You remember, when a common enemy attacked America or the world, everyone forgot personal issues and all helped defeat the enemy whatever it was. Not today. Our large corporations are like one of the 007 villains who hold the World hostage for millions or billions of dollars and promise tragedy will strike the World. They now have figured out that they don't even need to build the threatening weapon. Look at the latest hurricane that has allowed the oil companies to hold all of us for ransom because they hold the keys to the gas (oil and natural gas) we need for our daily lives. Remember Exxon Mobil recently posted their highest profits this last quarter of $9 billion. If we could smell them they would leave a foul stench in our nostrils. Did I mention greed breeds greed, and did I mention that America needs, well you know?

Our School System Needs Revival

Let me talk a little about our school system. Our teachers have stopped teaching our children. All they want is more money. They hated our previous governor, Arnold Schwarzenegger, not because he wanted to balance the budget that was bankrupting the state, but because he wanted to cut funds from the schools and the fire department and because he didn't want to add anymore money from the budget to their institutions. They wanted the budget balanced but not in their areas. The school children in California are ranked at 46% among others in the nation. We have the highest funding per child in the nation and still teachers and their unions want more money. The following scenario is typical.

This happened to me at a coffee shop recently, however, I have embellished it somewhat. I purchased a coffee for $1.58. The counter girl took my two dollars, but I found some change so I gave her 8 cents. She stood there, holding the nickel and 3 pennies, while looking at the screen on her register. I sensed her discomfort and tried to tell her to just give me two quarters, but she hailed the manager for help. While he tried to explain the transaction to her, she stood there and cried. Why do I tell you this? Because of the evolution in teaching math in our country since the 1950's. In the 50's the teaching would have gone like this;A logger sells a truckload of lumber for $100. His cost of production is 4/5 of the price. What is his profit? In the 60's a logger sells a truckload of lumber for $100. His cost of production is 4/5 of the price, or $80. What is his profit? In the 70's a logger sells a truckload of lumber for $100. His cost of production is $80. Did he make a profit? In the 80's a logger sells a truckload of lumber for $100. His cost of production is $80 and his profit is $20. Your assignment: Underline the number 20. In the 90's a logger cuts down a beautiful forest because he is selfish and inconsiderate and cares nothing for the habitat of animals or the preservation of our woodlands. He does this so he can make a profit of $20.What do you think of this way of making a living? This is the topic for class participation after answering the question: How did the birds and squirrels feel as the logger cut down their homes? (There are no wrong answers.) And finally in the 2000's: Un lendor vende un camion con madera por $100. El coste de las produccion fue de $80. Que opinas? This says it all. Not quite. The teachers are not totally to blame.The system that sets the curriculum carries far more blame. Many of the teachers who want to teach cannot because of a system that has lost its moral compass.

I questioned a teacher friend of mine when he said that the money for the war in Iraq should have been spent on education. My question to him was did he think if we spent another \$2 or \$3 billion on education would that be enough to bring the ranking of our children from 46% to up to 45%? I got no answer. I told this same teacher that I would like the Bible taught and read in the public school system. He said, "That would be disruptive because it is a religious book". I told him that the school system had just purchased thousands of Harry Potter books to be read and studied in the schools and they espouse witchcraft which is a religion.I asked my friend how come the schools would read and study the religion of witchcraft but not the Bible? As always, he had no answer. It was easy for him to have no answer because we were communicating by email, so he just didn't answer when he had no answer.

The Bible Is The Word Of God And Does Not Need Anything

The Bible was written thousands of years ago. There are 66 books written by 40 writers in 3 languages, Hebrew, Aramaic and Greek. There are no contradictions and there is a continual theme running throughout the entire book. The Bible was the first book ever translated from one language to another. The Bible was the first book to be printed on a printing press, the Gutenberg invention. It's the best selling book in all of history, it is translated into more languages than any other book, and it is still being translated daily into obscure languages in remote parts of the world. Unbelievers and believers alike have read and studied it for years and freely admit we have not totally understood all of it. Yet it is not good enough to be read and taught in our schools. America is in a spiritual battle and America and the school system desperately need Revival. If you don't think America and the school system needs revival and that the battle is a spiritual one I don't know how to convince you. I could write about the schools system and what ails it and who ails it for the rest of this book, but what I have already written will have to suffice.

Chapter Thirteen

The China Solution/My Solution

People say, "We import everything from China. " I know ethics seem non-existent in China. It seems that everyone in China is only concerned about himself or herself. Their people are rude. Many Asians bring their own culture here and seem slow at adopting our culture or assimilating in that they treat America as an extension of their country. These cultures are mostly non-Christian and are full of prejudice, superstition and non-Christian and non-American ways. They don't seem to add much to our culture, save a good work ethic and great food. The more that come, the more our culture is diluted. Our country has come so far from our Christian principles and so politically correct that we are afraid to even recognize we have a problem because we do not want to offend anyone. I don't want to belittle the Chinese; I am only pointing out what I have seen in our country and theirs. Americans can teach them plenty on how to be rude.

In Beijing

As I write this I am in Beijing, China. I have never experienced a more superstitious and gambling prone race of people. Almost everything they do is motivated by some plan to bring them good luck. They don't seem to believe in a supreme being. I watched while people were burning hands full of incense sticks in front of an idol of some sort (I have pictures). The person explaining it to me did not even know whom they were worshipping. He said they burn incense to get good luck. My theory is no one ever loved an idol. They worship it to get something from it. This seems exactly what is done in China. They almost seem like they are a society of superstitious people who won't step on the cracks in the sidewalk for fear of having bad luck. This culture is being exported to America by some Asians that arrive in our country. The above description is not of the 200 million Chinese born again Christians that are underground in China. They are the salvation of China and possibly America. I have discussed my thoughts below.

Classes in China

The society in China is agrarian to a large extent and that is where the poor are. They are very open to evangelization by the Chinese Christians who are evangelizing 15,000 people per day. The middle class is another element of their infrastructure that work in factories and are somewhat better off. I visited a city in China called Chongqing (pronounced Chun King). It is the city that has the Flying Tigers Museum. It also has has a population of about 29.2 million. While I was there I asked one of the people I was with what their manufacturing product was and he said we make 3 million motorcycles a year. I mention this because none of the workers could afford to buy any of these motorcycles. In fact, hardly any of the general population of China can buy the fancy electronic items they make for the rest of the world.

I have a story about the upper class group. They are the super rich. I have a friend in China who has a large business. He used to do some business in the USA. While here working with my friend but they lived far apart and my home was in the middle so they met at my home a number of times. While I was in China, my friend said that our mutual friend wanted to see me; he said he owed me for my hospitality. When I got to Beijing I called him. He now owns a six-story building and has 2,000 tenants. The tenants have booths about 8'x8' selling many of the items made in China to tourists. We went to dinner and we talked. After dinner my friend invited me to stay at his home during the Olympics. He said he had a 12,000 square foot home. I thought he was exaggerating. I could not go but my friend in the US did and he told me yes, it was at least that big. I said this to say that there is an upper class in China.

Another interesting story regarding the upper class in China was related to me by my son who travels to China many times during the year as he has partners and a manufacturing factory there. He related a story to me about the last time he was there. He was at dinner at a new restaurant. My son is a wine enthusiast, so while at dinner he asked sommelier' for the wine list. He brought it and my son asked if he had any better wines than were on the list. The sommelier' said, "Follow me."

My son thought, "I am in Shanghai," but that can't happen here now can it?" He took a chance and followed the fellow and they went to an elevator which went down a few floors. When the doors opened there before them was a huge wine cellar with very good wines with commensurate prices. After looking over the wine for a while, the sommelier' went over to a large cabinet and pressed a button underneath the rim. The cabinet slid away reveling the real wine cellar. The wine in this room had prices at around $10,000 a bottle. My son asked who could afford these wine prices, maybe the Arabs? "No", the sommelier' said, "the Chinese." I saw a statistic stating that China rivals the U.S. in billionaires.

China: Our Model For Christianity

Does the above heading seem contradictory after reading the previous paragraphs? It is to some degree, but remember there are around 2 billion people in China. Having said the above, I will still say that China is in the midst of a Christian revival that I covet for America. I will spend an inordinate amount of time on this revival since the China solution is my idea of the solution for America so I will begin. When Mao came into power he abolished all the temples to any god, he said he was god, and his wife (remember the gang of 4) continued Mao's wishes after his death. This left an opportunity for the Gospel of Jesus Christ to flourish because the people had no religion and were open to the Gospel. I have been to China many times and some of my comments are from my own experiences.

How Could They Have A Revival?

While in China I asked certain people that I knew what religion they were. They said that they had no religion because Mao banned all religion. Today there are around 150 to 200 million real Christians in China. I use the word real because they are suffering persecution for their faith. They are multiplying at the rate of 15,000 per day. This is significant because for the first time the conversion rate exceeds the birth rate. In the past, the Western missionaries like Hudson Taylor never believed that China could ever be evangelized because the birth rate greatly exceeded the conversion rate. However, Mao installed the one baby law in China and now the Christians say that law has opened the way for the rate of conversion to make it possible to evangelize the nation.

Read David Aikman's, "Jesus in Beijing", "The Heavenly Man", the story of Brother Yun, and David Aikman's, " Back to Jerusalem". These books will bring you up to date on the move of Christ in China. Check Google. It states that there are 200 million Christians in China in 2013. There were books in the hotel gift shops throughout China with titles like, "Mao, a Man not a God." This is a complete departure from the time of his reign when he claimed to be a god. (Update: 1-10-07: For the first time the Chinese government stated publicly that there are 150 million Chinese born-again Christians. We would not expect that number would be an inflated number as it would not be flattering to the Communism Government, in fact it probably was under-inflated.)

China an Enigma And a Conundrum

China is an enigma (contradiction) and a conundrum

(puzzle/mystery). I will explain and I believe you will agree. China is the second largest human population in the world, second only to India, with a landmass that is the largest country as well. They have a nuclear capability, yet they could be considered a third world country. American Christian ministries send medical and humanitarian aid to China. Organizations like Christian Broadcasting Network (CBN) with its Operation Blessing and World Reach arm, send medical teams and help with water needs in remote areas for the farm people. That is an enigma. America has borrowed billions upon billions of dollars from China and this is a third world country? The Bible says, "Just as the rich rule the poor, the borrower is slave to the lender" (Proverbs 22: 7 NIV). This above paragraph is an enigma.

While the Communist government is arresting Christians when they find their meetings and even torturing them and putting them in prison, they are allowing this underground revival to continue and are allowing American Christian Ministries to financially help their poor agrarian people. This is an enigma. A conundrum is defined as a puzzle. So, China is an enigma wrapped in a conundrum.

The Heavenly Man

I read Brother Yun's book, "The Heavenly Man", and it changed my thinking in many ways. I dreamed of meeting him but thought it would never happen as he was considered one of the leaders in the underground church in China and was always arrested whenever he was found. Eventually he moved to Germany and now has come to America. My pastor at the church I attend read Brother Yun's book and it changed his life, so he looked into finding out where he was. He found him and invited him to our church. My dream to meet him was fulfilled. In addition we received current information which I have put in this book.

What is the Agenda of the Chinese Church?

They are very evangelistic, both to their brothers, the Chinese and to certain parts of the world. For example, because they are Asian and are from a Communist country, they have open access to North Korea and they are there. They also have missionaries in the Muslim countries (no one expects Chinese Christians). They also have a movement called the 10-40 Window. The 10/40 Window is a term coined by Christian missionary strategist Luis Bush in 1990 to refer to those regions of the eastern hemisphere plus the European and African part of the western hemisphere located between 10 and 40 degrees north of the equator. These numbers are geographical locations generally believed to be the places where the Gospel of Christ has not been preached. These geographic locations include the Muslim countries and Jerusalem. They also have a specific program to bring the Gospel to the Jews in Israel called The Back to Jerusalem Movement. Their agenda is the command of Jesus, "Go into all the world and preach the Gospel to every creature" (Mark 16: 15 NKJV). Again an enigma wrapped in a conundrum.

Why would God use China to do what the Western Christians should be doing? Did America drop the ball? There is more to going into the world and preaching. There needs to be prayer backup at home, along with resources, and more backup at home. This is not to say that the Western Body of Christ is doing nothing; they are doing much in many parts of the world, but not at home. While we are away evangelizing the world others are ransacking our very faith in God at home. We need a revival at home like the Chinese are having. There will be persecution, hardship and even death at home. When we talked to Brother Yun, he said that the underground church in China does not want the persecution to go away. He says this statement is true, "The blood of the martyrs is the seed of the church." If the persecution goes away, the church will get soft and become lukewarm. America is now beyond lukewarm, and needs a revival before it is totally a pagan country and it needs the Chinese Christians to help us out of this situation as well as our financial problems. And that is another enigma.

How Did America Lose its Faith And Will it Return?

How did it get this way? How much longer will it go on? What can we do to change it? I have stated the problem ad-nauseam and now anyone reading this is as depressed as me. So how did this get this way? Psalm 10:2, "The wicked in his pride doth persecute the poor: let them be taken in the devices that they have imagined." Psalm 37:12(NIV), " 12 The wicked plot against the righteous and gnash their teeth at them;. . ." The battle for the soul of America is spiritual.Man left to his own devices will always choose his selfish way. These scriptures sound like today.

Chapter Fourteen

Confusion Breeds Confusion

I was recently in Danbury, Connecticut at the church site where it all happened. What and how did it happen? The phrase, separation of church and state does not appear in the Constitution, but rather is derived from a letter written by Thomas Jefferson to a group identifying themselves as the Danbury Baptists. In that letter, quoting the First Amendment of the United States Constitution, he writes, "I contemplate with sovereign reverence that act of the whole American people which declared that their legislature should make no law respecting an establishment of religion, or prohibiting the free exercise thereof, thus building a wall of separation between Church and State." The letter to Danbury Baptists (1802) is a speech in a meeting at the site of the Danbury Baptist church in response to the letter that was penned to Thomas Jefferson regarding the separation of church and state.

The United States Supreme Court decided a case called

Everson v. Board of Education in 1947. It was this decision that opened the floodgates of hell upon us by commencing the removal of truth, mercy and the knowledge of God from America. They took a phrase, separation of church and state from the letter President Thomas Jefferson wrote to calm the fears of the Danbury Baptists who were struggling with rumors that Congress was working on forming a national Church. This phrase is not in any of our Founding Documents. The words separation of church and state do not appear in our Constitution, Declaration of Independence or Bill of Rights. In 1947, the Hugo Black Court divorced the phrase from Jefferson's own explanation and used it to create a new, and completely arbitrary, interpretation of the First Amendment.

On the heels of this monstrosity, one disastrous Supreme Court decision after another followed in its wake to the point where evil is now good and good is now evil. The Bible has been removed as the cornerstone of America's education, the prayers of our children have been silenced. The Ten Commandments have been stripped from our walls and our schools. They have been replaced with culture, political correctness and government. The knowledge of God has been replaced with condoms, police officers, metal detectors and unprecedented violence and perversion.

In light of this predicament, Psalms 11:3 asks a critical question and that is, "If the foundations be destroyed, what can the righteous do?" For one thing, we can go back to God's blueprint found in His Word and rebuild the foundations being destroyed under our watch. This is what Nehemiah did when he found Jerusalem with its walls knocked down, gates burned, and God's people perplexed by these deplorable conditions. He assigned workers that handled both trowels and weapons to go to the exposed areas and rebuild the walls and gates that had been decimated which made them a prey to their enemies.

No Change Equals No Change

In order for the modern day Church to accomplish this great task in our lifetime, there must be a fundamental shift in the emphasis of the Church. We must move from being program orientated to the prophetic. We must move from the Motherhood nurturing aspects of God to the Fatherhood justice aspects of God. Jeremiah 23:22 defines the prophetic ministry as such, "But if they had stood in my council, they would have proclaimed my words to my people and would have turned them from their evil ways and from their evil deeds." I love the Father, but it is not an excuse to not follow the commands of Jesus. I love my children and grandchildren, but there are rules to keep them from harm, and I believe that God has rules for the same reason as well. The Church needs to change from managing sin to preventing it, and from closing the gate after the horse is gone. It is like having a divorce recovery group instead of marriage counseling or ministries that deal with prevention. One provides a cure after a disastrous event, while the other prevents it from happening in the first place. It is better to be healthy and sound than to need an operation to save your life. I would rather pray for health than for healing.

America needs revival because the Church needs a revival. Something that needs reviving means it must be brought back to its original state. I believe here's how to fix it. The churches have lots of programs that help people after the fact. We have AA meetings, divorce counseling, and many other programs that close the gate after the horse is gone. But we have few to keep the horse from getting out such as preventing divorces or preventing addictions. If the Church does not fix it, then what is the Church for? Is it to build the kingdom of man or the Kingdom of God?

God is Speaking. Do We Know How To Hear?

I know a pastor who says we have the Holy Spirit living within us and thus we should have the mind of Christ. I say the Holy Spirit within us is talking as loud as He can, but not many have been taught to hear so we only hear the sounds of the flesh, the world and sometimes the whisperings of the devil. The Holy Spirit speaks to our heart; the devil whispers in our ear. It takes practice to hear the Lord. It also takes experience in hearing to know when the Spirit of the Lord is telling us what He wants us to do versus something the enemy of our soul is telling us to do, because he sometimes tells us to do good things particularly "religious" things. But it may not be what God wants us to do .(Can You Hear Me by Brad Jersak). A good way to hear who is talking to you is when you sin, the one who says to you, "You call yourself a Christian, look what you did" is the devil, the accuser of the brethren The One who says to you, "Come on, let's go to Jesus", is the Holy Spirit. The Holy Spirit convicts us of sin; He does not condemn us for our actions. Romans 8:1 says, "Therefore there is now no condemnation to them who are in Christ Jesus." The heart of man is most deceitful and desperately wicked. Who really knows how bad it is?" This statement is alive and well in our country. Man needs God and man must find God before it's too late. The problem is that if something does not change soon we will be dragged down with the world because the spiritual needs of America are not being met. I've said it before, "If man is left to his own devices having no God he will even kill unborn babies."

Abortion has killed over 50 million babies.Ever wonder why it is so important? Who is really behind all of this infanticide? Joseph was his father's favorite son and the devil knew that Joseph was going to be a deliverer and preserver of Israel in the land of Egypt, so he tried to kill him but he failed. Likewise when the devil knew that Moses was going to be raised up to be a deliverer and take the people out of Egypt, he killed all the babies while trying to kill Moses, but he failed. When the devil knew that Jesus was going to be the Jewish Messiah/Savior/deliverer of the World, he tried to kill Him by killing all the innocent babies in Bethlehem,-he failed. Today God has said through His prophets that He is raising up an army of youth to usher in the endtimes so the devil again is trying to thwart the plan of God by killing the potential army of God. He is also using his tool AIDS to kill millions of babies in Africa and America. Why?

Who Do We Blame?

Because the battle for America is spiritual, it is a battle we must win with spiritual weapons. First the soul of America is at risk. The founding fathers laid the foundation of America on the Word of God. The devil knows he must break the dependence on that foundation and on the Word of God. So far he has done a good job because he has had good students who have flunked out of the school of God. Or more likely, the school, the Church, has failed the student/believer. I am concerned that the Christian is as guilty as the non-Christian because the Christian who has not totally turned his life over to the Lord and has one foot in the world and one in the Church is succumbing to the desires of his heart (flesh) which are the same as desires of the world. He has not let God fill the void. Nothing fills that void but God. Nothing can soften the pain of injustice but Jesus. If this is true, why are they not going to Jesus for His help? My opinion is that the Church is partly to blame. The Church has not matured the people under its care. Walking close to the Lord in the midst of sin's pleasures and the desire for more and more is difficult. It will take more than church programs to change a person. And if you get changed or blessed outside of your church, the church often won't accept your blessing. They will consider what you got competition for their resources. The Bible says that judgment will begin with the House of the Lord. God help us.

Chapter Fifteen

Judgment Will Begin at The House of The Lord

I believe that God is not happy with the church. Notice that I am using large "C" and the small "c" to differentiate between the Body of Christ and the local church. The church has been so busy doing its own thing for so long it doesn't even know what the Lord wants .I believe that anything that is not born from a communication with God is idolatry or legalism. A Bible teacher I know, Lance Wallnau says, "The churches have been teaching the Gospel of church not of the Kingdom of God." God has left many churches. The churches must stop doing the works of Martha and begin doing the works of Mary. As long as the Church is tied up in church politics, budgets, buildings, programs, even evangelism or anything else that produces church as usual, there will be no revival in the America church. The rain falls on the just and the unjust. Someone asked a friend of mine who was teaching on the Kingdom how many kingdoms there are. His answer was, "as many as there are pastors."

I Peter 4:17 (ASV) says,"For the time is come for judgement to begin at the house of God:and it begin first at us, what shall be the end of them that obey not the gospel of God?". Ezek 34:10 says, (God speaking) "My anger burns against the shepherds, and I will punish the leaders."

A Better Way

I want to borrow a page from a wonderful book by Rolland and Heidi Baker, "Always Enough." They are from a small church in California and work as missionaries in Mozambique, Africa. Since 1982, they have worked in Africa and now have over 7,000 churches there. They see miracles like raising the dead which are commonplace among their churches. They come to American churches and speak in some local Spirit-filled churches. They could teach us a lot on how to change the world we live in. From the forward in his book Rolland said, "I always wanted to believe the Sermon on the Mount, but I was usually told that it did not mean all that I thought it meant and that I needed to be practical. I would read the Scriptures longingly, trying to imagine how wonderful it would be to not worry about anything, safe and secure in the presence of Jesus all the time. Miracles would be normal. Love would be natural. We could give and never lose. We could be lied to, cheated and stolen from yet we would always come out ahead. We would never have to take advantage of anyone or have any motive but to bless other people. Rather than always making contingency plans in case Jesus didn't do anything, we could count on Him continually. We, our lives and all that we preach and provide would not be for sale, but would be given freely, just as we have received freely. Our hearts would be carefree in the love of our Father in heaven, who always knows what we need, and we could get on with the glorious business of seeking first His Kingdom and His Righteousness. There would always be enough." We should try to emulate this, but instead we do this:I Corinthians 6:7, (Living Bible)"to have such lawsuits at all is a real defeat for you. Why not just accept the injustice and leave it at that? Why not let yourselves be cheated? But instead, you yourselves are the ones who do wrong and cheat even your own Christian brothers and sisters."

Love God, Forsake Your Rights

We are so interested in getting our rights that we do not even think of God. How many of us would just let ourselves be cheated like it says in verse 7? Try it sometime. If you realize that freely you were given and the Scripture says, "freely give," you will actually feel freedom. Have you ever had someone take something from you and you feel taken ? You find out the person stole out of extreme need and you said, " take it". You changed your attitude from "I want my rights" and "I want justice" to thankfulness. If we all practiced this in one form or other, we would begin to change the way of the world to the way of the Lord. Small things are important. The other day while waiting in line at a small fast food restaurant before I got up to the counter, the phone rang and the girl started to take an order. The next cashier took someone who just walked in. I failed my own test and complained to the cashier, demanding my rights. A small thing you say? Yes, but important. God says if we are faithful in small things, He will trust us with more.

The way of the world is to grab all you can for yourself.

When Hurricane Katrina hit the Gulf Coast, in the midst of all the pain and suffering, the gas stations of the country were price gouging as high as .80¢ or .90¢ per gallon more than standard prices, even though they had not received shipments of higher price gas from their suppliers. How is this not looting? The looting that was going on in the streets of New Orleans was not for food and water; it was for anything that could be grabbed. The offering box was pried open in a church devastated by the storm. Those of us who were not in immediate danger of the hurricane will get to share the suffering in home energy prices, natural gas and electricity, and any other thing that the greed of Americans can blame on the hurricane and can put upon us to fatten their purses. Their greed has no mercy. Only God can provide mercy and justice.

I have written about this twice before in this book but it needs to be said again here. Reports are starting to come regarding the insurance companies that have been collecting premium payments from the people in the hurricane areas for years. Now that it's time to pay, they are coming up with all sorts of reasons to leave the people with no benefits while they are the most needy and are the most unable to fight for their rights. The city of New Orleans has a rule in all of the casinos and it goes like this; "When you put your money on the passline and 7 is rolled, you pay." The insurance companies don't seem to be part of that rule. They are part of a better crap game. They lose but don't need to pay. Is this a great country or what? Yes, for the insurance companies. You know the ones, they are those who have TV commercials that tell how they are right there when you are in need. Only God can deal with this kind of greed.

The way of the Lord is to give away what you have, starting with your life. The good news is that the faith based ministries are providing fresh water, food and shelter needs for thousands of Americans. James 2:16, (NIV)" If one of you says to him, 'Go, I wish you well; keep warm and well fed,' but does nothing about his physical needs, what good is it?" Romans 6:13 (KJV), " Neither yield ye your members as instruments of unrighteousness unto sin: but yield yourselves unto God, as those that are alive from the dead, and your members as instruments of righteousness unto God." Romans 12:1(KJV),"Therefore,I urge you, brothers, in view of God's mercy, to offer your bodies as living sacrifices, holy and pleasing to God—this is your spiritual act of worship"

Our Society Needs Revival

Our society is morally corrupt. We have almost no moral resistance left to battle sin and corruption. Our conscience is seared and calloused and does not prick us for the same things that it did even 10 years ago. We are slowly leaving God, our Christian heritage and our moral ethical foundation behind. We have twisted our Constitution so much that it doesn't even sound like the original. The judges, especially the Supreme Court Judges, are ruling America and we now have an oligarchy. The framers of the Constitution set up a protection against such a situation. Unless we go back to God, judgment will surely begin at the house of God because the battle for the soul of America is a spiritual one. It must be fought with spiritual weapons, not carnal ones. Our enemy is spiritual, not flesh and blood; therefore we must fight with spiritual weapons. The Christian must learn. He must learn on his own if he cannot get the correct teaching in his local church. The Christian must seek out good extra church Bible teachers that are teaching the basics again. We don't need to know how to receive the Lord again and again because we already have salvation. We must learn what God wants next from us and how to do it. It may not be going on a short mission trip or some job needed in the church. It may be to love our wives better than we do now before a crisis hits.

This responsibility rests on the church, but if it does not do it, the believer must do it for himself. God in His mercy has provided for the believer through ministries not available in the local church. These ministries are mostly rejected by the local church because they consider them competitors for the support they need to sustain their church budget. The emphasis is on the their budgets. This speaks of a lack of faith in the Lord by not believing He will pay for what He raises up. If He does not support their ministries, perhaps they should seek the Lord and see if their ministry is doing what He wants.

Our Weapons: Not Guns And Knives, What Are They?

Sending wounded soldiers to fight will not work. Sending soldiers who are not living the Christian life into a spiritual battle will not win any battles. Christians who have invited the devil into their lives six days a week by living in the world and doing the things of the world, cannot fight the devil and his demons on Sunday. He will not leave. He knows you too well and he knows just what temptations to use against you. He will defeat you and then condemn you so you are defeated mentally and spiritually. We must be overcomers. In Revelation 2 and 3 God says to all seven churches that they must be overcomers. Overcoming is not easy and must be learned through trials. We must prepare for war during a time of peace. The Church needs preachers who will challenge Christians to do the things that are hard but are needed for the maturing of the Saints. Drill instructors are not known for being easy on their charges. They are known for raising them up in the way they should go. The Saints need to be prepared to survive in the battle for their maturity, and the Church needs preachers that will train like drill instructors.

Christianity was made for the storm, not for the calm. If we never train believers to deal with the storms that come in their lives, they will drown in sin and every sort of perversion and never be a witness for the Lord to attract unbelievers into the Kingdom of God.

James 1:2-8 (NIV) says, "Consider it all pure joy, my brothers, whenever you face trials of many kinds, because you know that the testing of your faith develops perserverance. Perserverance must finish its work so that you may be mature and complete, not lacking anything".

Chapter Sixteen

Are They Really Saved?

In America the Church's overemphasis on evangelism has not done much to mature the Body of Christ. It has only crowded the sheepfold and required the building of bigger buildings and more staff and then more evangelism giving the false impression that the Church is growing and maturing. This might sound like I am against evangelizing. I am not. I am against using evangelism as an excuse for not maturing the Body of Christ. I believe that this is the main reason why we are now in the state we are in and why America needs the shake up I have been talking about. Leading people to the Lord doesn't automatically make them honest, get them off drugs or alcohol and make them a better father, mother or spouse. They will look like the rest of America except they will have Jesus in their heart. They will be so busy they won't even know when judgement has arrived. I believe 1 Peter 4:17 is coming, now is the time for judgement to begin. The Church will always give the Body tangible Martha things to do. They do this because the results are immediate and satisfying, e.g. a soul gets saved, food is collected for the food pantry, baskets are collected and sent to needy people etc. The Church keeps its people so busy they leave their first love. "Martha was distracted by all the preparations that had to be made. She came to him and asked, 'Lord, don't you care that my sister has left me to do the work by myself? Tell her to help me!' 'Martha, Martha,' the Lord answered, 'You are worried and upset about many things, but only one thing is needed. Mary has chosen what is better, and it will not be taken away from her.' "

The New Pharisees

I was complaining to my wife that I was tired of trying to preach this new gospel to everyone in the church. She said something that released me from my discouragement; she said that I was preaching to the Pharisees. Even Jesus couldn't teach the Pharisees a gospel of change. They had their traditions, their methods and above all, their rules, which were all set in place to protect their positions of power and authority, not unlike the minions of power and authority in the organized Christian church today. Above I said a "new gospel" but it really isn't new, it's the old Gospel that has been perverted and changed. "Even from your own number men will arise and distort the truth in order to draw away disciples after them." Acts 20:30 (NIV). Our hope is in the Lord; 1 John4: 4, ". . . greater is He who is in me then he who is in the world." This is a great scripture, but it is like having a more powerful weapon in our arsenal, but without the know-how to use it. American Christians are the ones who need to go back to the principles we have left behind. We cannot expect the world to return to godly principals because they never had them to begin with. We also cannot expect the world to look at a carnal Christian and be jealous for the Christian life.

The Church Needs Extra Church Ministries

There are great Christian teachers on television who are teaching the whole council of God. The Church must accept these Bible teachers and not look at them as competitors for their pews. I recently visited my daughter in Michigan in the Dutch farm country. While there we attended the Christian Reform church that my daughter and her family attend. They are very similar to the Baptist church, except they're bound up much tighter than the Baptists, more do's and don'ts. The Pastor said he believed that their church teaches the full gospel of God. However, he only talked about salvation and the ramifications of salvation. They do not believe in the work of the Holy Spirit in this day.

Anything that takes our focus away from Jesus, whether it is legalism, good works or any form of religiosity, is an idol. We Christians need to drop our pet doctrines and join other Christians here and in the rest of the world and do what Jesus said just before He left which is, "love one another.". That is the first thing we need to do after doing Matthew 22:36- loving the Lord our God with all our heart, soul and mind. John 13:35 (NIV), "By this all men will know that you are my disciples, if you love one another." John 13:34 (NIV), "A new command I give you: Love one another. As I have loved you, so you must love one another." This is not a suggestion!

A Bible teacher/minister that I think a lot of, Carol

Arnott, said that if someone would have asked her if she lost her first love before she started to seek the Lord and listen to Him quietly each day in what she calls "soaking", she would have denied it. However, since the time she positioned herself before God to experience His love and to give her love to Him with no agendas or shopping lists of her needs, she began to have an intimate relationship with Jesus and the Father. Soaking is what some call marinating in the Lord. Like you would marinate something, we soak in the essence of the Lord. Psalm 46:10 says, "Be still and know that I am God. . ." God is love and wants us to be lovers of Him before we even try to love others. From early childhood we have been taught to accomplish more, to finish a task, and always be on duty. I have seen people say they want to get prayed for and in a few minutes they are up and gone. They miss the point. A practice of spending time soaking in the presence of the Lord opens your heart to receive visions and dreams. Jesus has lots of servants, but not many lovers.

We have a long way to go to come back to the ways of God. We must start now, and we must start with the House of the Lord. We cannot expect Americans to change their wicked ways, give up their greed, give up their godless cultures and their pursuit of pleasure and follow us if they do not see Christians united, loving each other and changing their way of life. Psalm 133 (NIV), "How good and pleasant it is when God's people live in unity." This scripture is not just a nice saying because without unity, the power of the Holy Spirit will not fall on the Church. They were in one accord. (See Acts: 2)

We Must Cause The World to Want What We Have

If we do not cause non-Christians to be jealous of our lifestyle, of our peace and confidence in God in times of trouble, if they cannot see God healing the sick in our churches or our lives changing by following the values in the Scriptures, we are wasting our time. If the Holy Spirit is drawing the world to a saving knowledge of God through Jesus, we at least, should show the world that there is some benefit to a saving knowledge of God beyond our salvation. The definition of revival is to take something that was alive but is now dead and revive it. This definition of revival does not fit the world because it was never alive in the sense we are talking about here. The definition fits the Church perfectly. What was alive and vibrant with activity inspired by the Holy Spirit of God is now mostly dead or slightly alive in some places. Living as authentic Christians has been replaced with programs, building mega-churches and buildings and striving to have the largest church and the most programs and staff. Thus, ". . . Having a form of Godliness, but denying the power. . ." as stated in 2 Timothy 3:2-7; the scripture continues in verses four through six as follows: "For men shall be lovers of their own selves, covetous, boasters, proud, blasphemers, disobedient to parents, unthankful, unholy, Without natural affection, trucebreakers, false accusers, incontinent, fierce, despisers of those that are good, traitors, heady, highminded, lovers of pleasures more than lovers of God; Having a form of godliness, but denying the power thereof: from such turn away. For of this sort are they which creep into houses, and lead captive silly women laden with sins, led away with divers lusts, Ever learning, and never able to come to the knowledge of the truth."

America Needs Revival, But the Church Needs it First

America needs revival but the Church needs revival first because the battle is a spiritual one. The Church is the army that fights with weapons that are not carnal or fleshly, but spiritual weapons. We cannot expect the world to fight because it doesn't have any belief or understanding of the weapons we use. John 3:3 (AMP), "Jesus answered him, 'I assure you, most solemnly I tell you, that unless a person is born again (anew, from above), he cannot ever see (know, be acquainted with, and experience) the kingdom of God." Thus the world has no weapons, no leader and no goal. If the Church does not know how to use its weapons, it will be overrun by the forces of evil. A God initiated revival such as the Welch Revival will save thousands or even millions of people as has happened in China, but revivals like that seldom come to a carnal, greedy, self-serving mega Church that is always in a mode of buying more pews, sound equipment and God forbid, a building program that has its feet half in the world, being so seeker friendly that the Gospel is compromised. Revival will not come to a Church that is not praying for revival. Acts 20: 30 (NLT) says, "Even some men from your own group will rise up and distort the truth in order to draw a following."

We don't believe we are compromising or perverting the Gospel, but when we do not preach the full Gospel, it appears we are. It seems that every event, whether it is an ice cream social or a thank you get together, is a time to ask for money. The ice cream is the bait. The innocent sheep are fleeced again with the promise of all the things the church wants to do.

Untrained Soldiers Don't Win Battles

If an army sends out all of its men to do everything except fight, they will be overrun by the enemy. In the U.S. Marine Corps, a fighting Marine has a basic MOS (military occupational specialty) of 0100. He is issued a rifle and he is proficient with it. He is not made a cook or office person; he is a Marine and he only has one overall military designation, that of a rifleman. He may cook, but he carries his rifle with him and he knows how to use it. During the TET Offensive in Vietnam this helped save the day because every man had a rifle and was able to keep the enemy from overrunning the camp. This is an important perspective for the Church; it must teach all its members how to fight using the spiritual weapons the Lord has provided for use against the devil, the enemy of our soul, and ultimately the enemy of the soul of America.

The army of the Church is weak from sin and living a worldly lifestyle. She gives in to the sins of the flesh such as hate, unforgiveness, pride, lust, debauchery, greed, selfishness and finally the sin of rebellion, which is the same as witchcraft. I would almost want to add a lack of faith as a sin, but I would lay it at the feet of the leadership of the Church. If a soldier is not trained it is not his fault. It is the fault of the leadership in charge.

The Church of Laodicea

URGENT PRAYERS NEEDED FOR HELP.

I just lost my mother, my husband is sick from Hepatitis C and taking therapy for it which has been making him very sick, my children are still concerned about their father's illness and our finances are suffering tremendously. I just need someone/ everyone to pray for strength, courage, patience, and guidance that God will provide for us, so we can meet our financial needs, that I can stay strong and continue to keep going through all this, and my that husband and will be healed. Thank you

God Bless,

Karin Billingsly (Name changed).

This prayer request appeared in an email sent to the church members of a local church in Orange County that I attended. It was part of many requests for prayer sent to the prayer team by members of the congregation. It was repeated everyday for a while. When I read it I wondered who would help. . . I wondered where the "church" was. The scripture in the Word came to mind; James 2:16 (NIV), "If one of you says to him, 'Go, I wish you well; keep warm and well fed,' but does nothing about his physical needs, what good is it?" Be filled, be warmed and blessed. I am not minimizing prayer, but God is asking us to do more. Prayer is easy and puts the responsibility on the Lord and it seems to absolve us from any further responsibility. I want to say that someone did step up and do more, but it was not the "church." However, if I use the strict definition of the Church as the Body of Christ, then the Church did help. In this application I mean the organized local church as the definition of the church. So using that definition, the church did not help. What was this lady's local church doing besides responding to her need? Maybe it was trying to raise money for offices and laying money aside for future expansion. I think it is appropriate to mention Matthew 9: 36 again. Somehow I don't think that Jesus would be as interested in facilities as He is in His people being fed and cared for. I believe that Jesus had passion for His sheep that were already in His pasture and He was not saying pray to the Lord of the harvest to bring more uncared for sheep into His pasture. He wanted workers to be sent to care for His sheep. I believe He is still saying that.

Chapter Seventeen

This Church Does Not Need A Revival

I recently saw a video of a small Catholic Church in El Paso, Texas. The members decided to go to the trash dump across the state line in Juarez, Mexico. They took the scripture that said, Luke 14: 12 (TNIV), ". . .'When you give a luncheon or dinner, do not invite your friends, your brothers or relatives, or your rich neighbors; if you do, they may invite you back and so you will be repaid. But when you give a banquet, invite the poor, the crippled, the lame, the blind, and you will be blessed. Although they cannot repay you, you will be repaid at the resurrection of the righteous.' " Including the scripture James 2: 16 (NIV), "If one of you says to them, 'Go in peace, keep warm and well fed. . .' "

Armed with those scriptures, they went to the trash dump on Christmas day and brought enough food for about 125 people. When they arrived there were many more people at the dump working, digging through the trash for bottles, cans etc.. They did not have enough food. They had 125 burritos and two hams. As they began passing out the food, they fed over 350 people and the people kept coming back for more and took much food home. There was more than enough for all. There was so much food that they had to go to three orphanages to get rid of the rest of the food.

This miracle was exactly like the multiplication of the fishes and loaves that Jesus did in the Bible. Jesus is still in the business of multiplication of food if we will give Him a chance. He is also in the healing and saving business. He healed all of the people who worked at the dump, from Tuberculosis, Cancer, Diabetes, and all sorts of childhood diseases. Hundreds were saved. How many people would we attract if we fed the 5,000 without money? We don't attract as much when we take an offering and then feed the people. What would you rather do, pay to feed 5,000 or feed them by the power of God as Jesus did? A side note; Jesus is multiplying food on a regular basis at that dump. I have the video entitled ,"The Miracle at Juarez". I know the people taking the video because that church was a Catholic Charismatic church and as I have mentioned my wife and I were involved.

This church meets in a small facility with hardly any seats. That seems to be okay since the people spend most of their time in church singing, dancing and praising the Lord. Many do not need to be seated; they are lying on the floor under the power of the Holy Spirit. This ministry is going on in Mexico and we send missionaries to Juarez! We need to receive missionaries from Juarez. I wonder if we would we receive them or would we think that they don't dress well enough or don't smell good enough? Would we even receive their theology? Their theology is fine in Mexico or Africa and we can receive it there, but not in Orange County. Most evangelicals do not believe that Catholics are saved, but if you saw this video you would be embarrassed. In the beginning you would believe that you were probably saved and at the end you would say, "If they're Christians, then what am I?"

Feed My Sheep, Love One Another, Go Make Disciples

Our theology is messed up. I am worried at what Jesus will say to the American Church when He returns. I don't think He will care about our facilities or our sound equipment or what we wear in church. He won't care about our busywork programs or our money raising events. Would He care about His sheep? Would He care that they have not been cared for and have not been pastored? Would He be discouraged if they haven't been matured and still need milk and don't understand the deeper things in His Word? Would he care that His people have not been taught to receive His Holy Spirit? Would He care that in most denominational and non- denominational churches His Holy Spirit's work beyond convicting souls for the need for Jesus has not been received? I believe that He would care.

It would be hard to believe that the American Church will be saved by the spiritual growth and maturity of the African or Latin American Church. Jesus will not say, " Because of the righteousness of my Body in Africa, Latin America and China, America, enter in". I am not speaking of salvation; I am speaking about ruling and reigning with Christ. To whom much is given much is required and America has been given so much. When I think of the Church in China, 200 + million Christians who cannot worship freely, who cannot have Bibles openly and cannot easily obtain them, who have no church buildings, yet are growing and maturing through the trials they endure (James 1), I think that we need revival in America. We have taken for granted all that we have been given. We don't believe the entire Bible and we disagree with most of the Body of Christ who do.

The Black Church In America

There is an interesting phenomenon in America. It is the Black church. Black churches are as large or larger than many of the White churches. Whenever the world wants an answer to a black problem they call the Rev. Jesse Jackson or the Rev. Al Sharpton. These gentlemen have Reverend before their names; I do not know if they have churches or congregations, but CNN, ABC or CBS and other worldly media seem to go to these men for answers to spiritual to political questions. They not even recognize a Black Pastor with a church of 25,000 members or any number of others with similarly large churches.

Part of the phenomena is that the Black pulpit is and has been the freest pulpit in America. I have always known it, but I always attributed it to the most liberal Black churches. However, the entire Black church is free to say anything they want to their people without fear of any loss of tax-exempt status or any other curb on their speech. The Black conservative Christian and Charismatic Black churches understand this and are using this freedom to preach the Gospel of the Kingdom.

They are not hindered in teaching what sin is and how their people should vote their beliefs. If the Government was not in fear of being discriminatory, they would apply the same rules to the Black church and the Black church in turn would be as fearful as the White church. However, the Black church is a powerful praying and worshiping body of believers.

Winning Battles Makes Us Stronger

During the Katrina disaster the church did marvelous Martha things. It was like a spiritually dead church doing wonderful really needed things, but in the end it was still spiritually dead. Mathew 7: 8 comes to my mind. When Jesus returns for His Church, and when the Church says we did these wonderful things. "He will say be gone from me. I don't know you." God will return for His bride and His bride will be without spot or wrinkle. He said He would make it so even if the church does not do it. The Church of Christ will prevail with or without the shepherds. Ezekiel 34:10 (NIV). Revelation 19:7, "Let us rejoice and be glad and give him glory! For the wedding of the Lamb has come, and his bride has made herself ready."

Chapter Eighteen

How Do We Pray for America?

If America is Under Judgment, How Do We Pray?

After writing the previous chapters, I have questions on exactly how we should pray for our nation. It seems to me that my prayers over the years for our nation have been slightly amiss; therefore, I believe some things need to be cleared up. I may not be the one to do this, but I will do what I can. In Matthew Jesus was in a boat with the Disciples and a great storm came up. Jesus rebuked the storm and it was quelled. Someone said that He was able to rebuke the storm because His Father did not bring the storm and Jesus would never rebuke His Father's command to send a storm or anything else. (See Matt. 8: 24-26)

I agree that Jesus would never countermand His Father's orders. However, if we think that God did not call the storm we automatically assign the event to the devil. There are three reasons that could cause this event. I am not saying that I am correct, but I think they are plausible. The first cause is

God Himself, the second is the devil and third is the natural order of our planet set in place by God to manage the Earth and the seasons, for the growing of our food etc. Thus our praying against any event we don't like or that harms people like earthquakes, storms etc. is saying that it is caused by the devil might not be correct. I believe also that it would be wrong to think that God sends every tornado or earthquake for judgment or punishment. There doesn't seem to be any simple answers for this.

Who Has the Power?

I don't believe God ever gave the devil the power to change the natural elements. He never gave the devil the power to change gravity, or to send tornados into the midwest or tsunamis around the world. If He had given him that power, he would have used it beyond the natural occurrences we see now. The devil does not have the power or authority to raise the dead. The world and the Church seem to want to attribute more power and authority to the devil than they do God. I know of a Muslim man who came to Jesus because he said Allah or his Prophet Mohammad never raised anyone from the dead, but Jesus does. I have read testimonies where God has changed the elements to save the life of a person. I would register that as a healing miracle.

God (Jesus) has all power and authority and He can change the natural order of things like storms. While Jesus was on the Earth He said that all power and authority was given to Him by His Father, and that He would share some of His power with us humans. In fact, the Bible states that Jesus said that we would do greater miracles than He did. The Scripture says we are empowered through our union with Christ. The devil has no union with Christ. Ephesians 6:12 (AMP), "For we are not wrestling with flesh and blood (contending only with physical opponents), but against the despotisms, against the powers, against (the master spirits who are) the world rulers of this present darkness, against the spirit forces of wickedness in the heavenly (supernatural) sphere."The Scriptures never said that God would share those same powers with the devil . He won't even share the powers given to us. Our power comes from calling on God in faith to do wonderful miracles and even applying these rules, God is still in control of the power.

Do All Christians Believe We Have The Power?

Do all Christians believe this? Unfortunately, not all do. We have Christians that have seen more than 100 certified raisings from the dead. The devil has none. Life and death is in the hand of God. The devil cannot create anything. Granted, humans do the devil's bidding for him, but without the power and authority of and from God, they are powerless to cause earthquakes, tornados, droughts or change any other natural occurrences that are part of the natural order. 2 Corinthians 10: 4 (AMP), "For the weapons of our warfare are not physical [weapons of flesh and blood], but they are mighty before God for the overthrow and destruction of strongholds." We are the ones with the power. The devil wanted desperately to cause Jesus to sin but the most he could do was to use the spiritual weapon of temptation to tempt Jesus after His baptism and then again against Judas to betray Jesus. When the devil saw that Jesus was going to the Cross in spite of his tactics to prevent it, he knew he was defeated for eternity. If he had the power to cause an earthquake that would have swallowed up the three crosses or sent a torrential rainstorm to stop the crucifixion, he would have done it and it would still be raining.

Prayer in The Old Covenant

As I read Daniel 2:21, "He changes the times and the seasons; He removes kings and sets up kings. . ." I realize that Jesus would not countermand any of His Father's orders, so if we pray for our country and our president and since the Scriptures clearly state that God sets up kings and He brings down kings when he sees fit to do so, am I praying amiss to pray that this authority set up over our nation and our life be taken down when it is obvious that God raised him up for a purpose? The people of Israel fell into sin when they worshiped the golden calf. It would not be the last time God's people would fall into idol worship. They had forgotten the great things God had done for them. This angered God so much that He was going to destroy the whole nation. Only one thing changed God's mind in the matter -- Moses. Psalm 106:23 (NASB) says, ". . .had not Moses His chosen one stood in the breach before Him, To turn away His wrath from destroying them.." Moses was a man willing to stand in the gap, sacrificially, for those who were not deserving of such sacrifice. This sacrificial love by Moses is called for among God's people today. The prophet Ezekiel described another situation in which God's people fell into sin. God was ready to destroy the nation when He spoke to Ezekiel, asking him if there was a man willing to stand in the gap so that God would not have to destroy His people. Is God asking us the same question?

This scripture is clear and it is key and it fits into my request as how to pray for our Nation. Romans 13:1-7 (NLT), "Everyone must submit to governing authorities. For all authority comes from God, and those in positions of authority have been placed there by God. So anyone who rebels against authority is rebelling against what God has instituted, and they will be punished. For the authorities do not strike fear in people who are doing right, but in those who are doing wrong. Would you like to live without fear of the authorities? Do what is right, and they will honor you. The authorities are God's servants, sent for your good. But if you are doing wrong, of course you should be afraid, for they have the power to punish you. They are God's servants, sent for the very purpose of punishing those who do what is wrong. So you must submit to them, not only to avoid punishment, but also to keep a clear conscience. Pay your taxes, too, for these same reasons. For government workers need to be paid. They are serving God in what they do. Give to everyone what you owe them: Pay your taxes and government fees to those who collect them, and give respect and honor to those who are in authority." I covered this in a previous chapter but I believe that there is a caveat. In Acts 5: 29, Peter said we must obey God, not man. If the ruler demands that you do something that is contrary to the Word of God, we have a caveat in Acts 5:29. God raises up kings for His various purposes; some for Judgment, some for blessing in Romans 9:17 and some to show His power. We do not need to be very astute to realize that God has raised up this particular president to rule over America because we Americans have gone away from God's rule for our country and over our individual lives. I don't mean to say that all

Americans have gone away from God; however, enough have to cause God to act to save America. I have said that He wants to save America by sending an evil king which again speaks of a plan of God. Do we want to thwart God's plan by praying for the president to be impeached? If the answer is no, then we need to figure out God's plan, agree with it and pray for its completion. The Lord's Prayer fits this nicely. Are we a people who will stand sacrificially in the gap like Moses did? What else would be a good prayer since we do not really know exactly what God's plan is? We know what He wants to accomplish, but we do not know how He wants to accomplish it. The Lord gave me a prophetic word through my wife on December 9, 2012. The word was: "Do you value your comfort and security above what I want to accomplish in the Earth? I must stir up complacency in the Earth to motivate people to look to me for help and deliverance. Will you go on this journey without further complaint?"

Are We The Main Attraction?

I have agreed to this. So again how do I pray? I believe I have made it fairly clear by now. God has said in 2 Chronicles 7: "14- If My people, which are called by My name, shall humble themselves, and pray, and seek my face, and turn from their wicked ways; then will I hear from heaven, and will forgive their sin, will heal their land." I believe that this is very clear. There are a few things in this scripture that make it clear that God is speaking to us at this time in our history. He says, "If My people", that's us Christians who need to turn and stop sinning. We are the main attraction here. This is difficult to explain, but I will try to make my point. The words that follow in John 3:17-21 are sometimes forgotten or overlooked because of the importance of John 3:16 " For God sent not his Son into the world to condemn the world; but that the world through him might be saved. He that believeth on him is not condemned: but he that believeth not is condemned already," So it is not about the world, it is about us.

The world is already condemned and God doesn't expect them to repent. By not having accepted Jesus, they are not in the family of God. 2 Chronicles applies to us, not the world. We alone can change judgment. This scripture applied to the chosen people of God and now it applies to us grafted in people of God.

God had a plan in those days because there was grave sin in the land among the Hebrews. They were making their children walk through the fires as a sacrifice to their idols. They were committing adultery in the name of the Lord; they were listening to false prophets. This sounds like America today. The interesting thing here is that I am sure Jeremiah was innocent and so was Daniel as are many Christians as well. While we are sinners and need to repent to maintain our relationship with the Lord, our eternal punishment is covered in Romans 8: 1 (KJV), "There is therefore now no condemnation to them which are in Christ Jesus. . ." Daniel's prayer includes corporate prayer which we may not be specifically responsible for. However, we will suffer as the guilty will suffer, if God allows judgment to come to America. If we will stand sacrificially in the gap for America, will God change His mind and spare America the punishment due us? The reason is that our sin that has caused the judgment is ongoing and we have not satisfied 2 Chronicles

7:14. I believe that is the very reason for our "captivity" under this evil king.

I want to speak to something that may sound strange, but when we confess our sins and the sins of America, take responsibility, repent and ask for forgiveness, we believe that God has heard us and answered our prayer. That being the case, we are understood and are forgiven, is repeating this same prayer again and again speaking of a lack of belief, faith and understanding? So as we pray for our nation, either individually or corporately, we should pray Daniel's prayer - Daniel 9:1-18 once and move on to The Lord's Prayer because The Lord's Prayer can be repeated daily as it is an outline for specific items that include daily repentance, forgiveness, petition and also agreement with God and His plan, even if we do not know specifically what it is.

Moses was innocent, but he stood in the gap for the people of Israel. Exodus 32: 11-12 (NIV), "But Moses sought the favor of the Lord his God. "Lord," he said, "why should your anger burn against your people, whom you brought out of Egypt with great power and a mighty hand? Why should the Egyptians say, 'It was with evil intent that he brought them out, to kill them in the mountains and to wipe them off the face of the earth'? Turn from your fierce anger; relent and do not bring disaster on your people." What Moses was doing was trying to quell God's fierce anger after sin was committed. Moses stood in the gap to prevent further punishment against the people of God. Moses was such a friend of God that God listened to His plea. However, he still was not allowed to enter into the Promise Land. There is another scripture that shows the just will suffer with the unjust. See 2 Samuel 24:10-17 where King David counted his horses and chariots proving that he trusted in them rather than the Lord his God, which to God was a grave sin. So David was guilty but seventy thousand innocent people died for David's sin. Hardly seems fair? Jesus was not guilty, but He died for the sin of many…Hardly seemed fair? David was the only sinner, only David counted his army; however, he did stand in the gap for the people.

There is a model for standing in the gap for the sinner. It was Jesus. Isaiah 53:11-12 (NIV) says it clearly, "After he has suffered, he will see the light of life and be satisfied; by his knowledge my righteous servant will justify many, and he will bear their iniquities. Therefore I will give him a portion among the great, and he will divide the spoils with the strong, because he poured out his life unto death, and was numbered with the transgressors. For he bore the sin of many, and made intercession for the transgressors." While Jesus was not guilty, He stood in the gap and bore our sins. It was not His sin as He was sinless. So Daniel stood in the gap for the people of Israel and Moses stood in the gap for God's people while neither was guilty of the people's sin. We might say they were a type of Christ in their actions to cover the sin of God's people. What is interesting is that all of these men, Moses, Daniel and Jesus suffered for the sins of the people, and they stood in the gap for the people with God. Jesus, though He was and is God, suffered death for us.

Yes We Are Sinners

Another scripture that speaks to this problem of God's

people suffering for the sin of others is 2 Samuel 21: 1b. David knew that famines could have a spiritual source so he inquired of God and God answered. The source was Saul's murder of the Gibeonites. Once David knew the source of the problem, he took action. He repented on behalf of the nation and made restitution. Even though David was innocent, God allowed him to stand in the gap and the famine was then lifted. I have mentioned that I believe we will suffer punishment for the sins of America. We are sinners; we have all sinned, but because we are washed in the blood we still have our salvation. God has a plan for us just like in Jeremiah 29: 10-11, but He was mindful of the suffering saying to the Hebrews to cultivate the land and work and you will prosper, but they still had to suffer the seventy years of captivity. If some of us do not see that many of us are already suffering, we soon will. How bad will it be and when will it end? I don't know; however, I have changed my mind, I believe this is how we should pray. We will not necessarily know how much and how long this captivity will be. As we notice that the issues mentioned in 2 Chronicles 7: 14 are meant exclusively for us Christians, we bear the responsibility for the length and severity of the judgment we are facing now. If "we" who are called by God's name continue to violate the requirements in this scripture, I believe that the way of shortening the time of captivity is to adhere to the requirements of 2 Chronicles7: 14. So while we pray The Lord's Prayer and have an idea of God's plan, we should also pray that the Christians in America would turn toward God and away from their wicked ways. We will have the perfect prayer and solution to our captivity.

How Do We Turn From Our Wicked Ways?

We have lost our compass; we think we can find God in our wants and desires. Our focus is not on God as it should be. It is on our wants and desires, some benign, but some not. We think if it does not hurt anyone, it is okay to do. Sometimes even if it does hurt someone but we want it bad enough and even if it's a fetus, it is okay. Our churches are part of the sin for which we are being judged. I came to realize that there are more unbelievers percentage-wise in America than in many third world countries, yet our churches still consider the third world as the place where we complete the Great Commission by sending missionaries. They don't see the need to evangelize our own country even while America has been named a non-Christian country by the evil king God has raised up to govern His people. When third world countries send their missionaries to evangelize America, we know we are in trouble.

The Prayers We Need to Pray

My first prayer is The Lords Prayer. My second is to pray for our brothers and sisters, our churches and for ourselves to turn from our wicked ways. This agrees with God's will being done, and if they seek forgiveness and repent, they speak to our needs and they remind God of His promises. This also speaks of remediation. It speaks of pleading in prayer, fasting and sackcloth and ashes (today we might think of that being on our knees) and finally, it pleads for God's mercy. Each of these prayers allow for the changing of God's heart. We are not countering God's plan as Jesus would not have rebuked the storm if His father had sent it.

What is happening here is we are saying, " Lord let us be

part of the solution to this problem, let us help you complete your plans so we can end the suffering of your children". We are in a slightly different situation however, than David, who was the only one guilty.We and other Christian people, individually and corporately, are guilty as well. We share the same sin and guilt and some responsibility for the judgment in America. We need to show great repentance which means turn away from the sins that God is angry about. In summation, I want to say that I believe we Christians need to stand in the gap for America through prayer, as it is under judgment from

God as was Israel in the examples above. We will suffer because we are all guilty of the sin in our country. Daniel, Moses and Jesus were not guilty, but they also suffered. Suffering has a benefit. Hebrews 5: 8 (NLT), "Even though Jesus was God's Son, he learned obedience from the things He suffered." God can and will be merciful if we do our part.

Has God Changed The Game? Has A Tipping Point Been Reached?

Dr. David R. Reagan, founder and director of Lamb and Lion Ministries, proposes that we have reached a trigger/tipping point. I disagree. After reading the scriptures below it would seem that the game has changed or at least another component has been added. See Jeremiah 30:13, Jeremiah 15: 1, Jeremiah 7: 16 and more see the bottom of this chapter. Obama asks God to bless Planned Parenthood! Mr. Obama, who is the evil king that God as raised up for judgment on America, has invoked Gods' name at the Planned Parenthood gathering he spoke before recently, in blessing them. During his speech Obama noted that there are those who want to turn back the clock to policies more suited to the 1950's than the 21st century. They've been involved in an orchestrated and historic effort to roll back basic rights when it comes to women's health. Basic rights? Isn't it amazing that killing unborn children is now categorized as a basic right? Was it not okay to kill the unborn in the 1950's, but now it is ? I guess we should not be amazed at that, but many of us are , and often appalled because of the result of abortion. To make matters worse, Obama ended his speech to the group with the following words, "Thank you, Planned Parenthood. God bless you. God bless America. Thank you." Excuse me? How dare he take the Lord's name in vain as he has done! God will not bless Planned Parenthood or America if we continue to murder unborn children at unprecedented numbers simply because it's more convenient than doing what is right! The idea that Obama can glibly invoke God's blessing on a group of godless individuals who are only concerned about maintaining their alleged "right" to destroy life is unconscionable. In fact, it is satanic. In Romans 1 Paul lays out the logical, gradual, downward spiral of what happens to people's hearts when they reject God over time. They come to the point where, "although they knew God, they did not glorify Him as God, nor were thankful, but became futile in their thoughts, and their foolish hearts were darkened." From there, unbelievably, they come to think themselves wise, but in truth, they are fools (Romans 1:21-22 NIV) The fact that President Obama can take the Lord's name in vain with a group that wants no part of God or His moral absolutes makes it even worse for our country.

Has Our Nation Reached The Tipping Point?

Rhode Island has become the 10th state to allow gay and lesbian couples to wed, as a 16 year effort to extend marriage rights in this heavily Roman Catholic state ended with the triumphant cheers of hundreds of gays, lesbians, their families and friends. Delaware could be the next state to approve gay marriage. Legislation legalizing same-sex marriage has narrowly passed the Delaware House and now awaits a vote in the Senate.

Now the pentagon does not allow religious proselytizing. Once that open sodomy was allowed in our military, you could no longer have real Christianity. They do not mix. So now the homosexuals are out in the open and the Christians are heading into the closet. This is all because many churches and many Christians have been playing religious games in America. The Church is, for the most part, powerless and a coward in the face of the hard left spirit of antichrist. I am not talking about individuals, but the collective body of the Church who have not been discipled. What will the nation be like a mere three years from now? God knows and He wants us to change. The statement I make above is my opinion about what God is trying to show us. We Christians can only stop this craziness by turning and repenting.

When a nation begins to rebel against God, He will send prophets to call the people to repentance. If they ignore the prophets, He will then send remedial judgments. If the people persist in their rebellion there will come a "tipping point" when God will deliver the nation from judgment to destruction. The tipping point is revealed in the Book of Nahum. In Nahum 1:11 God reveals the reason for His unalterable decision to destroy the city and its empire, "An oracle concerning Nineveh, From you has gone forth one who plotted evil against the Lord, a wicked counselor." Thus, the tipping point, the point of no return. God's wrath happens when neglect or rejection of Him turns to war against Him. In response, God declared, "Your wound is incurable" (Nahum 3:19). In short, their fate was sealed. A contemporary of Nahum's, the Prophet Jeremiah, spoke of the same principle regarding God's relationship to Judah. He proclaimed that the nation's wound was incurable (Jeremiah 30:11-13). He added, "There is no one to plead your cause, no healing for your sore, no recovery for you" One chilling point is that the Bible teaches that when a nation reaches this point of no return — this point where "the wound becomes incurable" — prayer is no longer of any avail.

What About the American Church?

Thus, Jeremiah was told by God that he was not to pray for the deliverance of Judah! "Do not pray for this people, and do not lift up a cry or prayer for them, and do not intercede with Me; for I do not hear you" (Jeremiah 7:16 NASB). Later, God made this same point again in even stronger terms: "Even though Moses and Samuel were to stand before Me, My heart would not be with this people; send them away from My presence and let them go!"(Jeremiah 15:1)...Have we ignored the prophets and the remedial judgments? Has God responded by giving us the kind of leader we deserve? Are we now positioned to be delivered from judgment to destruction?

Ezekiel was told the same thing when he tried to pray for Judah, but in even stronger terms. God named three of the most righteous men who had ever lived, Job, Noah, and Daniel. He told Ezekiel that even their prayers could not deliver the nation from His wrath (Ezekiel 14:12-21). "I have set My face against them," the Lord concluded. (Ezekiel 15:7). God is patient and longsuffering but He cannot be mocked. "Whatever you devise against the Lord, He will make a complete end of it" (Nahum 1:9). God will ultimately deal with the sin of every nation. "The Lord is slow to anger and great in power, and the Lord will by no means leave the guilty unpunished" (Nahum 1:3 NIV). I believe that God is talking about Obama here in these scriptures. It is Obama that mocked The Lord. He will be judged, not Gods' people. How can we, Gods' people, stop Obama from mocking God? I am sure Obama will continue to mock Him. If God will not allow us to step in and pray for our country then a lot of innocent sheep will be hurt. I don't believe a just God would allow that to be the case. All the people of Sodom and Gomorrah were involved in the sin. Abraham could not find any to stay God's hand of destruction. However, we are different. There is a large remnant in America. Sinners yes, but Romans 8:1 says we are protected by the Blood of Jesus. In Jeremiah 30: 10-11(HCSB) God speaks of judgment, "For I will be with you— this is the Lord's declaration— to save you! I will bring destruction on all the nations where I have scattered you; however, I will not bring destruction on you. I will discipline you justly, and I will by no means leave you unpunished."

All the above scriptures are in the Old Covenant. I believe since we are in the age of grace, the New Covenant with all of God's mercy and grace will prevail to those who love Him, again, that's us born again believers. We have not mocked God.

I still remember that Nebuchadnezzar is the one who ate grass like a cow for 7 years, not the Hebrews. Daniel 4:24-25 (NIV), "'This is the interpretation, Your Majesty, and this is the decree the Most High has issued against my lord the king: You will be driven away from people and will live with the wild animals; you will eat grass like the ox and be drenched with the dew of heaven. Seven times will pass by for you until you acknowledge that the Most High is sovereign over all kingdoms on earth and gives them to anyone he wishes." All this happened to Nebuchadnezzar the king. God also requires responsibility from the king.

Chapter Nineteen

*Are You Thinking Of Counting
Your Horses And Chariots?*

I know you don't have any horses and chariots, but there is a modern day equivalent to horses and chariots. I'll say more about that later. King David in 2 Samuel 24: 3-9 counted his men, horses and chariots and God was not pleased with him. The punishment (See 2 Sam 24: 15-17) seems a little high for just taking inventory of his fighting men and equipment. However, was that all David was doing? The obvious question is why did seventy thousand innocent Israelites need to die for a little accounting on David's part? David asks the same question himself. David also asks God to take the punishment away from the innocent people and put it on him and his family in verse 17. We don't get an answer in the Bible, but we can make some assumptions as to why this made God angry enough to punish as severely as He did. David was king and responsible for all the people. He did not trust God. God gave David a choice of the punishment (2 Samuel 24: 13). I believe

He gave David a choice because He loved him in spite of the sin. David chose to be in the hand of a merciful God.

Do we have horses and chariots to count? Obviously we do not, so what is the modern day equivalent of the same sin that David committed, and what does it represent in our lives? Does it represent the same as the sin David committed? I believe that the equivalence is our resources that we depend on to help us live our lives in a comfortable manner. When we depend on them more than we depend on our God, we are bordering on the sin of David.

We all need resources to live in our modern world, so how do we know when we could be in trouble? Does God want us not to do any accounting of our resources, e.g. balance our checkbook, look at our savings account, consider investments to make more money, look for a better job or start a new business? That is not what God is concerned about. With God it is always about faith and trust. David had a serious breech of trust and faith in his God. Why was it so serious? I believe it was because David had a special relationship with God. He experienced God's favor, His trust-worthiness, His faithfulness and most of all, he had an intimate one-on-one talking relationship with God. After all this, he was a man after God's own heart. The reason I am saying this at all is because I have been trying to discover why God would consider David counting his horses and chariots such a grave sin.

I thought of the difference of being unfaithful to a close friend, one that would cause the relationship to be strained to the breaking point. Then I thought of being unfaithful to your spouse. This would be the ultimate hurt to the relationship and many times it is the destruction of the marriage and the family and is very personal. I believe that was what God experienced when David stopped trusting in Him, and began to trust in how many weapons of war he had to win the next battle. He began to trust in himself and his natural abilities, which included his warriors, horses, chariots, and his weapons. While God, his closest friend, his faithful, trustworthy God who never allowed David to lose a battle in his life, must have felt betrayed, hurt and deserted.

So where do we fit in this story? When we do not seek God to allay our fears or for the solutions to our problems, when we stop trusting in God and begin trusting in our own abilities and the money we have in the bank, when we trust our good ideas to resolve the issues in our life, then I believe we are approaching David's lack of faith. A caution, first of all, this is the age of grace and God loves us. We are His kids and He loves us more than we love our kids. He is a gracious God, a long-suffering God and a just God. He isn't waiting for an opportunity to punish us. Will God punish us? If we use our own resources He may reduce them, if we move on an issue using our own ideas without seeking God for His wisdom, He may allow the plan to fail. Our assignment, whatever it is, is not bigger than the covenant and relationship we have with God. I have personally experienced both. Sometimes He will put us in a valley or desert experience to check our faith and trust in Him. He already knows how we will do, but the test or desert experience is to show us what we will do. He also wants to remind us of our lack of trust in Him and to correct our actions.

Today we face problems on many fronts. Some are financial, some spiritual and some health questions are more complex than we as Christians have ever had to deal with in our generation. We face a government that is unChristian and even hostile to us as Christians. We don't know where it will end or when it will end or what to do. We have sought God for His wisdom, but we must be able to hear God to know what He is saying. Hearing comes with practice on previous issues of less importance. If we haven't learned to hear the voice of God through the logos written Word, the Bible, or the rhema word from the prophets, along with our own impressions given by the Holy Spirit then we will miss God's direction.

If you are reading this and think that I have written this word for the reader alone, you would be only half right because it is for me as well. I struggle with the faith to trust God completely in areas of our country and what will become of it with the current king that God has raised up to govern America. I know that God raises up good kings and bad kings as He has done for thousands of years, some for judgment, some for blessing. I also know that we as the Body of Christ have fallen into a way of life that is not pleasing to God. We tend to think that it is the world that displeases God and He wants to judge it. However, the world is already judged and condemned because they have rejected Jesus. John 3:18 says, "Whoever believes in Him is not condemned, but whoever does not believe stands condemned already because they have not believed in the name of God's one and only Son". (NIV) God could easily end the devil's reign on this Earth himself, but that is not His plan. He has us and He has given us His power to defeat the devil. When Jesus walked the Earth, He was under the same rule. He had to deal with fear, discouragement and betrayal just like we must. Fear, uncertainty, and lack of trust are the same things that cause us to want to run away and hide from the enemies.

So I ask how much havoc will God allow this wicked king to do before God's people repent and turn from their wicked ways? Does faith and trust in God have anything to do with changing the punishment or the length, or do we need someone to intercede for the Body of Christ? Who can do it? The Body of Christ can intercede for the judgment on America. However, we must be right before God, and I am not talking about being born again. That is just the first thing; the next is We must repent and turn from our wicked ways.

The Lord gave me a prophetic word through my wife on December 9, 2012, the word: "Do you value your comfort and security above what I want to accomplish in the Earth? I must stir up complacency in the Earth to motivate people to look to me for help and deliverance. Will you go on this journey without further complaint?" I am repeating this again for the benefit of this chapter.For those who do not know, the above is a rhema word from the Holy Spirit to me through my wife; it is a prophetic message for me. What does it mean? It is the Lord cautioning me to trust in Him and not in my own resources or wisdom and not to make a decision based on what I see around me, no outcome based decisions. Businessmen usually make decisions based on our perceived outcomes without considering God. I must stop worrying and complaining (mostly worrying) and stop trying to do something with my own resources as King David tried to do. It cost him seventy thousand of his people. You might be saying what could I do? I could move out of the country and move to a safer place with my wife and family. That is counting my horses and chariots. If you are thinking of counting your horses and chariots, don't. Seek the Lord in every situation, listen carefully and ask the Lord for instruction, talk less and listen more. That will take practice but remember that He is faithful to answer. He hears every time we call. We all experience fear many times in our lives. We have all kinds of fear. Most fears are because we are human and when circumstances that we have no control over attack our peace, fear strikes our heart. When we hear of things that we cannot control, things that impact our lives and the lives of the ones we love, it brings tremendous fear upon us. It is very difficult not to experience fear when you love your family and they are in jeopardy. 1John :18 says, "There is no fear in love. But perfect love drives out fear…".(NIV).

I realize that the Bible is saying that the love of God will cast out all fear because there is no punishment and because God loves us. I also understand that if I am close enough to the Lord in a relationship like my children had with me when they were young and completely dependent on me, there was no fear. They knew that I loved them and would take care of all the fearful situations because of past experiences they had with me. When we come to that same relationship with the Lord because of our experience of past saves from God for past problems, we begin to trust and love God more. It is all about faith and trust in God. It doesn't come easy. It takes trials when we see God move on our behalf and faith and trust are built. Soon we see that God is trustworthy and we know that His love will cast out all our fears. We can be relieved from our fears through the love of God.

When I feel like I want to run and hide from what I see going on in our government, I think David must have felt the same fear as he began to count his horses and chariots to help God save him from his enemies. Even with all the battles David won. I can see how easy it is to have fear of the unknown. However, God is our source and our resources are not. I remember when my little daughter was standing on the edge of our swimming pool. She wanted to jump as I was encouraging her to do but she was afraid. But soon, with my encouragement, she jumped and I caught her in my arms. I got a kiss and each jump after that was easier because she now trusted me and knew I would catch her. The same goes with the Lord. We trust God a little more after each catch.

Chapter Twenty

Is America Disingenuous?

I wrote this on December the 19th of 2012. I decided to put it in this book of my Journey. I mentioned in the Preface of this book that God has directed my journey on the issues about which He is concerned and this chapter is one of those issues. I have been disturbed about the things that I have seen in this last week in America. The more I heard, the more disturbed I became and I decided to talk about my thoughts, so I wrote this and I didn't know what else to call it. I named it, "Is America Disingenuous?"

There are flags at half staff all across America, the country is in mourning and the politicians are weeping in public. The world is sending its sympathies. Millions of mothers and fathers are crying over the loss of potential of the children, the President is overreacting and up in arms and wants to eliminate the cause of this terrible loss and everyone is asking "why?" Why did this tragedy happen? Who is to blame? What can we do now, who can we punish, how harsh should it be and how and who should mete out the punishment?

If you are thinking of the 56 million babies we have aborted at birth or near birth in America, you are wrong. This national concern is for the 20 children murdered in the recent tragedy at a school in Connecticut. Does this seem as strange to you as it does me? Why the concern for one small group and not the other? I will try with God's help to answer some of these questions.

First, do we in America really know or care that we have killed 56 million live babies? All America seems to know that twenty children were killed in Connecticut in less than a week. However, for the sake of this writing I will assume that some do know and care as I do. That question must be answered or we can go no further. I will try to answer the question of who is responsible, who has committed both of these hideous crimes and why some will recognize only one as a crime.

I believe that there is more than one individual or entity involved and responsible. I also want to add to this question why do Americans think that the two types of baby killings are different? We all consider the murders in Connecticut to be bad, hideous and unconscionable by any standard. This includes the people who think it is acceptable to murder thousands of babies that are alive, but not birthed. The statistics show access of 100,000 babies are aborted each month. This seems to be a contradiction. I agree it is. Abortion is the leading cause of death in the world. It kills as many people as all of the other causes of death combined. We have lost more Americans through abortions, 64 times more than we did in all of our 12 wars combined. This is more than all the other deaths combined. (See the bottom of chapter for link) However, if we cannot discover the answer as to why there is a disconnect in the minds of some Americans who consider a difference between the two types of murders, then we will not be able to find a clear understandable reason for this opposite thinking. Now we are faced with another contradiction wrapped around a conundrum.

The answer may be found by looking at the people who consider that both types of baby killings are bad, whether killing kids in a schoolroom or killing them in a doctor's office. I fit into that group and again I am sure you do as well. It would make more sense if we could discover what makes us different. We may be able to discover the disconnect in them. Are they less caring, less compassionate, less spiritual or less American? It may be a combination of these. Let's start with the heart of man. The Bible says that the heart of man is desperately wicked. Jeremiah 17:9 (NKJV), "The heart is deceitful above all things, And desperately wicked; Who can know it?" This being the case acknowledging the fact that we are triune beings, body, soul and spirit, may help the discussion. We are familiar with our physical body. That is the part, simply put, that carries out the decisions made by our mind. These decisions either offend or please God, please ourselves or they please the legal authority over us. Our soul is the unique part that separates us from the animals and is considered our intellect, heart and conscience. Our Spirit is the part that is most like God. It will live forever with God or wherever we choose for it to live for eternity. This is dependent on actions based on our beliefs. Christians believe that when we accept the blood sacrifice of Jesus, we have chosen where we want our spirit to spend eternity. I have not mentioned Hell; some do not believe that there is a Hell. I believe that if there is a God, there is a Hell. That is the other eternity we can choose. Some do not even believe that there is an eternal component to the issue of sin. In fact, some do not believe that there is sin. "I have seen that fools may be successful for the moment, but then comes sudden disaster" (Job 5:3 NLT).

God is against the killing of our children whether we do it or hire someone to do it. "Then you took your sons and daughters—the children you had borne to me—and sacrificed them to your gods. Was your prostitution not enough" (Ezekiel 16:20 NLT)? While I recognize that not all people agree with the above paragraphs, that is partly the problem. If we think that we human beings are nothing more than a lump of flesh with no other qualities except our free will and no consequences other than breaking the law of the land and no fear of an eternal punishment or reward at the end of life, then the discussion would end here. When temporal authority over us allows us to do this or any horrible deed and, in fact encourages it, then we feel we have permission. The permission even carries empowerment with it. Therefore, we have no problem with killing 56 million live children as long as the reigning authority over us approves. There are historical similarities; the people operating the gas chambers and ovens in Germany would be a good lesson to ponder. This time it is not Jews; it is children. Who's next? I once wrote that it amazed me how a woman who has been given the most precious job ever given to a woman, the birthing, nurturing, raising, and loving a baby would trade it for a choice. It also is difficult to understand how that same mother, after a baby is born to her and after she has nurtured the baby for a while would arguably give up her own life for the life of the baby. That is a dichotomy which I do not understand. It is also the real mystery. God gave us the gift of free will to choose what we want but does He want us to choose death over life? No, He says in His Word, choose life. "Today I have given you the choice between life and death, between blessings and curses. Now I call on heaven and earth to witness the choice you make. Oh, that you would choose life, so that you and your descendants might live!" (Deuteronomy 30:19 NLT). "Then I will arrange to take you to another land like this one—a land of grain and new wine, bread and vineyards, olive groves and honey. Choose life instead of death!" (2 Kings 18:32-A NLT). What makes the difference?

Who is holding down the mercy and the compassion? Who says it is wrong to kill 4 or 5 year old children, but says it is acceptable to end the life of a child in the womb? If you do not serve the true God, then any authority will suffice. This may be the answer to some of the questions. Let's go back to my premise regarding the heart of man. If the heart is not changed by some higher power, then we will be left with only our willful desires and the free will to express those desires through our actions. I define a willful spirit as doing what I want without consequences. That doesn't mean that there will be no consequences, it just means you are not going to worry about them . "I have seen that fools may be successful for the moment, but then comes sudden disaster" (Job 5:3 NLT). It would seem that this issue all turns out to be a person without God as his guide. This leaves his heart open to the pleasures of the world. This type of person will do what is right in his own eyes. The Scripture tells us to live following the law of the land because God says that He sets up all authority in the Earth. If we refuse to obey those laws because they are contrary to the laws of God, we will suffer the consequences from the authorities over us. Those who do not have God in their heart will obey any law that fits their want. If the authority over us wants to remain in their position of authority over us, they will give us all the wants and desires of our heart. We will have authority for the murdering of babies or whatever else we want, and then we will want to mourn only for the 4 and 5 year old children murdered at the school house. We will have no thought to mourn for the others.

Maybe I have answered some of the main issues. It really all boils down to one main issue. Without God we will do only what satisfies our own desires and pleasures. I think the question now is why did God raise up an evil king in our country? I believe it is because He knew the desperate condition we were in and He knew that He had to bring some judgment on the sin to draw people back to Him.

I was thinking about the time in the scriptures when the Israelites sacrificed their children to false gods/idols. God punished Israel for 70 years. Jeremiah 29: 11 is a verse that we Christians quote all the time, but we do not read and quote Jeremiah 29:10. Jeremiah 29:10-11 (NLT), " This is what the Lord says: 'You will be in Babylon for seventy years. But then I will come and do for you all the good things I have promised, and I will bring you home again. For I know the plans I have for you,' " says the Lord. 'They are plans for good and not for disaster, to give you a future and a hope.' " My point is that God punished His people for killing their babies by throwing them into the fire as a sacrifice to idols. They did not kill as many babies as we have. We have been sacrificing our babies to our idols of choice, self, greed, sexual perversion, same sex marriage, homosexuality and any desire our ungodly heart's can imagine. So to the question, is America disingenuous? The answer generally speaking is no. They are doing exactly what is expected of a Godless nation. God help us all. However, there are some who are blatantly disingenuous. Are the abortion doctors and nurses among the mourners for the murdered babies in Connecticut? Have they lowered their flags to half staff? For the abortion doctors and nurses to mourn for the Connecticut children is hypocritical. I notice that the very politicians who are yelling the loudest about the dead babies in Connecticut are yelling just as loudly for the laws to allow abortions and the pill that makes it clean and easy to kill fetuses.That is the highest form of disingenuousness, as well as outright idiocy. They call for punishment for whoever is to blame. They want to abolish the weapons (guns) used to do the killing. Our President, while he is weeping alligator tears on television over the Connecticut children and using the example of his own children being killed to engender sympathy, all the while he is signing laws making it legal to murder children in the womb and laws to force Americans to provide abortions pills to their employees. Is that disingenuous?

He is using the dead children in Connecticut for political gain. It appears no one is either watching or cares as long as they get their wants and desires met, which is the very reason he was elected. It is difficult to choose righteousness over the pleasures of life, even for the people of God. One last footnote: The president must know which ethnic group has the highest percentage of abortions. They are African America babies. Some call it Black genocide. Over 13 million Black babies have been aborted in America. This is over 50% of Black pregnancies. The most dangerous place for Black babies is the womb.

Several years ago, when 17,000 aborted babies were found in a dumpster outside a pathology laboratory in Los Angeles, California, some 12,000 to 15,000 were observed to be Black. Minority women constitute only about 13% of the female population age 15-44 in the United States, but they underwent approximately 36% of the abortions. According to the Alan Guttmacher Institute, Black women are more than 5 times as likely as white women to have an abortion. On average, 1,876 Black babies are aborted every day in the United States. The rest of the statistics among Blacks are: Aids: 203,695; Violent Crimes: 306,313; Accidents: 370,723; Cancer: 1,638,350; Heart Disease 2,266,789 and finally Abortion: 13 Million. All statistics are from the US Center for Disease Control. Some have referred this as a countdown to extinction.

http://www.wickedshepherds.com/abortioncounterandstats.html

www.topix.com/forum/afam/TIONS6TLED4M2M8HJ

http://www.abort73.com/abortion/abortion_and_race/

Chapter Twenty-One

*The Effective Prayer of a Righteous
Man Avails Much*

I wrote this message to the pastors I have known and those I felt have the same beliefs. I felt this was heavy on God's heart because He has given me this burden for a long time. I hope that I have done it justice and have not overdone it. I hope I have not missed God on this subject and have made my comments with love.

I once was involved in starting a church that we were planning to co-pastor. I called a friend of mine who had experience in planting over fourteen churches and I asked him where the pattern was in the Word, as I could not find it. He said The New Testament used the word "church" in two different ways. Sometimes it refered to people of God gathered together in congregations and that is the traditional idea of the local church. But other times it means believers in general (the Body of Christ) wherever they might find themselves. I believe that we have chosen the former and we believe that the Church/Body of Christ is a building, and the bigger the building the better the church. My friend ended by telling me that I should see the way the book of Acts had church and consider that as there was no definitive model for church as we are used to. He also said the Church is called to impact the world for change. The Biblical definition of "church" is not an institution or building, but rather is made up of individuals. Jesus said, "Wherever two or more meet together, I am in the midst of them." The Father's idea was for His Church to change the world. There were, however, some requirements. Before the Lord went to the Father, He asked Him in John 17:23 for the Church or Body of Christ or assembly of believers to be united to be able to complete this task that He was leaving for them. What was the task? The task was to change the world. The means was unity; the reason was so that the world would know that Jesus was sent by the Father and that would show that the Father loved Jesus and also loved the Church.

A Couple of Questions

Are we united? In my opinion, we are not. Have we changed the world or has the world changed us? In my opinion, the world has changed us more than we have changed the world. We have the only truly powerful God. The world has the pleasures of sin without a conscience and no Ten Commandments to constrain them. We have created a system that feeds, builds, expands and changes core beliefs to fit into the goal of the particular local church and pastor and have ignored the full meaning and purpose of the Great Commission. We accept what we want of the Scriptures and leave the rest. We build the kingdom of man and not the Kingdom of God. " Sometimes Christians need to leave the church to find Jesus." (Steve Thompson) I mentioned the Great Commission in this book a number of times and my point is that it states that we go into the world and make disciples. Discipleship speaks of change, teaching, mentoring and ultimately, maturity. Paul knew this was not happening. (See 1 Corinthians 2:1-5) Why are the statistics on divorce, homosexual life styles, pornography and alcoholism not what they should be, and what are we doing about it? What can we say to the world when they say, "We are doing as well or better than you are without Jesus than you are with Jesus?" The church does sin management, or how to have freedom from addictions, like programs for recovery after divorce and AA groups to stop drinking. There is nothing wrong with that, but wouldn't it be better to have teaching on how to have a Christian marriage and how to prevent alcoholism? It seems like all that the churches do is lock the barn door after... well, you know.

Is The Devil Winning?

Is the devil winning the war for the souls of Americans? If so who is helping him? And if this is correct, what can we do about it? When did you last preach a sermon on the evils of sin? If you never did, was it because you were afraid that people would leave? The Apostles were very stern with the sin found among the early believers, evidence Ananias and Sapphira. Because of the punishment of this husband and wife, two things happened. The people understood that the sin of lying to the Holy Spirit was not acceptable and there was a new respect and not a little fear of the Apostles. Acts 5: 11(NIV), "Great fear seized the whole church and all who heard about these events. The apostles performed many signs and wonders among the people. And all the believers used to meet together in Solomon's Colonnade. No one else dared join them, even though they were highly regarded by the people." The Apostles were not afraid of dealing with sin in the Church. Do you deal with sin in your church?

I have named this chapter "The Effective Fervent Prayer of a Righteous Man Avails Much" for a reason. The reason has to do with basic core belief in the Scriptures. If they are not accepted as the true and inerrant Word of God and appropriate for this age, then my question as to what are we doing about our problem of not changing the world is answered. After discussing the above, my question now is do you believe that scripture in James 5: 16-17? If you do, what do you believe that those fervent prayers can avail? Do you believe that they can raise someone from the dead? If you say no, do you believe they can heal a headache? How about providing you a job if you are unemployed? If yes, what makes the difference? Would you say it was your faith? Would you say the other things did not happen because you did not have enough faith? Why did you not have enough faith? The Word says we are all given a measure of faith so how much faith does it require to provide a job and how much faith to heal a headache and how much faith does it take to raise a person from the dead? How do we increase our faith to do any of these things?

Isaiah 53:5 states, ". . .By His strips we are healed." That does not require any faith. It is the heritage of the believer. Do you think that if you prayed for a headache and the headache left immediately, that you did the healing or was it God? Do you think you provided the job if one was immediately provided or was it God? Do you think you would be the one raising the dead person or would it be God? If you believe that God has done all these things I have mentioned, where does your measure of faith begin and how far does it go and where does it stop? Is it faith for headaches and jobs, but not for cancer? If you want to move a mountain how do you increase your faith? The Word says, "So then faith comes by hearing, and hearing by the word of God"(Romans 10: 17 NKJV). It says in James 5:13-15, " Is any among you afflicted? Let him pray. Is any merry? Let him sing psalms. Is any sick among you? let him call for the elders of the church; and let them pray over him, anointing him with oil in the name of the Lord: And the prayer of faith shall save the sick, and the Lord shall raise him up; and if he have committed sins, they shall be forgiven him." Possibly you believe that you must pray "if it be Your will, Lord". I think that people who walk in this belief will not be able to explain any of the healings that have taken place since the Lord walked the Earth so it is easy to just say that they did not happen. I have also heard that the ones who do not believe sometimes consider themselves the keepers of the Word and profess that they teach the full council of God. However, we must leave those beliefs behind to really know what the full council of God is.

Healing Is For Today

I personally have been healed of serious problems three times over my 43 years in the Lord. I have prayed for a cancer patient and seen him miraculously healed of 29 diagnosed tumors in his lungs in less than a minute. I did not have the faith for that or for my own healings except I believed that God could do it because He said we could do greater things than He did. Not everyone I have prayed for is healed, but some have been. Just because I have been healed and you have not does not mean that I was not healed, and just because I speak in tongues and you do not doesn't mean it is not real.

John 14:12 (NIV), "Very truly I tell you, whoever believes in me will do the works I have been doing, and they will do even greater things than these, because I am going to the Father." This seems to me like healing is the heritage of the believer. It doesn't mean we all get healed as God is still in control, but it does not mean healing does not exist either. We use Isaiah 53 to prove to the Jews that Jesus is the Messiah, so why don't many Christians believe that Jesus heals by His stripes? Some call us cafeteria Christians, we take what we want from the Scriptures and leave what we don't want. Sorry about the cliché, but it fits. You may be happy with a powerless Church; however, Jesus, Paul and I are not. Paul said," I come not in the wisdom of man, but the power of God". 1 Corinthians 2:3-5 (NLT), "I came to you in weakness—timid and trembling. And my message and my preaching were very plain. Rather than using clever and persuasive speeches, I relied only on the power of the Holy Spirit. I did this so you would trust not in human wisdom but in the power of God." Are there still people on the Earth that need you and me to come in the power of God like Paul came to believers and unbelievers? Or shall we come in the wisdom of man since some believe that since the canon of Scripture is closed and the Apostles died the Holy Spirit is gone?

Who Does Not Want The Church To Move In Power?

The only person I can think of who wants the Church weak and powerless is Satan himself. I believe he has a very willing partner in those who want to deny the power of the Holy Spirit and the Spirit-filled Church. Even the Catholic Church has embraced the Charismatic and they have become Evangelistic, bringing people into the new birth and then into the baptism in the Holy Spirit. The Catholic Charismatics have no reservations when it comes to believing the Word of God in its entirety. Acts 19:1- 7(NIV), "While Apollos was in Corinth, Paul traveled through the interior regions until he reached Ephesus, on the coast, where he found several believers. 'Did you receive the Holy Spirit when you believed?' he asked them 'No,' they replied, 'We haven't even heard that there is a Holy Spirit.' 'Then what baptism did you experience?' he asked. And they replied, 'The baptism of John.' Paul said, 'John's baptism called for repentance from sin. But John himself told the people to believe in the one who would come later, meaning Jesus.' As soon as they heard this, they were baptized in the name of the Lord Jesus. Then when Paul laid his hands on them, the Holy Spirit came on them, and they spoke in other tongues and prophesied. There were about twelve men in all.' " While the Catholics have had some erroneous doctrines over the centuries, they are shaping up according to the Word. I know this as I was involved in teaching with the Catholic Charismatic renewal for years and because my unsaved background was Catholicism.

Some Christians Do Not Want The Victorious Life Promised

In John 14 25-27 (NIV), Jesus told His disciples that when He left He would be leaving the Holy Spirit and He, the Holy Spirit, would help them live victoriously for Him. " 'All this I have spoken while still with you. But the Counselor, the Holy Spirit, whom the Father will send in my name, will teach you all things and will remind you of everything I have said to you.' " Some Christians think the Trinity is Father, Son and Holy Scriptures instead of the Holy Spirit. There can be a tendency in Christianity to give so much focus to the Holy Scriptures that we fail to acknowledge the role of the Holy Spirit in our daily activity, the very one who wrote the Scriptures. When we make this mistake we are on our own and open to the influences of the world. We are also open to the whispering of Satan in our ears and he will condemn us every chance he gets. His motivation is to keep us defeated. He is, after all, the accuser of the brethren and the father of lies. Has he changed his ways or lost his power and is he still here since the canon of Scripture closed and the Apostles died? He whispers, "And you call yourself a Christian, look what you just did." This is contrary to the Holy Spirit who speaks to your heart and says, "There is therefore now no condemnation for those who are in Christ Jesus" (Rom 8: 1 NIV). Satan condemns us, the Holy Spirit convicts us of sin and righteousness and says, "Lets go to the Cross, let's go to Jesus." There is a difference between condemnation and conviction. Now let me see if I have this correct. Satan stayed when the canon of scripture was closed and the Apostles died, but the Holy Spirit left?

If the Holy Spirit only convicts unbelievers that they need Jesus, does he hang around and deal with believers on sin only, or will He inspire, heal etc.? If you have sinned now that you are a Christian, you understand the whispering of Satan in your ears. You feel defeated and think that God cannot love you after what you just did. That is exactly what the enemy of your soul wants you to feel. Jesus called the Holy Spirit "another comforter". John 14:16, "And I will ask the Father, and he will give you another comforter..." Was Jesus saying that the Holy Spirit would leave after the Apostles died or does He give the new comforter to all of us on the Earth until He returns again at the end? My point is that Jesus did not send the Comforter for a little while or just for the Apostles. He sent Him to minister to the Body of Christ for as long as we are here. "For John baptized with water, but in a few days you will be baptized with the Holy Spirit" (Acts 1:5 NIV). No longer would converts be baptized just with water, but now they would be baptized with the Holy Spirit as well. Baptism means we are immersed in water and now we will be immersed in the Holy Spirit too. Surely not just the Apostles and their group? Who will be immersed? There is no favoritism in the Lord so all can be immersed. Notice that I said, "can be" because you can reject the Holy Spirit's baptism and His work in the Church. Shamefully, some have done so to the delight of the devil.

What Is The Purpose of The Church?

The Church is called to impact the world. The Biblical definition "church" is not an institution or building, but rather it is made up of individuals. Jesus said, "Wherever two or more meet together, I am in the midst of them." The Biblical word translated, as "church" is ekklesia, which in the original Greek means "the people of God." Without the Holy Spirit in your church, you will not be following the purposes of God for His Church. You will be building your own kingdom and not the Kingdom of God. You may as well just start a secular business, then your business principles will apply and you will not need to change the world.

The Holy Spirit Who Draws Us Into Intimacy

It is the Holy Spirit who draws us into intimacy with the Father. He prompts us with a scripture verse to share with a friend or coworker. He endues us with the power to live for Him. We do not have to live by our own strength. Truly the Holy Spirit is the third person in the trinity who must be acknowledged and obeyed as we seek to live for Christ. He is also our teacher and guide. There is the story of the three legged stool. No one can sit on a three-legged stool with two legs. I feel the same way regarding the Father, Son and the Holy Spirit. Without the work of the Spirit we will fall. I don't believe you can have an intimate relationship with God or love the Lord your God with all your heart, soul, mind and spirit without the Holy Spirit.

If you have not asked the Holy Spirit to baptize you, why not ask Him to fill you afresh with the power to know Him, not just know about Him? Will you lose status in your church or be ridiculed by your friends? Maybe, but you will gain a new friend that will change your life.

Why Do Some Fight This Wonderful
Gift of The Holy Spirit?

To whom are they listening? In my opinion, only the enemy of the church wants the Holy Spirit, His power and His gifts nullified and forgotten. He tells us that they are not for the Church today. He is the father of lies and many in the Church are listening to his lies. Are you afraid of speaking in tongues, a heavenly language is that scaring you? 1 Corinthians 14:2-4 (NASB), "For one who speaks in a tongue does not speak to men but to God; for no one understands, but in his spirit he speaks mysteries. But one who prophesies speaks to men for edification and exhortation and consolation. One who speaks in a tongue edifies himself." The devil has kept many in the Body of Christ from being edified because of the fear of speaking in tongues. Are you one of those?

I refer to tongues as being a secret language that only our God understands and the enemy does not. No war can be effectively fought without a "command and control" that keeps the enemy from knowing your every move. I do not claim to understand all about this issue, but the Scriptures have a lot to say (1 Corthinthians14:1-39). Paul says, among other things, "I thank God I speak in tongues." He also says we are talking to God when we speak in tongues. Don't be confused by those who say all tongues need an interpretation. Paul says he speaks in tongues more than you all, but when in a meeting he prays for an interpretation for understanding to teach. That being the case, then where does he speak in tongues more than you all? It would be in his prayer closet to God alone. The devil loves confusion and he has worked his magic on many in the Church to nullify our private communication with God. The Church of Jesus Christ is in a war with darkness and our weapons are not guns and knives, but are spiritual to the taking down of strongholds. Communicating with our commander-in-chief is vital. I love that when I speak in tongues to the Lord, the devil does not know what I am saying. The scripture says the Holy Spirit hears from Jesus and will speak to us. Use your weapons, they are powerful.

Paul says he prays in the Spirit and also sings in the Spirit. Some things must be taken by faith. The Word says regarding Speaking in tongues in 1 Corinthians 14: 39b (NIV) , "Do not forbid speaking in tongues." I read two books by Jack Deere, "Surprised by the Power of the Spirit" and "Surprised by the Voice of God." Jack, formerly an associate professor of Old Testament at Dallas Theological Seminary, is a writer and lecturer who speaks throughout the world on the gifts of the Holy Spirit. Jack was a well-known evangelical. In fact, he was a professor at the seminary that is considered the bastion of dispensational doctrine. They had decided that the Holy Spirit was just to be around in power until the Canon of Scripture was closed and given for the benefit of the apostles alone. His books explain how and why he changed his mind to coincide with the belief that the Holy Spirit is alive and well and active in the life of the believer today.

Religion Works Both Ways

I have discovered that people who are not baptized in the Holy Spirit often do not raise their hands when they worship. King David worshipped God with abandon and God liked it.

His wife Michal did not agree with David's type of worship. God kept Michal barren her entire life, keeping her from possibly being in the lineage of Jesus. I have noticed that some non-Spirit filled people also applaud the musicians after each song. They seem to think that they are being entertained and that they are the audience and need to applaud the musicians. What they just do not seem to understand is that they have only an audience of One. After making this rather harsh point, I want to add that in many Spirit-filled churches they have made an idol out of a certain way of worshiping. I have noticed that many, if not all, will stand when they worship everytime they worship. It has become a religion, the same way non-Spirit filled people sit or don't ever raise their hands. The Spirit-filled people stand and they don't seem to think God can receive their worship if they don't stand. This may be splitting hairs here, but David worshipped with abandon without his royal robes and God liked it. David did not worship that way all the time or it would have become religion. When asked if I ever raise my hands in worship, I say I never raise my hands unless I cannot keep them down.

Do I Have a Suggestion?

Yes I do. If you are a pastor, most of the above is a matter of teaching or pastoring. Are you afraid you will lose your pastorate? Do you think God can't give you a better pastorate? I know a pastor who does not raise his hands, but encourages his people to worship as they wish. He has a very successful church by the world's standard and God's. I know many pastors that have turned all over to the Lord and He has done wonderful things in their lives. I sometimes think that the moneychangers are back and are working the tables again. What falls by the wayside is discipleship. Then we see the statistics for sins committed by Christians and they resemble the world without Christ. The churches need to change something. Bringing more converts into the churches and leaving them to be a bad witness for the Lord is not what Jesus had in mind. Why can most American men quote the statistics for their favorite sport team and players, but cannot quote a scripture? Where does the fault lie?

An Apology

I apologize for this writing because I have not been biblically taught in a Christian college or seminary. I am writing only from my forty plus years experience in the Lord and the Charismatic movement. I seem to be apologizing a lot for chapters in this book. But now you may be getting a hint of how I think God may feel about the large organized churches in the Body of Christ.

So is God mad at the shepherds with the largest churches, the ones who do not teach the full council of God? The same ones who have locked up the Holy Spirit so when asked, the converts will say, "We didn't even know there is a Holy Spirit?" There is time to change, and we need to change before it is too late. The Israelites had an evil king for seventy years, but we do not have that much time. Jeremiah 29: 10.

In watching the news lately, we are seeing Christians being killed in many parts of the world for no reason but their profession of faith in Christ. We may soon be experiencing the same persecution as the Chinese. Perhaps then we will grow in love and unity and will experience the same sort of miracles they do. However, we will need the Holy Spirit to survive and grow the Body of Christ. One of my favorite scriptures is Deuteronomy 28:7 (HCSB), "The Lord will cause the enemies who rise up against you to be defeated before you. They will march out against you from one direction but flee from you in seven directions." Seven is God's perfect number so your enemy will flee from you perfectly. Do you believe this is still true today? "For our struggle is not against flesh and blood, but against the rulers, against the authorities, against the powers of this dark world and against the spiritual forces of evil in the heavenly realms" (Ephesians 6:12).

Chapter Twenty-Two

We Are Called To Be Led By The Spirit

❝By day the Lord went ahead of them in a pillar of cloud to guide them. . .” (Exodus 13:21 NIV).How are you at waiting on God? How do you determine if God is giving you the green light to move forward? Many believers make the mistake of adding up all the pluses and then concluding that God has given them the green light. Several factors go into making a decision from the Lord. Sometimes I go ahead with what I feel the Lord has told me to do before I check it out with my wife and others. It is important to do a few things before I make a decision on any matter. First, I gather the facts and ramifications of my decision on my family and any other previous commitments. This allows me to determine all the realities of my choice. However, this does not ultimately drive my decision, but could put a stop to it. For instance, if I were planning to follow my heart on something I believed that God wanted me to do but I knew that God had called me to an earlier commitment that had not completed, then I should look at the people I would be affecting by my decision. Second, would God lead me to enter into a project or venture that would adversely effect other people or leave unfinished a previous venture or commitment? I don't think so. Third, is the Holy Spirit guiding me in my decision? "If the Lord delights in a man's way, He makes his steps firm" (Ps. 37:23 NIV). God puts hedges around us, but many times we bull our way through the hedges under the guise of tenacity and perseverance or personal want and desire. Many times it is difficult to tell the difference between a "now" time and a " wait" time. This is unrighteousness and I have paid a high price for doing it. A wise believer said that the greatest success one can have in doing what we want and what God wants is to know when it is time to commit or cancel, rather than keep forcing a situation until we get what we really want, not what God wants. Not all calls are yes and amen, nor are they all for now. I always need to remind myself that we do see darkly. 1 Corinthians 13:12, " For now we see through a glass, darkly. . ." I don't always get it right. It was a little clearer with the pillar of fire and the cloud. It is not so easy today. Fourth, has my decision been confirmed? God has placed others around us to be used as instruments in our lives to confirm decisions and keep us from the pride and deceit of our own heart. "Every matter must be established by the testimony of two or three witnesses" (2 Cor. 13:1b NIV). This is God's way of keeping us within the hedge of His protection. Proverbs 24:6 (NRSV), " for by wise guidance you can wage your war, and in abundance of counselors there is victory." "I should put my ideas in my computer and give God the eraser". (Faith Walk 365, Sarasota, FL). When we get a word we think is from the Lord, a rhema word or maybe an impression we think is from God, it should be thought-out thoroughly and not jumped into because it may be something we want or would like to do. If we treat it as a word that we would not necessarily want to do, surely we would check it out from many sources and wait for conformations before doing something, e.g., if I feel through a prophetic word that God is telling me to move my family to Alaska vs. moving to Hawaii, I would want clear direction from all involved including my family. It is easy to get myself into a "Fix" and then I need God to "Fix" a "Fix" to get me out of the "Fix" I got myself into (Bob Mumford). Proverbs 11:14,"Where no counsel is, the people fall: but in the multitude of counselors there is safety." When we have clear direction from a multitude of counselors (advisors),we have eliminated the confusion and now we can move in safety with belief that God has called us in our decision.

Psalm 27:14 (NIV), "Wait for the Lord; be strong and take heart and wait for the Lord." Hearing and doing God's will are two important steps that often get confused as one step. However, these are two distinct processes. When we hear God's voice this is only fifty percent of the process. The next important step is to know when to move. It is one thing to hear; it is another to know when to act. I may not be good at preaching like Billy Graham, Reinhard Bonnke or even my pastor.

I may not be able to teach like some of the teachers we know of in the Body of Christ, and God doesn't expect me to do any of these things. He knows my abilities and He knows what I should and should not do. He may give me the desire to do some of those things, but that desire should not resemble a green light to preach or to teach, or to go to Africa just because

I have the desire to do it. I might have a burden for the lost, the poor, and the hungry or to do any number of things. There are many ministries to support that already do those things. Airplane trips and hotel dollars can really help the professional already in the field. As I have previously stated regarding family, wives or husbands and kids are the ones who bear the burden for your time away from the family. This is the most important issue in your decision to go. Your commitment to what God has called you to do first is a priority above any desire you may have to do anything for the Lord that will conflict with that first duty or calling. The question must be are you achieving the God-given calling for your life? God has called people into all types of vocations and businesses to fulfill His purposes just as He has called people to be pastors or missionaries. It is time for believers to stop feeling like second-class citizens for being in business or being a mother or father. It is time for believers to stop working toward financial independence or other personal goals so that they can concentrate on their "true spiritual calling." This is the great deception for those called to a business or what some would think is a mundane calling. Significance comes from fulfilling the God-given purpose for which you were made.

In the non-Christian world many men have the desire to play football with the pros or with college guys. The world won't allow this to happen. The lack of exceptional ability will keep them from doing the thing they want to do. I have always felt that an untrained person trying to do the work of a trained person in a real life situation would be like a non-professional football player trying to help win a game. He would just get in the way of the professional who must take care of the untrained guest to make sure he doesn't get in the way or worse, doesn't get hurt. In the Christian world, we take our desire to do something we would love to do and say God called me to go and we go! Of course we can't go on our own so we do what the missionaries do, we raise money. As a long time Christian, I have been the target of many money raising letters from people wanting to take trips to foreign countries. Having the resources to go, whether they are your own or provided by others, is not the criteria. Your great desire is also not the criteria. We are all missionaries. Some are called to foreign lands. Some are called to the jungles of the workplace. Wherever you are called, serve the Lord in that place. Let Him demonstrate His power through your life so that others might experience Him through you. View your vocation as means to worship Him. Paul said it right, "Each person should remain in the situation they were in when God called them (1Corinthians 7:20).

Bob Hartley has said that the devil has an old weapon that he uses against the brethren. "The good is the enemy of the best." We want to do good for the Lord because it is a good thing, but in reality it is not the perfect will of God for us. So the devil pushes us toward what we know are good things. To me it speaks of being busy for the Lord when the Lord is saying, "Slow down and wait for me. I will direct you to do what I want you to do." Being led by the Spirit often means we must not use the world's standard for success as our measuring stick. You never know what an act of obedience will yield at the time. We must leave the results to God. Our role is to obey. His role is to bring results from our obedience. I sometimes make decisions based on evaluations of the facts of a matter, rather than being led by the Holy Spirit. This is called making outcome-based decisions.This is the world's way and it works sometimes. If our decisions are based on reasoning and not on the Spirit's leading, we may not have the benefit of God's protection on our success. I am not saying that 2+2 doesn't always equal 4. It does. However, most decisions or projects we encounter are not that easy and it is good to have confirmation from God that you are on the right path.

I have many examples of hearing God, moving with His direction and winning. I will say listening and asking the Holy Spirit is not always my first choice. I usually try my own intellect first and fail. Then I go to God in desperation. I will give two examples. The first was a crisis that arose in my dumpster business through no fault of mine. I had sold around 1,500 dumpsters to the Walmart Company through one of their contract haulers. I didn't know that they were going to overload the bins by almost three times the acceptable weight by putting wet organic waste in the bins (a normal 4 cubic yard bin weight allowance was 3,200 lbs.; organic is 8,600 lbs.). The bins began to fail. What could I do? I immediately began trying to figure out how I was going to save 1,500 bins. I could not come up with anything. After two days I turned to the Lord in desperation. I said, "Father if you don't help me, I am ruined". I went to sleep that night and the Lord awakened me during the night as He usually does to speak to me. He gave me specific directions on how to save the bins. I did exactly what He said and it worked and the idea became the way the entire industry is able to put organics in all plastic bins using God's idea. We called it an extreme weight kit and were able to market it as an additional product.

The second example that I remember is when God told me to move to Orange County from Sierra Madre, California. The Spirit of God was very specific and I, with great fear, required the Lord to be even more specific and He was. So I moved my wife, 6 kids and all my belongings. I put my home up for sale, rented a house and started looking for a home to buy in Orange county. I now was committed because I was following directions from God and my fears were low. There was testing along the way. I could not find a home in O.C. that could accommodate my 6 kids. So I decided to build a home myself that would be big enough, however, I had never built a house before. Oh well, not my problem. God told me to build one through a young girl in my Bible study in Sierra Madre. At the time I was tempted to believe that she was a false prophet because I was so scared!

God tested my trust and obedience by not allowing my former home to sell. I had found a lot to buy and in faith I took a swing loan out to buy it. I did not even know what a swing loan was until then. It was a loan on the home I was trying to sell. If it did not sell it was the Lord's problem, not mine. I bought the lot, got a construction loan and built the house. My other home did not sell until the day my new house was finished. Did I think that I had made a mistake in hearing God? No, because I was committed to following the Spirit. Being led by the Spirit is comforting when you hear correctly, and that is the rub. When you are used to hearing because of past history, you begin to know when you have heard the Lord and not your own thoughts, the world's or the enemy's thoughts. This only comes by becoming close enough to the Lord to hear His still quiet voice when He speaks. When you hear, then obey, you have thrown the ball to the Lord and it is His job to make the goal. Even when our doubts are relieved, we humans with our weak flesh always need assurances from the Lord in the process. These are lessens as we have more experience hearing the Lord and watching Him move on His word, both the Logos and Rhema word. I have found it is good to ask God to give you a willingness and ability to hear the Holy Spirit and to obey His promptings.

I have decided that you need to hear one more example of being led by the Spirit. It is very dramatic and again it required me to obey, only this time it was a desert experience that the Lord led me into. Desert experiences are when God is preparing you for a job or promotion as He did with Joseph. My brother and cousin came to me in Orange County after I built my house. They said that the oil drilling business needed a new rotary table that allows the driller to drill to extreme depths. They said that the current equipment was old technology and not capable to do it. This was the time in 1984 when we were having an oil crisis and cars were in line at the gas stations for gas. There were no rotary tables for sale as they were all sold or leased to drillers, and there was a great need. The cost for this project was over one million dollars. I was careful to do some due diligence before I committed to that kind of obligation. I had not heard anything from the Lord. So I decided that I would not do it. By the way, every place we checked, including going to Houston to the Off Shore Technology Show, we were told by the oil drillers that they needed what we had. At this time I attended a Christian conference featuring a prophet named Bill Hammond. While sitting in the back of the auditorium the speaker said, "You in the back, stand up." He said, " you have been considering a new venture and the Lord says do it". Well , I went away rather confused because I was used to hearing the Lord, but I had not heard for myself. So I said no again. A couple of weeks later I attended a one-day seminar at a Catholic church because we had been teaching in the Catholic Charismatic renewal. A prophetess who did not know me at all and I did not even know her name, pointed at me and said, "You in the back, stand up." She repeated the exact words that Bill Hammond said. Well, I said to myself, "This is the Lord," and I committed to the project. It cost me more than one million dollars and nearly bankrupted my company. Did I hear correctly, was this the Lord? If it was, why did I not hear like I usually heard? I don't know why, but I do know that it was the Lord who wanted me to get into the rotary table business. I learned much from the struggles. I was blamed for going into the business even after I was the only one who did not want to go into the business until I felt that I was supposed to from the Lord.

What happened? Well, we produced 10 tables, retail price $55,000 each. We sold 10. We were paid for 2, the industry reversed, oil dropped in price and tables were plentiful. We were told by the industry that our table was the best design ever made to drill oil wells for the deepest known depths. The Lord helped me and I set up a plan to pay all my debts. It was unique. My daughter shared it in her college class and I was asked to teach it. Do you think your life was planned even with that misstep figured in? Absolutely. Isn't it comforting to know that you cannot plan God out of the equation no matter how bad you mess up? He will always turn crooked places into straight places for those who are humble and contrite.

I still do not believe I know all the reasons I was told to go into that business, but I just know it was the Lord. Maybe it was for others to learn that God could lead them into a desert like He did to many of His people for training and developing them into people prepared to achieve their God ordained destiny. Don't be afraid to ask the Holy Spirit for all that you do. Don't ask for the things you should know because you are alive and breathing, God did give us a brain to use. However, there are many areas you will need God's help. Ask and obey and leave the rest up to the Lord; He is faithful. Ephesians 3:20 (NKJV), "Now unto him that is able to do exceeding abundantly above all that we ask or think, according to the power that worketh in us." I have experienced that scripture and it is wonderful when the Lord moves in your behalf and irrefutable miracles take place.

Chapter Twenty-Three

Stop the Bombing

T he battle plan is to bring the Kingdom of God to Earth. I wrote this in 2004. God began His plan to return to the Earth the second time and He set in motion a Master's master plan that would usher in the End Times and His return. He set into action specific things and ministries. The Evangelical movement started to obey the Great Commission. Other movements started to help prepare the Church for the coming of the Lord. In 1906 God visited a small group of people with His Holy Spirit and gave them a visitation not unlike the Acts 2 visitation. We called it the Azusa Street revival. They spoke in tongues. This was a small group of poor people that only wanted more of God. I believe that this was part of the Last Day master plan.

God moved on Chuck Smith and John Wimber and an unlikely fellow named Lonnie Frisbee and told them to begin to evangelize the youth. God called Billy Graham to win souls and Kathryn Kuhlman to show the world God's power and love. Many other ministries were called to prepare the way of the coming of the Lord. In 1965 the Catholics were called. The master plan was changing and it was more than these simple first steps. Jesus said He was coming back for a Church without spot or wrinkle so there was more to do to prepare. However, we were not told the complete plan all at once. God has given us bits and pieces over time. All of those who were called were just ordinary human beings , but great work was done by the power of God which was the new move.

There was only one problem. The Church and the ministries that were part of the very beginnings of the move thought that they were all that there was to the master plan. So they would not stop doing what they had been called to do, and would not even listen to see if the Lord wanted to change something. The biggest hindrance to the new move of the Lord is always the last move of the Lord. Many leaders trying to implement change used this phrase during in the early 1970's.

Some of the ministries diligently following the Great Commission did not even complete the most important part of the Great Commission. Matthew 28:18-20 (NIV), "Therefore go and make disciples of all nations, baptizing them in the name of the Father and of the Son and of the Holy Spirit, and teaching them to obey everything I have commanded you." The Church has done a petty good job of evangelizing. The world may have heardthe Gospel many times. That is not my point. My point is that I believe Jesus will be back on the Earth and these ministries will be too busy doing the Great Commission to realize Jesus is coming back.

God has moved beyond the beginning ministries and

wants to set more of the master plan into motion before He returns but the Church is so busy doing the last thing God told them to do. They have built a virtual fence around the last word of God so that they cannot hear, or more likely they don't want to change as though God has no more good ideas. Sometimes I think they are protecting their giant ministries and won't change and do the new part of the master plan because they are afraid God will say stop doing much of what they have built their ministries on. Does this sound like the Pharisees of old? They liked doing what they were doing. They liked the robes (suits) and traveling from town to town on their donkeys (now on their jets). They like the power and authority and money; it is the same today, just more extravagant and world wide and not confined to one area.

What's the Battle Plan?

This reminds me of the 2nd World War. The Marines were trying to take some islands in the Pacific, Iwo Jima and others. The master plan was to take the island for an airfield closer to Japan. The first part of the master plan was to bomb the island with Navy ships and planes. This was to prepare the way for the Marines to land on the shore. The purpose was to destroy any of the enemy that might hinder the landing. What if the Navy ships kept on bombing the island while the Marines were landing? What if the planes kept bombing? It is obvious what would happen. The Marines could not land on the island without the risk of being killed by their own forces. What if the Navy thought that their action was all there was of the master plan and there was not going to be any further action to take the island? I believe that is what is happening now in the Church. I also believe that we may be holding up the landing of the Lord because we are not allowing the next part of the master plan to begin. The Church needs to stop the bombing before the friendly fire of the disunity in the body gets worse than it is now.

What is the next move in the master plan? How do we know? God says in Amos 3:7 (NIV), "Surely the Sovereign Lord does nothing without revealing his plan to his servants the prophets." I believe we know a little of what's next. The prophets are speaking and some of the Church is listening. God wants to bring to fullness the power and direction given to the Church. He wants to reestablish the five-fold ministry in the Church with the pastor, teacher, evangelist, prophet and apostle with the emphasis on each part of this five-fold ministry and the gifts of the Holy Spirit. Some of these offices have been gone from the Church for centuries and God wants to bring back the command and control to the Church.

In a battle scenario, the first part of defeating an enemy is to defeat his command and control and to stop his ability to communicate with his people who are doing the fighting against the objective. You must stop his ability to tell them to change direction, to move left or right or in God's case, to stop the bombing, so He can implement the next move. In the war in Iraq, America destroyed the enemies' command and control in one day rendering the enemy deaf, mute and blind. The enemy was able to be defeated in a few days.

The enemy of the Church and of Christ's return has defeated the command and control of the Church. He has convinced much of the Church in America that the offices of apostle and prophet and the Holy Spirit's work of power with the individual believer, i.e. the Baptism in the Holy Spirit with speaking in tongues hasn't existed since the Canon of Scripture closed. The shame is that the enemy of our souls has found a willing partner in much of this work in a major part of the Church. In a real physical war these people would be called traitors.

Eph 4:11-16 (NIV), "It was he who gave some to be apostles, some to be prophets, some to be evangelists, and some to be pastors and teachers, to prepare God's people for works of service, so that the Body of Christ may be built up until we all reach unity in the faith and in the knowledge of the Son of God and become mature, attaining to the whole measure of the fullness of Christ. Then we will no longer be infants, tossed back and forth by the waves, and blown here and there by every wind of teaching and by the cunning and craftiness of men in their deceitful scheming. Instead, speaking the truth in love, we will in all things grow up into him who is the Head, that is, Christ. From him the whole body, joined and held together by every supporting ligament, grows and builds itself up in love, as each part does its work." Wow! What a scripture! If we had this working in the Church in the last 100 years just think of what the Church would look like! We would almost look like a Church without spot or wrinkle. As I said, we need the prophets. Without the prophets operating in the Church, how can we know God's plan for His return? How can we know when He wants us to do something new or different from the status quo? How can we know when He wants to implement the next move to take the island so we could have an air base or to do the next thing required to prepare for His return?

Stop and listen to what the prophets are saying, and heed what they are saying. They are God's mechanism to change the direction of the Church for the preparation for the return of the Lord and the defeat of the enemy. I am not minimizing the Word of God in the least. I am just making a point that the Lord has already made (Amos 3: 7).

Have We Made an Idol Out of The Status Quo?

Have we become complacent in the battle rather than striving to win the objective? Have we forgotten the objective? The Church desperately needs the apostle, prophet, pastor teacher and evangelist. In order to continue with our war scenario we cannot send untrained troops into the battle. They must know who the enemy is, how to defeat him and what weapons to use. How can we train the troops if we have all jobs done by only one member of the five-fold ministry, the pastor? Our enemies are not carnal they are spiritual and we need to learn how to fight a spiritual battle. We need sheep and shepherds who are trained and committed to the Lordship of Jesus

The objective, the Island, needs to be taken, but everyone is still doing the old (last) direction given to them. Don't they think that God might want to change the battle plan? God has a plan, but He gives it to His children a piece at a time.

We don't need people who go to church just to be doing something good on Sunday, then go back to their busy life style on Monday. We need sheep and shepherds who hear God and are committed to doing what He asks. What if God asked His Church to only meet in homes, to give up the buildings, give up the mortgages on the church plant? What if He wanted to have a worldwide Church that operates out of the box as we know it today? What if it was an underground Church, one without walls? Would anyone hear? Could anyone hear? A prophet could. A prophet could then give direction to the Body of Christ. The apostle would implement the directions of the Lord. The Church needs to believe that the office of the prophet and apostle do exist today and it needs to listen to them. I have discovered again that the greatest hindrance to the new move of God is the old move of God.

Please understand that I am not only promoting the apostles and prophets, I am promoting the entire five-fold ministry and acceptance of the gifts for this age. The Body Christ must be mature and move in power to win the battle and even is more needed. The local Churches need to be related to all the other local Churches worldwide. When Christ left the apostles to go to His Father, He said to love one another (See John17:23). We cannot even decide what day is the Sabbath, let alone love one another or be united. We are a divided Church thus we are a weak Church. We are barely held together by the main doctrine of being saved by the redeeming blood of Christ. The baptism in the Holy Spirit is a great division in the Church. Can you imagine an army trying to win a battle with half of the army in disagreement with the other half? There seems to be a great fight in the churches to fill the pews from the pulpit. (J. Gerald Harris, Editor, Published June 7, 2007) The pastor's job is to fill the pulpit. The evangelist fills the pews. The pastor should pastor the sheep once they are in the pen.

In summary, I wrote most of this in September of 2004,

almost 10 years ago. I have updated it recently. I find that the Church of Jesus Christ is better than it was in 2004. It is stronger and God is moving sovereignly throughout His Body. The part of the Church that does not believe in the baptism of the Holy Spirit is getting smaller by the year. Unity, however, is not much better. The Lord is still in charge and His Word is still true and He will still perform it as promised (Zech 10: 3).

Chapter Twenty-Four

God Needs To Test Us

If we are going to be used by the Lord to go to the next level of maturity or for a new level of trust and authority we must be tested. The Bible has many examples of men of God who were tested before being allowed to take on a work of God. A great example was Joseph who was tested for 13 years before he was allowed to save the Hebrew people from starvation.Moses was another as was David who was not allowed to walk in the promise of God to be king until he was thoroughly tested and corrected.

However, we do not know how we will act. He knows whether we will act in faith without us having a history of personal experience in what He can do in our extreme need. So God wants us to know what He knows about us and about Him. Once we have been tested in battle and have acted in faith and trust, God can then send us out to do His will with confidence. However, this is not for God, it is for us. He already knows what we will do, but now we also know with confidence that God will be with us and that we can trust Him. Psalm 144 (NIV),"Praise be to the Lord my Rock, who trains my hands for war, my fingers for battle." David was trained in battle with the lion who attacked his flock so when it was time to fight Goliath, he was well trained. It wasn't physical training on how to sling a slingshot, but training that he could trust God in a battle, no matter who the enemy.

God knows all of this ahead of time and He does not want us to fail. We can fail even after coming out of our prison, trial, valley or desert experience, however, the likelihood of failure would be greater if we were untested. Even Moses failed after many years and he had a closer contact and relationship with God than almost anyone. We are flesh and blood and we are weak but God knows it and He doesn't expect more from us than we can do. My example is the soldier that goes into battle after being properly trained has a better chance of completing his mission and protecting his people than if he was not trained and thoroughly tested.

Another area in our relationship with God that we need to know about is how we will act when all is well when we have no fear of loss of resources or position. We are on top of the world in a non-spiritual sense. Oswald Chambers says, "Not every man can carry a full cup. Sudden elevation frequently leads to pride and a fall. The most exacting test of all is to survive is prosperity." So God, in His mercy, tests us even in a time of blessing so we will know that God is still our source, not our personal wealth or natural wisdom and abilities. It sounds like our Christian walk is all about testing. It's not, but those the Lord wants to use for His Kingdom will need to be people that look like Him and act like Him. I can't impress on you enough on how much God wants to put you on His team to prepare for His return.

Chapter Twenty-Five

Is Isis a Judgment From God?

T his may be a foreign idea to us Christians, however, I want to postulate it here because there doesn't seem to be a simple answer as to why God is tolerating the murders of innocent Christians. I decided to look in the Scriptures and found some of the same kinds of situations have taken place. I have found a lot of relevant scriptures in Habakkuk as well as 1Chronicles.

Is God allowing the deaths of the innocent Christians in Iraq as He did in Israel when King David committed a grave sin by counting his horses and chariots? God sent the death angel and killed 70,000 innocent people. Is this what is happening in Iraq? If so how do we stop the killing of the innocent sheep as David called them? David asked God to put the blame on him and his family and stop the killing of his people and God stopped the killing. David repented and stood in the gap for the people (See 1 Chronicles 21:14-15).Can we repent and stand in the gap and satisfy God for our sins? Repent means change so we must change. What grave sins have American Christians committed that could be contributing to these horrible deaths of our brothers and sisters and how do we help stop the killing?

What will it take to stop the killing of the Christians in Iraq by the ISIS death angel? First, what is our sin that caused this wrath of God upon us? I believe David's sin was to turn from God and trust in his own resources, forgetting his God. Have we turned from our God in favor of our own false gods or selfish desires for pleasure, wealth, power, worldly desires of all types, including greed? I believe God has had enough. He has put up with all our modern, sophisticated ways to move away from Him. We can spend time with anything but our God, yet we expect Him to meet our every need. God is a God of mercy, love and forgiveness. He showed it all on the Cross. Genesis 6:3a (NIV), "Then the Lord said, 'My Spirit will not contend with humans forever, . . .' "Habakkuk 1:2-17 (NIV-UK) Habakkuk's complaint. "How long, Lord, must I call for help, but you do not listen? Or cry out to you, 'Violence! But you do not save? Why do you make me look at injustice? Why do you tolerate wrongdoing? Destruction and violence are before me; there is strife, and conflict abounds. Therefore the law is paralyzed, and justice never prevails. The wicked hem in the righteous, so that justice is perverted. The Lord's answer 'Look at the nations and watch–and be utterly amazed. For I am going to do something in your days that you would not believe, even if you were told. I am raising up the Babylonians, that ruthless and impetuous people, who sweep across the whole earth to seize dwellings not their own. They are a feared and dreaded people; they are a law to themselves and promote their own honor. Their horses are swifter than leopards, fiercer than wolves at dusk. Their cavalry gallops headlong; their horsemen come from afar. They fly like an eagle swooping to devour; they all come intent on violence. Their hordes advance like a desert wind and gather prisoners like sand. They mock kings and scoff at rulers. They laugh at all fortified cities; by building earthen ramps they capture them. Then they sweep past like the wind and go on, guilty people, whose own strength is their god.'

Habakkuk's second complaint, "Lord, are you not from everlasting? My God, my Holy One, you will never die. You, Lord, have appointed them to execute judgment; you, my Rock, have ordained them to punish. Your eyes are too pure to look on evil; you cannot tolerate wrongdoing. Why then do you tolerate the treacherous? Why are you silent while the wicked swallow up those more righteous than themselves? You have made people like the fish in the sea, like the sea creatures that have no ruler. The wicked foe pulls all of them up with hooks, he catches them in his net, he gathers them up in his drag-net; and so he rejoices and is glad. Therefore he sacrifices to his net." This is so relevant to our situation today.

God started with our judgment by raising up an evil king over us. I believe we have heard enough from his own mouth that he is a Muslim or sympathizes with them. That being said, we can expect Him to act accordingly, as He has. The Scripture tells us to obey those who are in authority over you as God has raised them up. Romans 13:1 (ESV), "Let every person be subject to the governing authorities. For there is no authority except from God, and those that exist have been instituted by

God." Romans 13:1 is a very familiar scripture. There is another on the same subject that would seem a little contradictory. Acts 5:29 (ESV), "But Peter and the apostles answered, 'We must obey God rather than men.' " It would seem that these two scriptures are conflicting, however, they are not. The Word has declared that we must obey the authority placed over us as God did the placing. Since we have free will and so does the king, he can ask us to do things that would cause us to disobey the Word of God just as happened to the apostles in Acts 5: 29. This allows us to disobey the authority.

Another scripture that is a good example is in Daniel 6:10. King Darius decided that he was the only god that could be worshiped. Daniel disobeyed King Darius and he went to the lion's den but was saved by God, as was Meshach, Shadrach and Abednego. Another scripture in Matthew 10: 33 (NLT) also states, "But everyone who denies me here on earth, I will also deny before my Father in heaven." American Christians are being told today to obey laws that are opposed to the Word of God. We have seen some disobey with some major Christian companies regarding abortion. 1 Peter 4: 17 (NIV), "For it is time for judgment to begin with God's household; and if it begins with us, what will the outcome be for those who do not obey the gospel of God?" First Peter says that we are under judgment or at least could be. I believe that we are under judgment and it may be that the murders of our brothers and sisters in Iraq is the punishment. In military situations when the leadership makes an error, many times, others suffer. I believe that we are in a battle and some innocents will suffer as they did in King David's judgment.

Back to my question, how do we stop the killing of Christians in Iraq? If I am saying that the killings in Iraq are because of the judgment put on American Christians by God, what do we do to stop the killings? We must stop doing what God thinks is offensive and humble ourselves, repent, pray, seek the Lord regarding our sins and turn from our wicked ways, then God promised that He would hear us and forgive our sins and heal our land. Does this sound familiar? It should to all Christians, but sadly, many may not know this scripture in 2nd Chronicles 7: 14.

How do we implement the above scripture in the American Church? It must start in the heart of man. We must come back to God and we must give up our idols of pleasure and self- indulgences that take our focus away from God. Even things that are good and beneficial can be the very things that take us away from God. We always think the major sins are what keep us from God and that is true. It is sometimes easier to stop doing bad things because we know they are bad than it is to stop the more subtle sins. I could give examples, but I will assume the reader will understand. What am I talking about when I say bad sins verses good sins? Maybe the term sins is a bad name for these good things. I know people who have fallen in love with their ministries and have forgotten who they serve. There are people who work in the church in various jobs and miss the Bible classes and never mature. There are churches who do not mentor or disciple their people. They just use them for the good things. Then there are churches who build buildings but not people. Jesus said something in Matthew 28:16-17 about that in the Great Commission.Go and make disciples teaching all that I have told you. The churches have made many converts, but few disciples. I have said this many times in my writing , but it is true and this makes the Body of Christ weak and vulnerable to attacks of the enemy. By the way, the enemy is the devil, Satan himself. He is fighting God, but he cannot fight God directly, so he fights God's kids, trying to wound as many as he can.

Other than the Holy Spirit and the scripture in Zechariah 10:3, Christians will never mature on their own. We need help from the five-fold ministry of the church to be taught but they don't seem to be too interested in it. They do not seem to take the convert to the next level in of Matthew 22:36-8 of loving the Lord with all their heart, soul and mind.

Chapter Twenty-Six

The Compassion of Christ

The definition of compassion from the New Oxford American Dictionary is: the virtue of empathy for the suffering of others. It is regarded as a fundamental part of human love, and a cornerstone of greater social interconnection and humanism —foundational to the highest principles in philosophy, society, and personhood. Compassion is often regarded as emotional in nature. Not a bad definition, in fact it totally describes the multiple facets of compassion plus it identifies it as "a virtue of empathy for the suffering of others." Virtue is a behavior showing high moral standards, and something we should all possess as human beings.

My discussion will take into consideration all of the facets that I know or at least have experienced regarding this wonderful virtue called the compassion of Christ. Do I think all compassion is the compassion of Christ? Yes I do, even when the person does not know Christ personally because his or her membership in God's human experiment qualifies any act ofcompassion as the compassion of Christ. Because God is all compassionate, all love and all merciful, practicing the virtues of God is always good. I do believe that as we should all have compassion. I also believe that there is a gift of compassion, much like there is a gift of healing that is different than just our normal praying for people.

Do you have the compassion of Christ? Do you know what the compassion of Christ is? You may think that you do, but I have some comments concerning it. I have the Compassion of Christ, so I have been told. It is not as simple as it sounds. I always thought that it was Jesus seeing sick people and praying for healing. It is that for sure, but it goes further than that. Jesus had the will of the Father and the wisdom of the Holy Spirit so He made no mistakes. We, however, need to pray for the will of the Father and the wisdom of the Holy Spirit. Now you may be confused, but let me explain.

I think it is a gift from God and it is different than just compassion in general. Do I think all Christians have the gift of compassion? No, I do not. However, I think we should go back to the parable of the Good Samaritan where Jesus was showing that we all should have mercy, compassion, and show concern for the needs of others. He was not talking about just His followers because the Samaritan was not a Jew, yet he shows him as having great mercy and compassion for a stranger. He also showed that the Samaritan revealed genuine concern by returning and paying for the care he requested from the innkeeper.

So if Jesus gave an example of a non-believer who showed care when the priests did not, I think He was showing an example that all should follow as well. How many times have we crossed over to the other side of the street to avoid a beggar on the street? I admit that I have at times changed lanes when I see a begging person on a corner by a stoplight. However, I need to explain. 2 Corinthians 1: 3-4 (ASV), "Blessed [be] the God and Father of our Lord Jesus Christ, the Father of mercies and God of all comfort; (4) who comforteth us in all our affliction, that we may be able to comfort them that are in any affliction, through the comfort wherewith we ourselves are comforted of God." God always seems to have multiple purposes for all He does.

My wife says that I have "unsanctified mercy" and she is correct. I have had to deal with this. While it is not bad, it sometimes frustrates the will of God in a person's life. It delays the lesson and really extends the time and pain that comes with the desert experience that God is using to teach the person and to build trust and faith in their lives.

How do we deal with the people on the street begging? I have dealt with this in a number of ways. In the beginning I let my gift rule my actions. Soon I realized that was not a smart thing to do. Now I have come to the conclusion that the gift of compassion without the ability to hear the Holy Spirit is like a soldier going to war without knowing who the enemy is and is not. You must hear direction from your superiors. The Holy Spirit is our superior and He will give us our direction on how and when to move in compassion. I am better at hearing now than I was early on so when I see a person on the street begging I wait to hear from God for direction because I cannot trust my emotions, if I do, I might soon be bankrupt.

Recently I noticed an older man sitting on a bus stop

bench near my home. My compassion gene began vibrating (if that is what it does). He seemed different because he wasn't begging, he wasn't asking anyone for anything, he had no signs telling of his plight, he was just sitting on the bus bench. I was torn between should I stop or continue on. I knew that I was coming back that way and I thought that I would stop then if he was still there. I came back some four hours later and he was still on the bench, now sleeping. I knew that I would not be able to sleep if I did not stop and help. I did stop. I gave him money to eat and went through the sinner's prayer with him. He was not totally there mentally but that part is God's business. I felt that I had done my part. I almost felt that he might have been an angelic entity for some purpose God had for me because I never saw him before or again. It was a little like the bible story of the Good Samaritan. I sometimes think any time I am prompted to help that it is as much of a benefit to me as the person I help.

I have noticed that when I work as a team with my wife, God will speak to us both and give us the same word as a confirmation. I have seen this many times even revealing the exact same amounts that the Lord may want us to give to a particular need. In fact, we like seeing God do this. It makes us feel like we are in sync with the Holy Spirit and with each other and now we have permission to act.

My prayer to the Lord has been, "Lord if you like what we do with our money then keep it coming." It reminds me of the verse in Exodus when Moses asked the Lord a similar question. Exodus 33:13 (NIV), "If You are pleased with me, teach me Your ways so I may know You and continue to find favor with You." At this point I want to say that giving isn't always giving money. We all are needy in many ways and the gift of compassion reaches all those needs to the extent that we have the ability to meet those needs. If we are not in the Word, we will not be able to give a word to a person who needs one for a particular situation. I am not speaking about a sovereign prophetic word or word of knowledge. Those are separate gifts and we only need faith to move in those gifts if we possess them.

We all do not have the gift of compassion. I have watched others in situations where I was moved by my gift while others were not even touched. I have the gift of God's passion as well. I feel it is the trigger that helps the compassion gift in that it gives it the incentive to act without further instruction. We have all quoted the scripture where God owns the cattle on a thousand hills (Psalm 50:10 NIV) to demonstrate that God can provide for our needs. I say we are the cattle and God will call upon us as his cattle to help others.

When I speak of these gifts I think of the prophetic gifts and the scripture as "we see darkly." 1 Corinthians 13:12, "For now we see through a glass, darkly. . ." We learn to use all the gifts as we move in them. We are all given a measure of faith, but we must increase our faith by studying the Word of God and building our faith through trials of trusting God and seeing God's hand in our life and the answers to our prayers.

Our Blessings are Meant to be Shared

If we feel that the harvest God provides through our hard work, our wisdom or our good fortune is all ours, we again frustrate the plan of God for our lives and for those He wants us to bless. In America, the pressure is always on to move up the ladder of material accumulation. However, anything that takes away our focus from Jesus is an idol. Jesus warned us about this. If your focus is to gain more and more, ask the Lord if you have an open hand when it comes to finances. Our Biblical example is 2 Samuel 24:10 (NIV), "David was conscience-stricken after he had counted the fighting men, and he said to the LORD, 'I have sinned greatly in what I have done.' " What David did was trust in his wealth and accumulation of horses chariots and soldiers instead of the Lord and the punishment was severe.

I hope that this has explained my gift of compassion. I know that I have much more to learn and I look forward to learning it. Proverbs 11:24-25 (NIV), "One man gives freely, yet gains even more; another withholds unduly, but comes to poverty. A generous man will prosper; he who refreshes others will himself be refreshed."

Having the passion and compassion of Christ is a career/ministry in itself. Join the fun, you won't be sorry.

Chapter Twenty-Seven

When Will Righteousness Return To The Church?

"For I, the Lord, love justice; I hate robbery and wrongdoing." Isaiah 61:8a (NLT))

"I know, my God, that you test the heart and are pleased with integrity" (1 Chronicles 29:17a). God tests His children to know what is in their hearts. God's desire for each of His children is to walk in relationship with Him and to uphold His righteousness and integrity. It is a high calling that we will fail to achieve without complete dependence on Him.

Sometimes the greatest tests come in times of prosperity. When we are prospering we can begin to lose our close connection with the Lord and lose our recognition of sin. We don't have the same motivation for change that adversity brings us. When we are in trouble, we are always seeking the Lord. When we have few problems, we may just be satisfied with the status quo. When righteousness returns to the Church, the healing mantle that the apostles had will return. Then healing will happen when people pass by as when Peter's shadow touched people and they were healed. Jesus wants us to follow Him and not the world. He wants us to act like we are different than the world by following God instead of our selfish desires.

The righteousness of the Apostles was so pleasing to God that He was compelled to apply His justice to unrighteous and unjust situations as in Acts 5:1-11 (MSG), "But a man named Ananias—his wife, Sapphira, conniving in this with him— sold a piece of land, secretly kept part of the price for himself, and then brought the rest to the Apostles and made an offering of it. Peter said, "Ananias, how did Satan get you to lie to the Holy Spirit and secretly keep back part of the price of the field? Before you sold it, it was all yours, and after you sold it, the money was yours to do with as you wished. So what got into you to pull a trick like this? You didn't lie to men but to God.' Ananias, when he heard those words, fell down dead. That put the fear of God into everyone who heard of it. The younger men went right to work and wrapped him up, then carried him out and buried him. Not more than three hours later, his wife, knowing nothing of what had happened, came in. Peter said, "Tell me, were you given this price for your field?" "Yes," she said, "that price." Peter responded, 'What's going on here that you connived to conspire against the Spirit of the Master? The men who buried your husband are at the door, and you're next.' No sooner were the words out of his mouth than she also fell down, dead. When the young men returned they found her body. They carried her out and buried her beside her husband. By this time the whole church and, in fact, everyone who heard of these things had a healthy respect for God. They knew God was not to be trifled with.' "

When I asked God how He could let the lying and the injustice and the killing of babies continue in our day when He dealt so harshly with Ananias and Sapphira, God showed me that the righteousness and obedience of the Apostles was so perfected that He had to deal with the sin of other believers. Then God showed me 2 Cor.10: 6 "… and we will be ready to punish every act of disobedience, once your obedience is complete." This verse is saying that when we begin to walk in righteousness like the Apostles, God will give us the same authority to punish all disobedience as the Apostles had.The obedience of Peter and the Apostles was complete and God was forced to deal with all sin, even what appeared to be a small sin of lying by changing what was previously agreed upon. When our righteousness is complete like the Apostles was and when this comes about in our churches today, we may see liars drop dead at the communion table. We will understand what taking the body and blood of Christ unworthily means. 1 Corinthians 11: 27-30 (NIV), "Therefore, whoever eats the bread or drinks the cup of the Lord in an unworthy manner will be guilty of sinning against the body and blood of the Lord. A man ought to examine himself before he eats of the bread and drinks of the cup. For anyone who eats and drinks without recognizing the body of the Lord eats and drinks judgment on himself. That is why many among you are weak and sick, and a number of you have fallen asleep." Acts 5:13(NIV) says, "No one else dared join them, even though they were highly regarded by the people." This is why no one wanted to get too close to the Apostles. It appears that it wasn't God who caused judgment on Ananias and Sapphira. It was the authority given to the Apostles by God. If we expect to see judgment on the sin in

America, we must become obedient to the Lord and not be as unrighteous as the world we live in. Then God will give us the power and authority to deal with sin like He did for the Apostles. We are in a time of crisis in our country. As the people of God, we must stop sinning, believe God and practice 2 Chronicles 7:14.

At this point I said to God, "Don't do anything until I call you." (Ha!) I need much more time to get my obedience complete and so does the rest of the Body of Christ. I think this is what Christ means when He says. "I am coming back for My Bride without spot or wrinkle". I titled this chapter, "When Will Righteousness Return to the Church?" The reason I did is because as a businessman in modern day America, I have experienced more unrighteousness in the last few years than ever. There does not seem to be any limit to what people will do to gain an advantage (which is a euphemism for money).I have been lied to, stolen from, cheated, and betrayed. And the next day it got worse, ha, ha. Business today is dangerous. Even the government will lie, cheat and steal from you as they have me with impunity. How do you put your government in jail? So when we also get all of the above from brothers and sisters in the Church, it is disheartening. I recently completed a seven- year lease in a facility I was using to run my business. I left the building in perfect condition and had put a couple of hundred thousand in the building to accommodate my particular needs. This enhanced the building to a full power building and broadened the relisting ability of the building. However, the landlord (a brother) decided that he would not return my considerable deposit. I talked with him, but he decided there was too much wear on the facility. So I wrote him a letter and quoted 1 Corinthians 6:7-8 (NIV), "The very fact that you have lawsuits among you means you have been completely defeated already. Why not rather be wronged? Why not rather be cheated? Instead, you yourselves cheat and do wrong, and you do this to your brothers and sisters." I ended the letter by saying. "I am okay with being cheated". I mentioned that I would pray for his buildings to be leased, as there were many empty because of the local economy. We had no further contact. However, four months later I received a check for the entire amount. I mention this because I believe that this is rampant to one degree or more in the Church. God is not pleased with it and He wants it to change. I believe it is the fault of the shepherds in the churches. I don't remember hearing a sermon on 1 Corinthians 6:7-8.

As I mentioned before, then God showed me 2 Cor.10: 6…" and we will be ready to punish every act of disobedience, once your obedience is complete." I think we are safe for now since the shepherds are not close to the righteousness of the Apostles. That doesn't mean that God likes my unrighteousness or yours either. We are supposed to change the world not the other way around. Hard times cause people to do drastic things. Christians should go first to the Lord for the help needed. If we have a relationship with the Lord, He is faithful to help. I realize He will not answer every need to meet our desires. God has a more perfect agenda for our lives than meeting our every wish and need. Walking with the Lord is an adventure. I have been on it for a long time and I have a good testimony of His graciousness, love, mercy, faithfulness and trustworthiness. By the way, this is one way to build our faith in God. Our faith rises after each time God answers a need.

Chapter Twenty-Eight

Trust

Trust is another word for patience or waiting. If you don't think so, you haven't been trusting God for something. God loves us like we love our kids, although more like us old folks love our grandkids. We like giving gifts to our kids. I have been fortunate to be able to do that with my kids and grandkids (grandkids are more fun and cheaper). God loves giving gifts to His kids as well.

In Matthew 7: 11 (NIV), it says, "If you, then, though you are evil, know how to give good gifts to your children, how much more will your Father in heaven give good gifts to those who ask him!" Usually when we think of gifts, we think of things such as clothes, homes and money .However, God also gives spiritual gifts 1 Corinthians 12:1 (NIV), "Know about spiritual gifts, brothers, I do not want you to be ignorant." We don't normally think about The Lord not answering our requests for spiritual gifts when we ask Him. But when we ask for something we want in the worldly realm, it seems that we almost do not expect to get an answer .Why? I have been asking myself that question for years.

However, God has worked with me in this area for a long while. I learned hard and long. It was not easy for God. I am sure he wanted to answer me quicker than He did. I just wasn't ready for the blessings I was asking for. That sounds strange, but you do not see it until after it is over, although we need to leave room for God's agenda and realize that it is not always our agenda. Now this is hard to do when you are praying for a brother or sister's healing or one of you kids or your spouse.

The best story I can think of to explain this is a story I heard Bill Johnson who is the Pastor of Bethel Church in Redding, California tell about his dad. He said that he actually needed to hire a person to keep track of all the healings happening at the church and in Redding at the mall. He said that in the midst of all the healings that were happening at the mall, at church and on the streets, his father died of cancer. God did not heal him. That will shake your faith and teaching and I would need an answer to continue moving in the Spirit.

The answer is that God sees the engine and the caboose at the same time, and we only see the engine. Another answer is that it is not God's agenda, not His agenda not to heal, it is His agenda to heal, but not this person, not at this time. Sometimes we get a little insight later from God, but most of the time none at all.

I have been on both sides of this scenario. I have prayed for people and they were healed, one instantly of cancer. I have also travailed for a long time and the person died. I prayed for a young sister who had cancer and she was healed. A few months later she died in one day and not from cancer. A well-known minister friend when asked this very question, explained that he was called to the hospital to pray for a close friend. He prayed and while he was praying someone from the next room heard him and came to him and asked if he would pray for his friend in the next room. He prayed for his own friend with all the faith he could muster, but God did not heal him. When he prayed for the man in next room, his prayer was perfunctory and with hardly any faith and you guessed it, God healed him!

I don't like the human excuses as to why God didn't heal this particular person or why He did not bless a person with a particular thing that they wanted. Excuses could be like God saved him from a worst fate, he was in so much pain, or he is in a better place now. One of the classics is that God loved him/her so much He wanted them in Heaven. All of these may be true and good, but they do not satisfy or answer the question. I personally like, "His ways are higher than our ways." That I can believe. My wife and I are praying the Lord's Prayer more now than ever before."Thy will be done on earth as it is in Heaven." With those words are we giving up our agenda to God's agenda. By the way, it is not really part of this word on trust, but as long as we are in the Lords Prayer, the words, "forgive me as I forgive others," make it pretty clear that we cannot have any unforgiveness in our heart toward anyone or we won't be forgiven.It has nothing to do with salvation just our relationship with The Lord.

I heard a testimony of a lady who had been in a wheelchair for 22 years. She is a spiritual lady, the wife of a Pastor and loves the Lord. She said that after her 10th year in the wheelchair and not being able to take a step, she confessed discouragement and that she had lost hope of being healed. She had been to so many healing services and not been healed that she put her expectation of being healed on a shelf and said," Jesus if you don't want to heal me, that is okay". She began thanking God for her illness. She said that she learned the true meaning of Proverbs 13:12 (NIV), "Hope deferred makes the heart sick." In her 22nd year in the wheelchair, she understood the rest of the proverb, "but a longing fulfilled is a tree of life." She was healed. I saw her being healed and then saw her give this testimony a few weeks later. She was running up and down the platform praising the Lord for about thirty minutes and giving this testimony.

Trusting and waiting are synonymous in spiritual things. You cannot have one without the other. This is a simplified answer to a very complex problem. God often births a vision in our lives only to allow it to die before the purest version of the vision is manifested. We saw this with Abraham and Isaac. It looked like God wanted to kill the promise. Abraham is called righteous by his faith. I always wondered why. I recently heard a good explanation. God knew Abraham would go through with killing the promise of making his seed multiply to be more than the sands of the sea. What was God's reason to tell Abraham to sacrifice Isaac? God is omniscient, so He knew what Abraham would do, but Abraham did not know. God looked way ahead and said. " I will show my Church a righteous man and a man of faith". Does God want to test us the same way? This has happened several times in my own journey. Romans 8:21-23 (AMP), "Fully satisfied and assured that God was able and mighty to keep His word and to do what He had promised. That is why his faith was credited to him as righteousness (right standing with God).Oswald Chambers observes, "God's method always seems to be a vision first, and then reality, but in between the vision and the reality, there is often a deep valley of humiliation, pain, suffering, trust, and temptation and ultimately faith and complete trust in God and His plan."

Remember the trouble King Saul got into when he couldn't wait for God and he made the sacrifice himself? He lost his throne. How often has a faithful soul been plunged into a like situation when after the vision comes, then comes the test? When God gives a vision, testing follows before the reality of the vision. Waiting on God will bring you into accord with the vision He has given . Otherwise, you will try to do away with the supernatural in God's undertakings and do it yourself. David could have killed Saul and became the king, but he did not. Even after Saul died, David waited for years.

Never Try to Help God Fulfill His Word

When God's vision is finally birthed, nothing will stop it. Our job is to allow God to birth His vision through us in His way and in His timing. Planning from God's view is a process. It isn't merely an exercise in reason and analysis. It requires entering into the mind of Christ together with using our minds to determine which course to take. I am guilty of not doing this many times. As a businessman I will use my mind, experience and sometimes consult an expert on the problem and forget God. I have an uncanny ability to make decisions based on my own needs and my own abilities, wants and what I think God wants for me mostly because if I want it, that means God should too. Right?

However, God desires that we seek Him to know His plans for us. Once you fool yourself into thinking you are doing God's will in a project, but you don't see God blessing it with success, you will need to go back and see where you took control. Then there is the vision that we can misinterpret. It can be a time of training, testing, trusting, watching, faithbuilding, and learning how to handle God's vision and nothing more. I have experienced many of these times. They were times when I was learning to hear God, times of teaching and times of spiritual boot camp. When you graduate you have the ability to handle the weapons of warfare and you can hear the command and control better than before. That is important because knowing the voice of God from the voice of the enemy or from your own voice is crucial. You will know more about God and you will have new intimacy with Jesus. Did I learn anything? Yes I did. Would I want to go through it again? Not unless the Lord has more training for me but it is still like asking Joseph if he would like to go back into Pharaoh's prison. One of the best things about boot camp is that when it is over you graduate.

God is all about our death so that HIS success can be realized through us! This is why the Church is having such little impact in our world today. Besides the lack of unity in the body there are too many believers who have not yet died to their old nature so that Christ can live fully through them. John 12:24-26 (NIV), "I tell you the truth, unless a kernel of wheat falls to the ground and dies, it remains only a single seed.

But if it dies, it produces many seeds. The man who loves his life will lose it, while the man who hates his life in this world will keep it for eternal life."

When believers come to the end of themselves, when they lose their lives to Him and live through the power of the Holy Spirit, when they begin to see the reality of a living gospel that impacts lives, workplaces, cities and nations, then things will change. God's ways are higher than ours. That scripture seems like an excuse, but it is still true. A side note , when I was in the Marine Corps I was in flight training and we were on a flight and I was trained slightly on how to evacuate the plane in an emergency. I was told to pull the canopy, roll out and aim for the wing, but that I would not hit the wing because of the speed. I experienced absolute trust in the colonel who was flying with me. If he said pull the canopy and jump, I would have done it without question. That is what God wants from us. I remember saying later that my government wouldn't hurt me would they? That is the kind of total faith and trust God wants us to have in Him. He will not hurt us.

I recently got a call from my daughter who lives in Kansas. She said, "Dad I have a scripture for you." She gave me Habakkuk 2:1-3 (NIV), "I will stand at my watch and station myself on the ramparts; I will look to see what he will say to me, and what the LORD replied: "Write down the revelation and make it plain on tablets so that a herald may run with it. For the revelation awaits an appointed time; it speaks of the end and will not prove false. Though it linger, wait for it; it will certainly come and will not delay." She did not know I was writing this. She knew we were praying for the prophetic word we had received. This is a rather obscure scripture, but she called later that day and said that she had heard it again on the radio. Sometimes we can hinder God in answering our promised vision. Psalm 106 (NIV), " The people refused to enter the pleasant land, for they wouldn't believe His promise to care for them."

If you don't like that one, how about Naaman who was promised that he would be healed if he went to see the man of God? Like many of us, Naaman expected God to perform his miracle through Elisha in a dramatic and "religious" way. Instead he was told to dip seven times. Sometimes we fail to recognize that God can work through a simple act of obedience that seems unrelated to the problem. God told Joshua to walk around Jericho seven times to win the battle. Jesus told Peter to catch a fish to get a coin to pay his taxes.

There are other times God calls us to use the natural to receive a breakthrough. Sometimes we simply need to change our diet or go see a doctor to see a breakthrough in our health. Sometimes we need to change the kind of work we have been doing to get a breakthrough in our career. Samuel, the prophet told King Saul that obedience is better than sacrifice. Learning to listen to the Lord and following His instructions may just work. I have a brother in the Lord that has throat cancer. My wife and I have been praying for him daily for over a year. When we see him and it is not often, we ask how he is. He answers, " I'm healed". We did not know if we should stop praying for him or not. But knowing him, he doesn't want to give a negative confession, so we kept praying for him. However, he died recently. These situations are a mystery.

They always require the question, why? The answer always seems unsatisfying. This brother was in the ministry and left a wife and young child. God is God and we are not. I am just thankful that He is a just God that loves us and has our best interest at heart. (Jeremiah 29: 11) It is difficult not be one of Job's friends at times like this who said to Job, "Why don't you just curse God and die?"

I have a personal testimony in this area. A little over three years ago, I was diagnosed with a disease called Myasthenia Gravis (MG). It is an autoimmune disease that has affected the muscles in my jaw and tongue. At its worst, it could effect my lungs and that is life threatening. What had happened to me was that I was only able to speak clearly for a short while and I was not able to eat without difficulty. I had lost over fifty pounds in my chronic phase. After having said all that, this paper you are reading was mostly written before I was diagnosed. Now the Lord is testing me on all that I have written here. I have been prayed for by many of my brothers and sisters in the Lord and have had many prophetic words over me speaking of my imminent healing. Well you guessed it, no healing yet. Do I expect healing? Yes.!When do I expect it? I don't know. I am trusting in the Lord. I can think of many reasons why He should heal me now and none why He should not heal me now. Well, maybe one or two reasons. However, I decided that I should thank the Lord for this disease. I needed to lose weight and I needed to draw closer to Him. I am sure there are many more reasons. I hope I am not sounding flippant or that I don't want to be healed desperately, because I do. I realize that healing is a spiritual thing and in the total control of God. I have been miraculously healed of Osteoarthritis. It took the

Lord two minutes to grow new cartilage in my knee but it took place four months after I had been prayed for, another mystery.

All that I have written about healing is still true as I live through this trial. By the way I have thanked God for this disease and I have said I do not care if You do not heal me and I meant it.I understand more now. It doesn't make it anymore pleasant , but it has confirmed that God is in charge. I've gained more insights such as there is more intimacy with the Lord in the valley than at the mountaintop, how to trust more when that is all you have and how to pray without ceasing. I also have more understanding and compassion for the pain of others in similar situations and predicaments. I find that I am more in submission to the will of God. I have found some comfort in two phrases, one spiritual and one not so spiritual. The first is, "It is what it is" and the other is 2 Chronicles 20: 12, "I don't know what to do but my eyes are on You, Lord."

I believe in a positive confession but a positive confession does not heal me. My faith is not in my faith. My faith is in Jesus who heals me. When I look at the scripture in Isaiah 53:4-5, which says, " we are healed by His stripes," I know it is the heritage of the children of God to be healed by Jesus' wounds. We do not even need to ask for healing; it is ours. Then why am I not healed? I have written a complete paper on that scripture, but in this book, I offer a very short explanation. God is sovereign and He gives us what we need when He believes we need it, much as we would give our children part of their inheritance when we believe it is needed and it won't hurt them.

Chapter Twenty-Nine

My Comments on the State of the Church of Christ

The Bible is the only book I know of where you can have the author come and live with you. The Bible is a book of truths but some people only know and study the Bible as literature. They sometimes know it better than most Christians do however, they do not receive life from it. We can make the same mistake if we do not have the author living in us.

Once we receive His life as in the born again experience, many of us think that is all there is for us. Our churches only teach how to be reproducers of that experience, never growing beyond evangelism, never going beyond John 3:16. Paul says in 1 Corinthians 3:2 (NIV), "I gave you milk, not solid food, for you were not yet ready for it. Indeed, you are still not ready." Paul wanted to feed them the meat of the Word, but couldn't because they were not able to receive it; they still needed to be fed milk. Some ministers in some denominations only preach from a limited number of verses, mostly the ones on salvation. If Jesus is the Word and they are preaching this "limited gospel", then they are missing a lot of Jesus. It's impossible not to have a better understanding of the Bible when we have an intimate relationship with Jesus because He is the Living Word. How can we get close to Jesus and not get closer to the Word and derive insights and revelation from it (Him)? He is the Word. One manifestation of the presence of God is His omnipresence which speaks of His presence everywhere.Another is His manifest presence. The dictionary says manifest means to reveal something or make something evident by showing or demonstrating it very clearly. The manifest presence of the Lord is when Jesus reveals Himself to us in a way we did not know before. This is not only to our spirits, but also when our mind and senses become aware of God. It is when His knowledge is revealed to our minds.This is what Jesus meant when He said, "I will love him and manifest myself to him" (John 14:21 NKJV).

I have experienced the manifest presence of God. The caution is not to seek the manifestations, but to seek Jesus. The manifestations don't satisfy but a close relationship with Jesus does. We are not being taught this and many don't even believe it can happen. Wouldn't it be good for our pastors, teachers, evangelists, prophets and apostles to be experiencing the manifest presence of the Lord? Wouldn't it be good if we had the whole five-fold ministry active in our churches to experience the manifest presence of God? " Now to each one the manifestation of the Spirit is given for the common good."

The State of the Church

The following remarks are my opinion of the state of the Church, at least in America. Some people have embraced Christ with the attitude of what He can do for me rather than that He is the Lord of Lords who is worthy to be worshiped and praised. If we do The former, we are no better than someone who worships an idol. No one ever serves an idol of wood or stone because they love it. They only serve it because they want something from it. We cannot just add Jesus into our sinful lifestyle. Acts 3:19 (NKJV), "Peter said to those inquiring, 'Repent therefore and be converted that your sins may be blotted out, so that times of refreshing may come from the presence of the Lord.' " We must have a heart change to have salvation. That's why some of our salvation tracts say, "Pray this prayer and mean it with your heart". I say that is a good start.

If our statistics on marriage, abortion and suicide are not what God wants from His people, we have missed something. Part of the problem is that people have not been taught that salvation is connected to repentance. We can pray all the salvation prayers we want, but if we do not have a change of heart, we have not achieved salvation. We cannot have a change of heart without an encounter with God. I am not limiting the drawing power the Holy Spirit in this statement or the power of the work of the cross, but I am concerned about man's desire to give up his will and submit to God's will. This is serious stuff and not as simple as we sometimes treat salvation. I know a minister who requires new converts to "cross the line." This speaks of changing your life and accepting the new life offered by God. This method is more than just a simple prayer that seems to leave out our will. I am not saying that the simple prayer won't do it, because I am an example of this very thing. I had a radical conversion by saying just a simple prayer. I think the difference is that I was in desperate need of salvation and I knew it. It also took six months of Q&A for me to get to a point of understanding that my Catholic works couldn't do it.

I have always considered the born again experience very similar to a natural birth. In a natural birth, the baby can have a perfect heart and lungs, but if it is not fed and nurtured, if it is immediately expected to start living on its own, even reproducing, which it obviously cannot do, it will die. I believe that the correlation to the newborn believer is the same. The church is the natural earthly parent to the new believer and has an obligation to have a means and ability to raise its kids before birthing more. The whole Gospel of God is sufficient to raise spiritual kids, one or two classes on spiritual growth are not. Their genuine conversion gives them their receptive heart. It just needs to be nurtured or it will experience a spiritual death. I must add that activity is not spiritual growth. Matthew 7: 21-23 (NIV) tells us that activities or works are not going to get God's attention, even good works. I believe that we are going to need an intimate relationship with Jesus for Him to accept our works. "Not everyone who says to me, 'Lord, Lord,' will enter the kingdom of heaven, but only he who does the will of my Father who is in heaven. Many will say to me on that day, 'Lord, Lord, did we not prophesy in your name, and in your name drive out demons and perform many miracles?' Then I will tell them plainly, 'I never knew you. Away from me, you evildoers!' "

So What is Going on?

1. We must not be hearing the Holy Spirit in our study of the Bible.

2. We don't have the Holy Spirit indwelling in us because we think He went back to Heaven with the closing of the Canon of Scripture.

3. Our teachers don't believe the whole Word of God therefore they are not teaching it.

4. The church is more concerned about the church than the sheep.

I believe that it is a mix of all four. However, I believe the biggest problem is that our teachers aren't teaching the whole Word of God. If Jesus is the Word, we are missing so much of Jesus and the Father. They are teaching us to be evangelists. There seems to be some benefit in having a church full of immature newborn babies, a church full of babies having babies. Jesus says, "I am not calling you servants, but friends." We work at all sorts of projects as though we think God is watching us from 9 to 5 to make sure we are busy. I believe two problems exist here. First, the activity stems from our erroneous belief that we must work for our salvation. Second, we have substituted the work for intimacy with God. We are leading other people to the Lord but can't keep our marriages together or our children off of drugs. There also seems to be some misguided benefit in keeping the new converts connected and as busy as the old converts making more new converts. And so the cycle goes on and on.

Jesus called Matthew 22: 37 & 38 the greatest commandment. We have been taught how to do the second greatest commandment instead. This is not the order in which Jesus wants the church to operate. It seems that we have been taught that the Great Commission is the greatest commandment. We have been taught how to build a food pantry, how to build houses in 3rd world countries, how to invite people to evangelistic meetings and many other worthwhile endeavors. We have not been taught how to keep from looking like the very people we are trying to impact for Christ. We do not have the power or knowledge of the Word or the intimate relationship beyond the new birth to help us from committing the very sins of the world we preach against. How can we have a permanent effect on the world when the evangelists, us, are no better than the people they are evangelizing? Keeping people busy won't necessarily keep them from sin or help them to know right from wrong. Sometimes the only Bible people will read is the life of the Christian, and in many instances it's a bad read.

Why do we reverse Jesus' teaching and begin with loving our neighbor as ourselves? Actually we have not even reversed it; we have not done the greatest commandment at all. Who knows how to love the Lord with all our might? Who knows how to have an intimate relationship with Jesus? I know many people who love the Lord but do not posses an intimate friendship with Jesus. I believe that they would welcome one if someone would just show them how. Please do not confuse raising hands or standing up during worship as having an intimate relationship with Jesus. I am not saying that you do not have that relationship if you do that, you may. I am saying that is not necessarily a sign of it but it is a good first start to begin your search for intimacy. It seems to me that the Church many times thinks that the only one with needs to be met is the Church itself.

The new denomination Christian Center, Christian Fellowship and the like , have become convenient alternatives to the old legalistic churches many of us have come from. When asked what denomination we are, we quickly answer that we are non-denominational. That way no one really knows what we believe in and what we do not believe in. We're evangelical, that's for sure, and because we are non-denominational, we can have agreement with those who believe in the Holy Spirit and we can agree that the gifts operate today in the Church. But this agreement without allowing and encouraging the Holy Spirit and the gifts to operate freely in the local church doesn't fool the Holy Spirit or anyone filled with the Spirit into thinking that anything has really changed. The dispensationist or cessationist position is very much intact in most evangelical non-denominational churches. Instead of dealing with the excesses that are sometimes found in churches where the Holy Spirit is allowed free rein, either by correction Biblically or by pastoring the excesses out of the churches, we throw the baby out with the bath water and continue the division in the Church. No one grows, not even the leadership. They just keep pointing to the excesses as an excuse for not allowing the Holy Spirit to move. Does anyone care about John 17:23 , unity in the Body of Christ? When churches are planted in Africa, India, Asia and South America the whole Bible is taught and the results are significant. In fact the center of Christendom is moving to those countries.

Is the Lord Returning?

How can the Bride of Christ, the Church, ever be ready for His return? Jesus said that He is coming back for a bride without spot or wrinkle. Is Jesus coming back for a church with the sins that are so prevalent in the people of God? Can Jesus come back for a Church that can't get agreement on basic issues like do miracles happen today and is the Holy Spirit present in a special way beyond salvation in the believer and the Church? When do we start preparing for the return of the Lord?

We in the church live like the Lord is never coming back. This reminds me of Israel at the time of Jesus. Israel talked about and was waiting for the Messiah, but when He came some rejected Him and some didn't recognize Him. Why? They were looking for a king that would deliver them from the Romans, among other things. How short-sighted and temporary! They had it all wrong. What are we looking for? Do we want God to bless and deliver us out of every problem? Do we want to be taken out of this earthly hell we're in, or do we want to rule and reign with Him? Revelation 2: 25 (NIV), "Hold on to what you have until I come back." Is it that we really don't believe Jesus is coming again? If we do, it seems peculiar to me since no one in the Church talks about it. It is an event that will impact the entire world with as many or more scriptures telling of the Second Coming than the First Coming, and no one is teaching us about it. Information is relegated to authors that have their own agendas. It would seem the Church should be concerned about how we get information about something that will affect us all.

When is the Church going to start to prepare for the coming of the Lord? We don't even hear about the coming of the Bridegroom or the fact that the Bride (the Church) needs to be prepared and what being prepared means.I wonder if we are holding up the return of the Lord because God can't get our attention about what needs to be done before His return because we are too busy. The status quo is okay with them. According to Revelation the rewards for overcoming are wonderful. The Church has enough theologians to explain these scriptures, why doesn't it do so? A few reasons I can guess are that without the inspiration of the Holy Spirit it may not be able to be done. Another reason might be they don't want to teach anything controversial because it could be that this kind of teaching will scare pew sitters away.

We seem to be practicing our own brand of church which is activity, activity, and more activity. No one seems to care about what Jesus wants His church to look like when He returns. We seem to think that all Jesus wants are big churches, the bigger the better, crowded full of baby Christians only drinking milk and all spotted and wrinkled with wet diapers. Repentance is a major part of salvation, yet are Churches emphasizing the turning away from sin and turning towards Jesus and the Father. Thus far, it has not given the help to make the change. It seems all it wants are notches on its salvation belt; salvation without change is not salvation. When Jesus comes will He look upon His flock in America and have compassion on them because they are like sheep without a shepherd, but have only an evangelist or administrator (Matthew 9: 36)? When Jesus spoke this He was not looking at unchurched people. He was talking about a people not unlike us. They had Synagogues in every city but the people were not being cared for. American churches fit the Matthew 9: 36 mold perfectly; we are full of saved people, but we are sheep without a shepherd.

The Answer?

The Church must give up its method of churching. The goals of the American church must change. Large churches are nice if they are filled with a mix of new believers being taught the basics and an ongoing maturation of believers by being taught the entire Bible. Mature believers should be mentoring young converts.

I know preachers who can preach a salvation message in at least a hundred different ways, and they do. Maybe the cliché, "you're preaching to the choir," came into use because of this practice. Preaching a salvation message for the benefit of a few unsaved people in the congregation while the others sleep and remain babies in the faith, is a misuse of the corporate meeting when so many believers are present and could be brought along in the faith. Some would argue that the preaching service is an evangelistic service. Fine. The Bible doesn't say it should or shouldn't be. The Bible does says that the Body needs to attain to maturity. Don't do one and ignore the other.

I believe the Pastors should be allowed to take care of the sheep. Let others take care of the church and its physical needs. Our church teachers need to stop teaching unimportant subjects that don't lead to maturity and understanding and do not give life to believers. Ephesians 4:14 (NIV), "Then we will no longer be infants, tossed back and forth by the waves, and blown here and there by every wind of teaching and by the cunning and craftiness of men in their deceitful scheming." How is the body supposed to keep from being tossed by every wind of doctrine if it does not know truth from error? If the Church was as interested in the maturity of the believer as they are in evangelism, the Church would probably be smaller but more mature.

Some time ago, my wife and I had occasion to tell some brothers and sisters that they should not read the DaVinci Code. They argued with us and could not understand why they shouldn't. Some had already read it. Who knows what confusion will arise as they mix truth from the Scriptures with the lie of the book? That is an indictment on the Church and its teachers. I don't necessarily think that a teacher should teach against a book that teaches lies about Jesus. I believe that the Christians established in a church should know truth from error without a teaching on the specific error. That's what attaining maturity is. I also believe that anyone who represents the Church should know the Word well enough to keep people under him or her from error. I believe that people in authority need to be under authority.

I believe in better qualifications for elders. Many are picked for their income level, status in the community or friendship to the Pastor, while their knowledge of the Scriptures is less than it should be. Some of their families are "out of order". The Church needs to stop worrying about filling the pews to pay the mortgage. If they want to run the Church like a business, then shouldn't spend money they don't have. It's not a badge of spirituality to spend more than what comes in. That's when we pray to God to fix a fix to get us out of the fix we got ourselves into. Then we do it again next year or we make an impassioned plea for money from the Body. The newest ploy is to look for a hired gun who has the experience to fill pews and bring in money. This plan does not seem to include any help for the sheep. This is done without apology or explanation as to how they got into the financial mess they're in or without any assurance they will not be asking for a bailout again next year. In a real business you cannot get a loan without a plan to get out of the mess you're in and the loan must be paid back. What a concept! If the believers saw the power of God operating in their church with the prophetic ministry active, they would be more likely to believe that an expensive project was called by God. They would also believe that if God wanted the project, He would provide for it. When the Apostles worried about the work needed to care for the widows and orphans, they appointed Deacons and assigned them to that work so that the Apostles were able to continue in the office to which they were called. The Apostles work was prayer and the ministry of the Word. (Acts 6:1-4) It would seem that the Church should copy that system and let the pastors take care of the sheep, the teachers teach and the administrators administrate.

I am not advocating running the church of Christ like a business. It should be run like it does not belong to us, but to God because it does;almost like a public company that must answer to the stockholders and ultimately to the CEO, God.

Another extreme is that many churches are run like private fiefdoms with founding pastors doing everything for themselves having no regard for the sheep, only considering what the sheep can do for them. They have perverted the term shepherd care to mean the sheep take care of the shepherd. They appoint elders that are not qualified to be elders, their only qualification being that they will rubber stamp anything the Pastor wants. One of my favorite sayings I coined out of frustration was, "the Pastor decides to paint the church purple and four elders run for brushes." In my experience, this model was very prevalent during 1970's during the last outpouring of the Holy Spirit. Thankfully it has changed, mostly because the government saw the graft, greed and chicanery of those churches and moved on some of the better known ministries. This stopped some of the bad practices. However, it was not totally corrected.

The lack of humility is the next thing that must go in the Church. I remember a local Pastor of a big church in our area relating that he had to control himself from bragging that he had 120 on his staff at a national conference. This kind of thing is also prevalent in secular business and I have succumbed to this myself. It is a sin of pride in either case. There are so many scriptures about being humble in the Bible that I believe it is a very important issue with the Lord with all of us. I don't remember hearing very many sermons preached on pride. God promises if we will give up pride, He will give us grace. He also said if we don't humble ourselves, He would humble us. He also said something about healing our land in 2 Chron. 7:14. All in all, the Church has a lot to do, and it doesn't look like it wants to.

The Catholic Church has its doctrines, its rules, regulations and its traditions. The Catholic Church has put a lot of emphasis on these. They do teach the Bible now and sometimes teach the born again experience. What they also have is unanimity of leadership and uniformity of belief. That has been maintained more or less for 2,000 years. My background is Catholic. I was born into an Italian Catholic family. Twelve years in Catholic education. Was I born again? No. Was I on my way to Hell? Yes, by Catholic rules, which I broke most of. But I was on my way by anyone's rules. Are all Catholics born again? Not always.

Having said this I want to tell a story of a friend of mine who was Messianic Jew born into a family of Messianic Jews. When he was a young man learning how to be a Christian Pastor he was required to pass out tracts. This particular day he was in a predominantly Catholic neighborhood. He knocked on the door of an elderly Catholic lady. When he was finished giving his little speech on how he found Jesus, the lady said, "I'm so glad that you found my Jesus," with tears running down her face. That was a revelation to him and to me when he told me the story. At the time I just thought that someone had given her the Gospel at some time and she responded to it just like I had. Now some thirty plus years later, I have different thinking about how this happened. My old thinking was to apply the Protestant formula to the situation and if it did not fit, I would question the experience. Today, in the light of my limited knowledge of the Scriptures and some of the things that God has shown me, I have a little different idea as to how this lady and quite possibly millions of Catholics have come to a saving knowledge of the Lord.

I believe we Protestants think that we have a lock on the born-again experience. The Protestant Church has abdicated in teaching the full scope of repentance required in salvation. Because of this we have people who are only what I call half saved. Who are the people Jesus is talking about in Matthew 7:21-23? "Not everyone who says to me, 'Lord, Lord, will enter the kingdom of heaven, but only he who does the will of my Father who is in heaven. Many will say to me on that day, 'Lord, Lord, did we not prophesy in your name, and in your name drive out demons and perform many miracles?' Then I will tell them plainly, 'I never knew you. Away from me, you evildoers!'"

If we were recruiting candidates into our CIA wouldn't we require an oath of allegiance? If they had been spies for a foreign power we would make them renounce that previous lifestyle before we would let them into our group? Wouldn't we check up on them to see if they believed all that we believed? You would think that we would do as much for the people who pray the prayer of salvation. If they do not have an encounter with Jesus, but only add Him to their sinful life style for whatever benefit they can obtain from Him, is that true salvation? I agree that legalism will not save you, but what it will do if it's all you have, is force you to find a god to love. Remember Catholics do not use the Bible much for direction. Protestants do, but if the church is not teaching the whole Bible, we are left on our own to discover the gems for life that are contained therein. Neither way is optimum. It seems that we have been told it does not require anything else but praying a simple prayer. It's true that the work done on the Cross by Jesus is sufficient, but in the light of Matt.7: 21 we must do the will of the Father. The Father sent His only Son to die for us all and that includes anyone who will do the will of The Father.

The greatest commandment is to love God with all your heart and soul and mind. Do we think that anyone can love Jesus with all their heart soul and mind and not achieve salvation? If the answer to that is no, then many Catholics have found the Lord like the elderly lady in the story.

As Jesus grieves over the deaths of His physical babies that are aborted, He grieves over the deaths of His spiritual babies that are left to die. I believe that Jesus is grieved over spiritual abortion as well as physical abortion. The Church and the evangelistic ministries have birthed millions of babies who have gone on to be spiritual milk drinkers. They have become part of the statistics that match the unsaved world's statistics, thus the church and those ministries bear some responsibility for their lack of maturity. The Church and the large ministries don't realize this, so they just keep evangelizing and exacerbating the problem. As any family knows, it's easy to have babies but difficult to raise them. They are not fulfilling the Great Commission as they think. Matt 28: 20 speaks of making disciples and teaching them to obey all that He has commanded. It also commands us to baptize them.

We have churches full of people who have not achieved an encounter or personal relationship with Jesus and have only prayed the simple prayer of salvation without repenting of their sins. They have not turned away from the lifestyle that they have come from and are using the grace given to them as an occasion to do whatever their heart desires. I understand why our divorce, abortion, suicide, pornography and alcoholism statistics are higher than they should be in the Christian world. Maybe it is because we are adding the people into the statistics who are attending our churches but are not really saved. Dietrich Bonhoeffer called this "cheap grace" in his book, The Cost of Discipleship. Cheap grace is the grace we bestow on ourselves. Costly grace is the Gospel that must be sought, the gift that must be asked for. "It is costly because it costs a man his life. It is grace because it gives a man the only true life" (Dietrich Bonhoeffer).

There is one last thing I want to mention. I don't want the reader to think I am saying that the church should be run like a business even though many are. My comments are in the form of a solution that could be applied to a secular business that could work for a church as well. I have owned secular businesses for fifty-five years so I might be qualified to make these comments. When a businessman sees that his customers going to another company for similar products, he is concerned. He knows soon he will not be able to pay his mortgage on his buildings or pay his employees. So he does what he can to discover why his customers are leaving and going to another company. He must figure out how to stop the exodus. It would be easy if he owned a restaurant and customers did not like the food, the prices were not competitive or he had a surly wait staff. Some companies are much more complicated and the cure may be subtle and difficult to discover.

What about a church? What if the people in a particular church begin leaving? What if it is people who have been attending for years or some who are new and stay only for a while? Soon the church cannot pay its mortgage and its staff and begins laying off trained staff and replacing them with volunteers. I don't want this to seem like it is all about money, however, it is to the Pastor and his elder board. Where does the Pastor look to understand why his congregants are leaving to go to the church down the street? Who does the Pastor blame? Who should he blame? How about the parking lot that may be too small for all the cars leaving long walk to the sanctuary? How about any number of things that are not the real issue? Let me see if there are some real reasons. How about the Pastor not feeding the sheep, the service is not relevant, or the entire service is too long or there is no personal communication with the Pastor for anyone except with certain people? The people may also feel that they are not being fed the whole gospel but just the salvation gospel .

What is the solution? For the congregant, it may be to leave. For the church, it is the beginning of the end. Someone would need to speak to the person in charge, who would be the Pastor as there obviously is no five-fold ministry to deal with these problems. Sometimes leadership in churches like these do not even realize that people are upset, discouraged, and have real personal problems that should be attended to by the shepherd. It seems that the church's needs take preeminence and that has created the cause for the problems that exist now. Who should speak to the Pastor, and will it do any good? If God is not in the middle of it and the Pastor has not shown care for the sheep he will not listen to anyone. The answer is people leave, and the church is in trouble.

In Conclusion, A Note: The state of the Eastern Church

In just 20 years, two-thirds of all Christians will live in

Richard Maggio

Africa, Latin America or Asia. We like to think of ourselves as the Christian West but there is growing evidence that the center of Christendom has moved.

Chapter Thirty

Why Christians Are Not Helping Our Country

Why are Christians not helping? When I read the statistics on he Christian involvement in American politics, I am disturbed and saddened. The statistics in 2012 show Christianity as the most popular religion in the United States at around 73% of the population, down about 5% from 1990. Of the Christians polled, about 62% claim to be members of a church congregation. The United States has the largest Christian population in the world, with nearly 247 million Christians, although other countries have higher percentages but fewer populations of Christians among their populations. (Statistics From Wikipedia)

Here are some sad statistics on the people in America from the PEW Research Center:

"This large and growing group of Americans is less religious than the public at large on many conventional measures, including frequency of attendance at religious services and the degree of importance they attach to religion in their lives. However, a new survey by the Pew Research Center's Forum on Religion & Public Life, conducted jointly with the PBS television program Religion & Ethics News Weekly, finds that many of the country's 46 million unaffiliated adults are religious or spiritual in some way. Two-thirds of them say they believe in God (68%). More than half say they often feel a deep connection with nature and the earth (58%), while more than a third classify themselves as "spiritual" but not "religious" (37%), and one-in-five (21%) say they pray every day. In addition, most religiously unaffiliated Americans think that churches and other religious institutions benefit society by strengthening community bonds and aiding the poor. With few exceptions, though, the unaffiliated say they are not looking for a religion that would be right for them. Overwhelmingly, they think that religious organizations are too concerned with money and power, too focused on rules and too involved in politics."

Beyond Statistics

What happened to the America I knew growing up? The answer to that question and the reason for the answer is very complicated. It has to do with many elements that have slowly affected the American attitude toward God, religion, war, peace, money, politics, crime, punishment or the lack thereof. There are other issues that affect the thinking of Americans. The young people today don't think like we did at the same age when we were growing up. Today we hear of a new group called millennials, people that have gained their adulthood around the year 2,000. At this age they should begin to think about things on serious levels and become part of America but they do not. Today some college students oppose anyone who thinks differently than they do to the point of breaking the law. We see some desecrating of the American flag. No one my age would have ever thought of doing that and if they did they would have been incarcerated, notwithstanding the protests against the Viet Nam war.

On December 7th, 1941 we saw lines all around recruiting offices across America to fight for our country. I am a baby boomer. My dad's generation fought in World War II. They would never have thought of not joining our military or not voting. They also would never have thought of voting only for their financial benefits at the expense of other Americans. That America is gone. The World War II generation is dying daily by the thousands from old age and the boomers are not far behind.

An Enigma or an Ulterior Motive?

Today we have a mix of peoples from countries that seem to have been unhappy where they come from but don't want to integrate into American society and do not want our way of life. It is almost like they want to duplicate the place they came from that they didn't like. That seems to be an enigma, unless they have an ulterior motive and we must believe that they do based on what we are seeing here and around the world.

These people say they want peace, forgiveness, understanding of other's religions and opinions and do not want to offend, however, that doesn't seem to be the case for many of them. They force their religion on us and want rights and laws that they had in their home countries. Have any other ethnic people done that here?

Our millennials are being converted to a new way of thinking that is really anti-religious and anti- American. Who is converting them? I believe that it is a combination of the current administration in America with its political correctness and revisionist history, allowing the Koran to be taught for extra credit in our schools but not the Bible, the total acceptance of Muslim customs and traditions while eliminating age-old American Christian traditions plus a progressive press corps unwilling to report the facts if they differ from their agenda. It would fill this chapter to list all the areas that have changed in our country.

Is This Possible in America?

Todd Starnes is an American conservative columnist and commentator for tv and radio. Quoted from FREEDOM FORCE: "Islamic indoctrination in Wisconsin School", April 15, 2015. He recently stated: "For quite some time, I have been exposing the Islamafication of American public schools. The Muslim faith has been given accommodation while the Christian faith has been marginalized. As I wrote in my book, "God Less America", Islamic advocates are waging what they call a stealth jihad in our school system. And if left unchecked, they will be successful in undermining the Judeo Christian values upon which our great country was founded". He also states: a Wisconsin teacher told her 10th grade class: "Pretend you are:

1. Muslim male/female in U.S.

2. Give 3 examples of what you do daily for your

religion

3. Any struggles you face.

4. Again, 5 paragraphs (intro, 3 body paragraphs,

closing.)

Keep in mind we've been doing work and watching documentaries that have the facts needed to write the essay."

Recognize that she is asking these students to think like and empathize with the U.S. Muslim. Feel their struggle, identify with their lives. What does this accomplish? It makes these students sympathetic to the Islamic viewpoint, and more likely to be receptive to their arguments. It causes the student to be receptive to the Islamic lifestyle and beliefs". Todd Starnes Is this the first steps to indoctrination? I wonder what this teacher likes about the Koran and what she doesn't like about the Bible?

Those Who Came Here Earlier

When my grandfather and father came to America from Italy, neither Italy nor America changed to accommodate each other. All the Italians adopted the American way of life. It was not easy but they wanted to be Americans. They did not give up being Italians or try to change America; they wanted what America had. The largest ethnic group that fought in World War II against Germans, Japanese and Italians were the American Italians. Would any current aliens from the middle-east pledge allegiance to America and fight for America against their own nationalities?

Other Issues That Affected Our Change

The other large issue is what takes away the interest of our youth from God/religion and politics? Again it is a multitude of things. To start with, I think the devices we possess and have added to our lifestyle are a big cause. The iPhones, Facebook, Twitter and emails take up most of our time on a daily basis. Pornography is easily available to all with no age requirement. I could write more about these, however, there are more things that take away and change us from the way we were in times past. I have written about this next item before but it answers the question so I will write about it again. Sports and the American interest in all sports seem to be a major item that captures the attention of our entire American culture. It doesn't seem to matter what sport we will watch. I noticed that the Final Four basketball season finally closed and the next day or two the baseball season started. Our men read, eat and sleep all sports. I call it climbing a ladder to nowhere.

What is the Benefit?

This activity doesn't seem to offer any monetary benefit to the people watching; in fact, it is very expensive if they physically attend these events. They have replaced what we used to get from our Church attendance with these activities. We used to get fellowship from friends on a personal level and learn about God and what He wants from His people. We discussed world issues that affected our lives. When I watch the TV interviews with people on the street, I am appalled at the incompetence of the average interviewees. The only subjects they seem to know about are the names of movie stars, pro-sports people and who they are married to or divorced from. Most cannot tell who the current vice-president is or who our first president was or who won the Civil War. I have not made this up. I viewed it on television. I also watched an interviewer ask adults if they would agree with Obama that he wanted Karl Marx to run for president after he left office. All but one person said," yes that would be acceptable and they would vote for him".

Who is Responsible for This Among our Youth?

Who is to blame for this shameful and dangerous situation? In my opinion, it is manifold. I will start with the parents of the young kids. I will assume that they have two parents. Many do not and that is the beginning of many of our problems in America. Single parent households unfortunately will almost always breed what we are seeing on the streets today. What happened to God and going to church? Moms and grandmas have power, but fathers have more. But they are busy doing…

More Major Issues

The other major issue that is affecting the change in our world is the Government we have been living under for these last years. It has changed all the rules we used to live by. I am referring to the religious traditions that were what we lived by. The schools have changed the teaching to the opposite of what we have had for over 200 years, and the constitution is being changed before our eyes. We have not been allowed to teach the Bible in our school curriculum, but now our president has just announced that he wants to encourage students to study the Koran for extra credit. Study the Koran in our schools? Is our president crazy or does he have an agenda we don't know about? We still cannot study the Bible in our schools. Why doesn't he encourage the students to study "Rules for Radicals" by Saul Alinsky or "Mein Kampf" by Adolph Hitler or one of Noam Chomsky's many books? We still cannot read the Bible in Americans' public schools. Our military Chaplains are being discharged out of the service with loss of their pensions for practicing their religion. I thought that is what they were supposed to do. That is backwards. The Bible says, "in the end black will be called white and white will be called black". Isaiah 5: 20 Woe unto them that call evil good, and good evil; that put darkness for light, and light for darkness; that put bitter for sweet, and sweet for bitter! This prophecy is being fulfilled before our eyes. The comment below is quoted from Chapter 12. I asked a teacher friend why the Bible could not be taught in our schools he said "it would be disruptive because it was a religious book". My comment was "the school system in California just purchased thousands of Harry Potter books and they are about the religion of witches."

What Can We Do?

We can expect more of the same in our country as long as we replace God with all of the things I have mentioned above and many more. Some of the things mentioned above are not all sins in themselves. Our job, our family, sports events or these other things are not all bad. They only become sin when they dominate us or become an idol. The things of God, country and family can and do suffer. The result is what we are seeing today in our country. God has a solution and it is in the

Bible in 2 Chronicles 7:14 (NIV), "If my people, who are called by my name, will humble themselves and pray and seek my face and turn from their wicked ways, then I will hear from heaven, and I will forgive their sin and will heal their land". Anything that takes away our focus from our God is an idol. You can name your own idols. They may be obvious things like any of the things we think of as addictions. It doesn't matter what it may be. If it takes your focus away from God, it has become your god and it is wrong and is considered sin. Again, the results are here now and we must change or God may continue the judgment we have caused ourselves.

Chapter Thirty-One

My Last Word

I am happy that my God moves among us in power. No other god does. They make a lot of noise, or rather their worshipers do. They claim many things and promise many things, but there is no performance of any kind. I recently saw on the news that one of the followers of the currently popular false god held a knife to a 19 year- old girl's throat and threatened to cut her throat if she didn't convert from her Christian faith in Jesus to his false god. She saw him kill others so she knew her life was at stake. How does that work for a "god" who needs his followers to convert to him under the fear of death. I would call that a loser god. Our God promises us a home in Heaven and a life in eternity with Him. Our converts come freely. I recently saw a picture of a Harvest Ministries Crusade at Angel Stadium in California. The stadium was full and when Greg Lori gave the invitation, nearly 12,000 people walked freely to the middle of the stadium to convert to Christ from whatever religion or no religion. Jesus is happy with freewill conversions. There is no fear of death to convert.

Our God Died For Us So We Don't Need To Die For Him

Our God forgives our sins, heals the sick, He even raises the dead, so we can ask questions of those who have come back. He gave us a book that has no lies in it. He has sent a comforter to stay with us and help us live in this world. The false god promotes the very things we call sin, like killing people who don't convert. Our God is a loving God.

I have been following the true God for forty-four years now. I have been on mountaintops with God. I have been in deep valleys and long deserts, I have learned to trust and believe that God is in control in all situations. He has taught me His Word. I have been physically healed 3 times for different issues. I have prayed for people and they have been healed. I have trusted God with my wife, family and my life. He showed me how to have an intimate relationship with Him and to love Him with all my heart, soul and mind and I have learned to love my neighbor as myself. Our God is faithful. God has taught me to hear Him when He speaks to me.

I have had an autoimmune disease for about three years. It is not life threatening with medication. I have thanked God for it. That may sound slightly crazy, but God has used it at this time in my life to draw me closer to Him and to teach me other things through this disease. However, one early morning I was awakened by the Lord. He said things that only He could know or say. This time I heard the words, "You are healed my stripes." I quickly said Lord I know that is Isaiah 53:4-5, are you going to heal me now? He answered me with a question as He many times does that seemed unrelated, "Do you love your grandchildren?" I said, "Yes, Lord You know that I do." Then He said, "When your grandkids come over to your home can they do anything they want?" I thought for a minute and said yes they can. He said, "Could they jump up on your lap and kiss you?" I answered, "Yes." He said, "Is there anyplace they cannot go in your home?" I said, "No." He then asked, "Where do you keep your candy?" I answered in the drawer in the kitchen island. I knew I was in trouble now. He then asked, "Can they have anything they want in there?" I said, "No." He said, "Why not?" I answered, "Because I love them and I only give them what I think will be okay; I control the candy". He then said, "That is what I do with healing you (Isaiah 53:4-5). Healing is your heritage, but I control it because I love you and I give you what is good for you at the right time." He also said, " Your faith has nothing to do with it, it is your heritage as a believer. When I walked the Earth, it was all about faith. Remember the centurion who had faith like I had not seen and the woman with the issue of blood, her faith had made her whole. That was because I had not died and resurrected yet. However, if you want to move a mountain today, it will take great faith". Isaiah 46: 9a-10 (NLT), "Remember the things I have done in the past. For I alone am God! I am God, and there is none like me. Only I can tell you the future before it even happens. Everything I plan will come to pass, for I do whatever I wish."

So it seems that God has the keys to the treasure chest of healings. He uses them when He wishes. My wife and I prayed for a sister in the Lord for over a year as did people across the country. We brought brothers with the gift of healing, we took her to a healing service as did others, but the Lord does what He wishes and He took her home. Yet, I as stated in an earlier chapter I prayed for a boy who worked for me with twenty-nine cancerous tumors and God healed him in an instant. God does what He wishes. He has the keys to the treasure chest of healing. His ways are higher than our ways. Isaiah 55:8-9, "For My thoughts are not your thoughts, neither are your ways My ways, says the Lord. For as the heavens are higher than the earth, so are My ways higher than your ways and My thoughts than your thoughts."

The benefits of knowing the Lord greatly outweigh the things we do not understand. I can't imagine what it would be like to have a God who did not answer when I prayed. God hears us each time we pray and He wants to answer us. We are his kids and He loves us more than we love Him. I have discovered that there is not much intimacy at the mountaintop. We get easily distracted with the goodies up there and that is why we need God to help even at the mountaintop. Without God's help and presence we will trade God for the pleasures of life. Then God will mercifully send a valley. Now when we need God at the bottom of the valley, He is there waiting for us, to comfort us and minister His love to us. He wants to show us how faithful He is. God craves relationship with us; He has called us friends. I like the song by Israel Houghton: "I am a friend of God"

Who am I that you are mindful of me,

That you hear me, when I call.

Is it true that you are thinking of me?

How you love me, it's amazing! (Who am I Lord)

I am a friend of God, I am a friend of God,

I am a friend of God,

He calls me friend.

Today we face problems on many fronts. Some are financial, some are spiritual and some are questions more complex than we as Christians have ever had to deal with in our generation. We face a government that is non-Christian and even hostile to us as Christians, and we don't know where it will lead or what to do. We have sought God for His wisdom but we must be able to hear God to know what He is saying. Hearing comes with practice on previous issues of less importance. If we haven't learned to hear the voice of God through the logos written Word, the Bible, or the Rhema word from the prophets and our own impressions given by the Holy Spirit, we could miss God's direction.

You and I, if we know Jesus and have made Him the Lord of our life, are among a select group that have all the resources of God at our disposal. Our prayers reach Heaven to a waiting God. Healing is our heritage and we have fellowship with the God of the universe. We have His words written for us and we have the only true God who performs miracles that no false god does or can do.He will meet all our needs in this turbulent time. He only requires belief and trust on our part. His promise is forgiveness of our sins. His ultimate goal is eternity and fellowship with us when we leave this turbulent Earth.

About the Author

Richard Maggio is a successful California businessman and a dedicated Christian. He is the oldest in his family with one younger brother. He lives in Orange County, California and is married to Judy Maggio. Together they have six children, fifteen grand-children and three great-grand children. Formerly a US Marine, his education includes attending colleges in California, including a short time at USC. From there, he joined the officer's candidate program with the US Marine Corps and went to Marine Corps schools in Quantico, Virginia.He completed their course and spent his remaining tour in the Marine Corps as a non-commissioned officer. As asuccessful businessman, he and his brother manufactured over a hundred products for the Home Depot chain of building supply warehouses. He also has patents on products that have been called "disruptive technologies." This book is his first endeavor at writing. He is well qualified to write this book as he has been a Christian for over forty-four years, studying the Word of God, helping found a number of churches and co-pastoring them as well. He calls himself a critic, but with solutions. Readers will find his writings honest, insightful and thought-provoking. He presents solutions to the Church through practical application of the Word of God using sound wisdom and doctrine.

Within these pages, the author also reveals his personal journey from over forty- five years of walking with the Lord offering an uncompromised view of Scripture. Presenting practical advice, this book speaks on many facets of the Christian walk as the author speaks openly on such subjects as being led by the Holy Spirit, the born again experience and the baptism of the Spirit. Readers will appreciate the author's candid, yet sound Biblical advice.

Richard Maggio

www.ingramcontent.com/pod-product-compliance
Lightning Source LLC
LaVergne TN
LVHW011910080426
835508LV00007BA/316